DYING WELL

DYING WELL

The Prospect for Growth
at the End of Life

IRA BYOCK, M.D.

RIVERHEAD BOOKS
New York
1997

RIVERHEAD BOOKS
a division of G. P. Putnam's Sons
Publishers Since 1838
200 Madison Avenue
New York, NY 10016

Published simultaneously in Canada

Library of Congress Cataloging-in-Publication Data

Byock, Ira.
Dying well : the prospect for growth at the end of life / by Ira Byock.
p. cm.
Includes bibliographical references and index.
ISBN 1-57322-051-5
1. Death—Social aspects. 2. Death—Psychological aspects.
3. Death—Case studies. I. Title.
HQ1073.B96 1997 96-32898 CIP
306.88—dc20

Printed in the United States of America
1 3 5 7 9 10 8 6 4 2

This book is printed on acid-free paper. ♾

Book design by Amanda Dewey

To Seymour Byock,
who taught me about living,
and to
Lila and Satya,
that they may know what
I have learned

"I had learned that all the greatest and most important problems of life are fundamentally insoluble. . . . They can never be solved, but only outgrown."

—Carl Jung, from the Introduction to *The Secret of the Golden Flower*

CONTENTS

Introduction
xiii

One
TEACHING ABOUT LIVING, TEACHING ABOUT DYING:
Seymour Byock
1

Two
QUESTIONING ASSUMPTIONS AND DAWNING AWARENESS:
My Journey
25

Three
LEARNING TO DIE WELL:
Anne-Marie Wilson
35

Four
SUFFERING AND BEYOND:
Douglas Kearney
59

Five
FINDING DIGNITY AMID DISEASE AND DISINTEGRATION:
Wallace Burke, Julia Rosauer, Hap Visscher
85

Six
THE HARDEST DECISIONS AND THE GREATEST OPPORTUNITIES:
Janelle Haldeman
119

Seven
WRITING A PERSONAL SCRIPT FOR DYING:
Steve Morris
139

Eight
ACCEPTING THE GIFT OF DEPENDENCE AND THE BURDEN OF CARE:
Jake Edwards
159

Nine
GROWING WITHIN TRAGEDY:
Michael Merseal
173

Ten
FACING UNBEARABLE PAIN, UNSPEAKABLE LOSSES:
Terry Matthews
193

Eleven
LETTING GO, GROWING ON:
Maureen Riley
217

Twelve
GETTING THERE FROM HERE:
Social and Cultural Dimensions
241

Appendix
WRITING YOUR FAMILY'S STORY:
Questions and Answers
249

Resources
283

Further Reading
285

Index
291

INTRODUCTION

While death may cast a long shadow upon us as we journey through life, Americans typically refuse to notice. We stride ahead, looking toward a bright future, concentrating on health and living fully. We exercise, eat fiber, know exactly how much fat we consume and exactly what type. We check ourselves for lumps. We make jokes about death to diminish its power, using laughter to insulate ourselves from fear. But, then, when death approaches, we are stunned and feel unprepared to deal with the situation we face. We don't know the right thing to do or say, and so we may retreat, turning over to professionals. In reflexively turning away from reminders of death, we have at times inadvertently isolated loved ones who needed our presence, and we have robbed ourselves of precious opportunities. Socially we have paid dearly, and culturally we are poorer for failing to explore the inherently human experience of dying.

But many of us have come to realize that death and dying are no longer mere abstractions. We have already taken care of a grandparent or a parent who was dying. Some of us have helped care for a dying sibling, others of us have lain beside a dying spouse. Some of us have even cradled children as they died. And some will be reading this book while facing, as we all will, death itself.

Through my years as a hospice doctor, I have learned that dying does not have to be agonizing. Physical suffering can *always* be alleviated. People need not die alone; many times the calm, caring presence of another can soothe a dying person's anguish. I think it is realistic to hope for a future in which nobody has to die alone and nobody has to die with their pain untreated. But comfort and companionship are not all there is. I have learned from my patients and their families a surprising truth about dying: this stage of life holds remarkable possibilities. Despite the arduous nature of the experience, when people are relatively comfortable and know that they are not going to be abandoned, they frequently find ways to strengthen bonds with people they love and to create moments of profound meaning in their final passage.

As a physician, being present as someone is dying tears the boundaries between the personal and professional realms of my being. The experience of a patient dying challenges me to accept a more intimate, and yet more deeply respectful, relationship with that person. I do not know how it could be otherwise. While I may bring clinical skills and years of experience to the task, ultimately I am simply present, offering to help and wanting to learn.

Over the years I have learned that the actual range of human experience of dying is broad. I have seen tremendous suffering, but I have also witnessed people who in their dying experienced a sense of wellness and peace that can only be called blissful. The stories I have chosen to tell in this book represent this wide range of experiences. Stories are the only satisfying way I know of exploring the paradox that people can become stronger and more whole as physical weakness becomes overwhelming and life itself wanes. The stories of patients and their families who appear on these pages show us how we can grow stronger within ourselves and closer to those we love as we confront the challenges of dying with honesty, caring, and commitment.

In each chapter, you will find a specific aspect of human development, or personal growth, associated with this inevitable phase of life. Each exposes another point on the continuum between suffering and grace. Readers should feel free to read chapters in an order and at a pace that seems right. Some stories highlight the interpersonal or internal conflicts that need to be resolved; others deal with the emotional skills or strategies that remain valuable even at the end of life.

INTRODUCTION

The events and circumstances in these stories are real. In all but one chapter, the names of patients and families and key identifying information have been changed to protect the privacy of the families. In chapter nine, actual names are used, both by request of the Merseal family and because Michael's story has previously been part of the HBO film *Letting Go: A Hospice Journey*. In a few instances, for the sake of simplicity, events from two actual cases have been combined or the chronology has been slightly modified. Care has been taken to preserve the context and meaning of the events.

Dying Well is a book about living. It is a book about realizing the human potential to grow—as individuals and as members of families—through the process of dying. Being with people who are dying in conscious and caring ways is of value to them and to us. Their reminiscences, our care, and the time we spend together all contribute to a legacy that enriches our lives. *Dying Well* tells stories about tragedy, but also about love, commitment, and courage; stories of people living in the shadow of death while growing within themselves and becoming closer with the ones they love.

In the ongoing research for this book and discussions with family members during its writing, I discovered that telling the story of a loved one's dying—and receiving the story of another—can be healing acts. In telling our stories we honor the person who has died, and, in a way, renew that cherished connection. In receiving a story as inherently intimate as the dying of a lover, grandparent, parent, sibling, close friend, or child, new connections are made and each person's community expands just a bit. I offer this book in the hope that it inspires others to tell their stories—and all of us to listen well.

—Missoula, Montana
August 1996

One

Teaching About Living, Teaching About Dying: Seymour Byock

I was the first person to know that my father was dying.

I realized it during a phone call eighteen months before he would die. I was living in California and in the midst of residency training required to practice rural family medicine. It was a warm winter evening; my wife, Anita, and I had just finished dinner and were preparing to snuggle in bed while watching *Lou Grant*, our favorite television show.

"Hello, Ira, it's Mom and Dad," came my mother's gravelly, unmistakable voice. "How're things in Fresno? How's Anita?"

"Fine, Mom, we're all fine. I'm as busy as ever. Anita's great. We've got lemons and oranges on our trees in the middle of winter! Hi, Dad, are you on the phone?"

It was almost eleven P.M. in New Jersey. I could picture my mother in the tiny office of their split-level home and my dad upstairs in the den, finally winding down from a day that probably started at six A.M. Anita picked up the kitchen phone; the four of us were now on the line.

"How are you, Sy?" I used my dad's first name intentionally, to speak as adults and let him know I wanted a genuine response. Often, while the rest of us chatted, he would get off the phone after just a few minutes.

"Oh, we're fine, I'm fine," he said, and then continued, "Actually, I have a question. What would make you itch?"

"I don't know, Dad. Where are you itching?"

"All over, I guess."

"More on your arms or legs or back?"

"Nope."

"Do you have hives or any kind of a rash?"

"No rash."

"Do you feel OK otherwise? I mean, do you have a sore throat or a fever or a cold or headache?"

"Uh-uh. I feel fine."

"How long has this been going on?" My father was hardly a complainer. I had seen him smash his thumb while moving a three-hundred-pound vending machine and not break into a sweat.

"Oh, four or five days, I guess."

"Are you itching a lot, Dad?"

"Yeah, a lot." Now I was getting puzzled and a bit worried. A side-effect of medical training is that you begin to imagine the worst when you or your family have any symptoms. I pictured the branching diagnostic diagram for pruritus, that is, itching.

"By any chance are you turning yellow, Dad? Are your eyes maybe a little yellow?"

"No."

"Uh, Seymour," my mother said.

I realized that she had not been competing for phone time. "I think they may be a little yellow."

"Really? Why haven't you told me?" he asked her.

"Is your urine dark, Dad?" I continued.

"Yeah, it is."

My heart sank. "And your stool has become lighter, sort of clay-colored?"

"Yeah, it's light; it's not right. How did you know that?" Thinking back on the sound of his voice, I imagine he was impressed at how astutely his son, the doctor, was zeroing in on the problem.

My mind was reeling. I leaned against the dresser in our bedroom, the phone to my ear, my forehead in my hand. He was dying.

He had told me enough for me to label his condition: painless jaundice. Jaundice is a discoloration of the skin that occurs when bilirubin, a breakdown product of red blood cells, is blocked from draining into the duodenum, backs up into the bloodstream, and gradually leaches into the skin. It makes a person yellow and itch. Not very specific, but enough to bring a familiar list of causes to mind. At the top of the list is cancer of the pancreas, and I was familiar with its diagnosis and typical course. When it begins to cause symptoms, it is predictably untreatable and uniformly fatal. Although other things can give rise to painless jaundice—tumors of the bile duct, gallbladder, and stomach, and an enigmatic condition known as primary biliary sclerosis—most of these are also lethal.

Occasionally, someone with painless jaundice will simply have scarring from peptic ulcers or obstruction from a gallstone, both of which are easily cured by surgery. It was possible, but the odds were not good. More honestly, at the time I knew it in my gut. Dad was dying.

My father was a remarkable, complex man, a study in contrasts. Born in 1918, he was the son of first-generation Jewish immigrants and grew up on the streets of Newark, New Jersey, during the twenties and thirties. Life was hard when Seymour was a boy, and it got a lot harder during the depression. My grandparents owned a small corner candy store that sold newspapers, magazines, cigarettes, and cigars and had a lunch counter and soda fountain. Mike Byock, my dad's father, also worked nights in the pressroom of the *Newark Evening News*. The family struggled to scrape by, and Sy's education took a back seat to getting the work of the store and the household done each day.

In the 1950s, when I was growing up in the New Jersey seashore suburbs, my father's motto was "It's nice to be nice." He was opinionated and could be stubborn, but his humor and kindness were what stood out. Morality and fairness were not just spouted for the sake of me and my sister. He went out of his way to help others. He was a mensch in the truest sense, instinctively and sincerely doing the right thing.

Our family owned a small cigarette wholesale and vending business that Sy had built from scratch. It was a modest operation, but it consumed endless hours of his time. As a boy I watched Dad glide comfortably through the bars, gas stations, and racetrack stables whose vending machines we routinely serviced. These were men's places, which could be crude and intimidating for an adolescent boy, but in physical stature and demeanor he was at home there. Yet he never went to bars, rarely drank, and abruptly quit smoking after the publicity about its ill effects began to build. Baking was his main passion and overeating his only vice.

Dad's other passion was people. Weekdays in the summer, while we rode between stops on the vending route, in an oversized step van with "S. Byock, Wholesale Cigarettes, Cigars and Vending Machines" stenciled on each side, he discoursed about the various characters who peopled his world. Tavern owners, public figures, relatives, shadowy friends from his past, guys he knew from the war: They were all grist for the mill. Dad was an astute observer of psychology and moral fiber; little escaped his attention, and his crisp assessments did not permit shades of gray. He was a man of principle who did not suffer fools kindly. Woe to him who wronged Seymour Byock or who was proven bereft of virtue. Sy chose mostly to avoid people he didn't like or respect, but their transgressions became teaching material for my ongoing moral education.

It would be wrong to give the impression that he was preoccupied with passing judgment on those around him. His preoccupation was business: taking orders, getting paid, making sure that the goods were delivered on time and the vending machines were functioning. Customers and suppliers knew Sy as honest, reliable, fair, and friendly. Family and friends who knew him well remarked on how much Sy liked people or, more accurately, how much he *enjoyed* people.

He especially enjoyed children. At various family gatherings Dad was a magnet for kids. With the infants he'd play "So, Big!" making eye contact and crooning until they smiled. With the older children he played games and little magic tricks, most notably "Acka Mazzacka!"

I had mixed feelings about this game, for it required an accomplice, which was usually me, and it became a nuisance before long. Prior to any family party Dad would grab a handful of pennies. My instructions were to discreetly slip a penny beneath lamps, ashtrays, or candy dishes on arrival at our relative's home. After the first few times we did this—and there were many—I didn't have to tell him where I had stashed them. At each family celebration, it wouldn't be long before a swarm of children formed—from as young as three to as old as twelve—all demanding to play "Acka Mazzacka!" Dad would show them a penny and make them blow on it or rub it. He would then slowly intone "Aaaa, kaaa, maaa, zaaa, kaaa," palm the penny, and point to the object beneath which it had been telekinetically projected. Squeals of amazement and delight greeted the discovery of the transported coin, followed inevitably by loud calls to "Do it again, Seymour. Do it again!"

My father was a handsome man in his youth, but World War II and years of worrying about the business and how, with only an eighth-grade education, he could support his wife and two children took a visible toll. My earliest images are of him mostly bald with deep furrows in his brow and a certain seriousness or reserve in his expression. Physically, Sy was distinguished by his big nose, which was easily the size of Jimmy Durante's, but what I remember most about his face were his eyes. The only expression he tried to hide was worry, although over the years I began to recognize a certain wounded darkness in his eyes. Despite the undercurrent of worry, which was usually over money, and tides of regret over his lack of education, Sy never lost his capacity for joy. When I was a young boy, my dad's smile was better than a new toy; his eyes became so warm and engaging that he was irresistible. No wonder the children loved him.

It seemed incomprehensible that all this could be lost. Before I hung up the phone, I insisted that my father see Stuart, his internist and a distant cousin, the next day. Two days later he had an ultrasound examination of his liver and gallbladder and a subsequent CT scan, which found a mass at the head of the pancreas. The next day he underwent exploratory surgery, during which the surgeon created alternate routes for food and digestive juices around the increasingly constricted intersection of the duodenum, pancreas, and biliary tree and took multiple needle biopsies from the mass.

Examination of both the immediate frozen sections and, four days later, the permanent microscopic specimens showed only inflammation; no cancer cells were found. Mom, Dad, and my sister, Molly, were all delighted and very encouraged. His doctors were evasive. I was furious, especially at Stuart. He knew exactly what was going on but was avoiding leveling with my father. Cancer of the pancreas often incites inflammation around itself as the blocked enzymes try to digest the glandular tissue that produced them. It's fairly common in these situations for biopsy specimens to be negative or inconclusive. My father deserved to know that his time was limited; instead, Stuart dangled a vague, faint hope and deflected questions by directing attention to postoperative issues. He said things like "You're going to get stronger and be back to feeling yourself before long."

Stuart's love for my dad, his favorite cousin, and my dad's trust in him, limited my ability to intervene. If I had it to do over again, I would press hard to change doctors then and there. Looking back, I think that Stuart should have been relieved of his responsibility for my dad's medical care and relegated to a supporting role as a member of our extended family. As things unfolded, the problem proved to be continuing.

After the surgery Dad indeed recovered rapidly, and within two weeks he was back at work. When I inquired about their plans for the future, Mom and Dad said that they were just going to wait and see. They made no plans to sell the business or to vacation and held no real discussions of end-of-life issues. My attempts to raise serious subjects were unwelcome, an assault on hope. So I kept my concerns to myself, and I was alone with the truth and my grief.

Naturally, the miles between us and my intense work schedule contributed to my isolation. I spoke by phone with Molly, who lived in New York City, and tried to express my concerns. She, too, needed to believe there was a chance that Dad would get well. Most of the time I was so busy that it was easy not to think about what was happening in New Jersey. The phone reports were all good—no signs of problems. Six weeks after Dad's surgery, Molly, Anita, and I surprised Mom and Dad by meeting them as they were walking into a Broadway show. We had given them the tickets as a Hanukkah present. During dinner after the show, their pleasure with our visit turned into jubilation when we told them Anita was pregnant. Their first grandchild would arrive in June.

Dad looked well—a little thinner from the surgery, but strong. He was eating well, had no complaints of pain, and seemed to have as much energy as ever. It was a happy time, and it seemed right to let it be. The only gloomy remark that week came from Dad, while he and I were driving to a bus depot to fix a jammed cigarette machine. He said, "I hope I'm around to see that kid of yours grow up."

"I hope you are, too, Dad. I really hope you are, too."

My father and I had become good friends. We usually spoke intimately while doing something or going somewhere, usually in a car, sitting shoulder to shoulder, facing ahead. This habit came from years of working together like this, after school, on weekends, and most summers. The transition from boy-and-his-Dad to father-son friendship had not been smooth. During my high-school years, the Vietnam War had been fought every night on a small screen in our kitchen and at our dinner table.

My father was a lifelong Democrat who simply could not believe that Lyndon Johnson and Robert McNamara could be wrong. "What about the Gulf of Tonkin?" he'd yell. I would yell back, "We need to make peace, not war!"

As a freshman in college in 1970 with the draft lottery number of 13, I studied Selective Service regulations, prepared my conscientious objector claim, and memorized maps of Canada. Dad hated war and lost no love for the military, but, as a veteran of World War II, he also hated draft dodgers. "This will follow you forever!" he'd exclaim. "You're ruining your life." Ultimately, it was my appearance, not my politics, that confirmed my moral degeneration in his eyes.

When I came home for spring break that year, my hair had passed my ears en route to my shoulders. My allowing my curls to grow was proof to Seymour that his son had been lost to drugs and rock-and-roll. For two years Dad and I rarely spoke and carefully avoided confrontation. My admission to medical school eased tensions; once again, he spoke with me rather than at me.

During vacations in medical school I still occasionally ran the business for a week to allow my parents to get away on vacation. I would hear from the customers how proud my dad was of me. "Really?" I'd say. "What makes you think so?"

"Oh, yes, he talks about you all the time!" And they would recount recent events in my life; passing some big exam or getting engaged. At first I was amazed; Dad never told me he was proud or seemed even to remember any of the details of my life. This was his way. Part of it, I am now certain, was knowing that his customers would tell me.

As father and son our wounds healed, and a new phase in our relationship began in April 1978 when I married Anita. As long as he lived, Dad spoke of our wedding day as "one of the happiest days of my life." His son was a doctor. He had a daughter-in-law whom he loved, and who loved him, and the promise of grandchildren. His dream, which had been his parents' dream and, before them, the dream of his immigrant grandparents, had been fulfilled. These were the best of times. But to me, those times now seemed long ago and brief.

In May, four months after his surgery, Dad began having a deep ache in the pit of his gut that the Darvon he had been given after surgery did not touch. A repeat CT scan showed that the pancreatic mass was much larger and metastatic nodules of tumor were in the liver. The diagnosis was now confirmed. While I was saddened by the test results, I was, I admitted to myself, relieved that the secret of his illness could now be shared. An oncologist encouraged Dad to take mild chemotherapy once weekly and referred him for radiation therapy "to slow the growth of the lesion." I managed a week off and flew to New Jersey.

Each morning I drove my dad to the cancer center and back. We usually took local roads made familiar by years of vending routes, slipping through the neighborhoods of Ocean Township, Eatontown, Little Silver, and Red Bank to avoid traffic and break the monotony. He began talking seriously about selling the business. During the two and a half hours or so our daily outing consumed, he also told me what it was like to be dying, as, years earlier, he had taught me about life and about right and wrong.

Twenty minutes into our wait at the cancer center one morning, as Dad sat resting with his eyes closed and I flipped through a magazine, he said, "They give you only six months to live, and then, little by little, they take it back from you."

Another lesson came on the way home from the cancer center when I suggested that we stop and have coffee with some friends who owned a luncheonette on the boardwalk in Long Branch. To my surprise, he declined.

"I don't want them to see me like this."

"Like what, Dad?"

"Well, like this. I don't look so good. I look sick, and I think I smell bad, sicklike, too."

"Dad, are you embarrassed by being ill?"

From the passenger's seat he turned his head to look at me. "Yeah, it's embarrassing. And it makes other people uncomfortable."

I kept my eyes on the road, blinked back tears, and tightened my jaw, hoping he wouldn't see. Here I was with the man whose very being defined pride for me. Pride was being at my father's side, pride was being seen with him in public; my personal pride arose from my father's approval of my accomplishments. It took a moment to make sure my throat was clear before speaking, "I don't think you should feel embarrassed about being sick. I'm still really proud you're my Dad."

Lila was born in June 1980, and three weeks later we flew to New Jersey. In spite of the radiation treatments and chemotherapy, Dad's health was continuing to deteriorate. He was losing weight and becoming weak. His strong tenor voice had become raspy and strained. I suspected that the tumor was robbing him of energy and appetite, something all cancers can do but for which pancreatic cancer is infamous. As we visited and celebrated the new life among us, I noticed that Dad's appetite was not that bad. My own evening forays to the kitchen uncovered another cause for his weight loss.

Dad had always been heavy, and he had been diagnosed years earlier as a borderline diabetic. He also had high cholesterol and a strong family history of heart disease, and thus, under doctor's orders, had long since given up eating eggs and red meat. When radiation therapy was started to his pancreas, the source of the body's insulin, Dad had been given special testing strips and told to check his urine for sugar. These "dipsticks" on occasion began to show that he was "spilling sugar" in his urine, so Mom had tightened up on his dietary habits, feeding him dietetic this and nonfat that. Seymour Byock, for whom eating was a central joy in life, had been sentenced to culinary confinement.

Dad and I began stopping for lunch on the way home from the cancer center. It was our guilty secret, but he enjoyed the hot dogs and pastries. Remarkably, his famous appetite had not yet succumbed to the cancer. For a few days I bought real ice cream and whole milk under the guise of wanting them for myself. While Mom understood why he should be allowed to eat anything he wanted, my arguments never quite swayed her. Medical degree or not, I was her son; it would require a call from the doctor for her to change.

I had not spoken with Stuart since the earlier trip home, when I had spent a few unsatisfactory minutes with him and had asked him in earnest, "Don't you think you should level with my father and let him know that we strongly suspect he has cancer and a limited time to live?"

He had answered, with quick condescension and a lecturing tone, "With a few years of practice, Ira, you'll understand that a doctor must not destroy hope. I know what I'm doing." I was too stunned, appalled, and exasperated to reply, but I immediately understood the arrogance of a doctor's paternalism. Hope? Hope for what—to live forever?! What about truth? What about respect for a person's right to make choices in his life? Who elected him to make critical decisions for my father that had nothing to do with medicine!?

Now I called Stuart at his office.

"Stuart, I came home thinking that the twenty-five pounds Dad has lost since spring was due to tumor anorexia. It turns out that he is literally starving to death because Mom is fixated on his diabetic and cardiac diet. She's certain that if she allows him to spill sugar in his urine, she will kill him. As a result, almost nothing he is eating has any real food value.

"I have been trying to convince her to change, but she needs to hear it from you. He should be eating any damn thing he wants, including ice cream and eggs and steaks, as long as he's able to digest them. If he needs insulin, and he probably will, then we'll deal with that." I spoke slowly and deliberately, explaining the events and the plan for care as I would to an intern under my supervision. I let hang the unspoken question: "How could you have allowed this to happen?"

"I'll call her tonight," he replied contritely.

Once he was fed, despite his cancer, Sy gained weight and regained a bit of his strength and sense of humor. His voice was less hoarse. Within a month of liberalizing his diet he did require insulin to keep his blood glucose in the nearly normal range. This was easily managed, with a single notable exception.

One evening in late September, now back in California, I was on call, writing orders at a patient's bedside in the ICU (intensive care unit), when the hospital operator paged me and told me to call home. Anita told me that Mom and Molly had just called from New Jersey and were very worried that Dad was acting strangely. I called them immediately. "He's become confused within the past half-hour or so," said Molly. "We called Stuart at home, and he said it was probably a tumor in his liver causing problems, and he wants us to come by first thing in the morning for a blood test. Is there anything we can do tonight?"

"Is he in pain?"

"No, I don't think so, Ira. He's here with me and looks comfortable, but he's not making sense," my sister replied.

"Mom, is one side of him weak? Is he shuffling one leg or not moving one of his arms?"

"No."

"How about his face, is it symmetrical or is one side sort of flat?"

"No, I think it's all normal."

"Is he sweating?"

"Yeah, Ira, he is."

"Put Dad on the phone, Molly."

All I could make out from Dad was "Hello." Everything else was gibberish.

"I think he's having an insulin reaction. I want you to get three or four teaspoons of sugar into him as soon as possible. Right now. He can have orange juice, too. If he's not better in ten minutes, call an ambulance. Is that clear? Got it?"

I called back in twenty minutes. "Oh, Ira, he's better, thank God!" my mother said.

Hearing my name, my father picked up the phone. "What the hell was that about?! That's the strangest thing that ever happened to me."

"An insulin reaction, Dad. Your blood sugar got too low. Remember the nurse told you about that when she was teaching you to give yourself the shots? It's not dangerous, as long as it's treated."

The immediate crisis was over, but I was not relieved. As I thought about what might have happened had I not been a doctor, I shuddered. I struggled to speak calmly. "Tomorrow morning, keep the appointment, but I want you to see Joel Shapiro." Joel Shapiro was a gastroenterologist and one of Stuart's partners. "I really want him to be your doctor. OK?"

"OK, Ira. Thank God you were there."

"Yes, Mom, thank God I was here."

"We love you," they said in chorus.

"I love you, too." I hung up. Now, I was sweating. I called Anita; as I told her the story, I began to cry.

In the early winter, a year after his surgery, Dad began again losing weight and becoming weaker. Although we put him on supplements like

Ensure and gave him vitamins and pancreatic enzymes to swallow, no dietary trick would work this time. He had already lived months beyond the norm for pancreatic carcinoma. He accepted that time was limited, but he wanted to make the best use of what remained. The business had been sold, fiscal affairs were in order, and visiting family and friends had become the highest priority. A trip to Fresno was hastily planned to coincide with his birthday.

Anita and I met my parents' plane late in the evening. As we greeted each other and walked toward the baggage claim area, I thought that Dad looked yellow. "Maybe he's just sallow," I thought to myself. "Maybe it's just the fluorescent lights." The next morning I knew he was jaundiced.

"Dad, you're yellow again," I said, as we were sitting down to have coffee.

"I am? Again?" he looked bewildered.

"What did Dr. Shapiro say when you saw him the other day?"

"He had an emergency at the hospital, so I didn't see him. They just drew my blood at the office, and we're supposed to call in a few days."

I was glad he had not seen the doctor, because he would never have let Dad make the trip. Now that he was here, I could take care of him in my medical universe. This, at least, was comforting. As a senior resident, I was convinced that our dingy, underfunded, overcrowded hospital gave the best medical care in the world. While other centers might have famous names and reputations, I *knew* the faculty who constituted Valley Medical Center (VMC). Together we had walked, time and again, into the chaos of blood, agony, or despair, and together, time and again, we had brought order: cure, or at least comfort. I would have trusted them with my life; now I trusted them with my Dad's. Before noon Dad and I were at the VMC lab having his blood drawn for a blood count and chemical panel. While we waited for the lab results, I gave him a nickel tour of the hospital and ducked in to talk with one of the faculty attending physicians who was an expert in interventional radiology. I explained my father's case and we discussed the need for an ultrasound study to look at his liver. The blood test results came back within an hour. His serum bilirubin was elevated, consistent with his jaundiced appearance, and the liver enzymes were elevated in a pattern that suggested obstruction of bile drainage with secondary hepatic cellular inflammation. All, unfortunately, as expected. The ultrasound examination revealed that the obstruction of bile was within the liver and from a metastatic tumor. This news was particularly bad, because it meant the obstruction could not be treated by placing a plastic channel, or stent, through the obstructed bile ducts.

By four o'clock we were home, relating the news to Mom and Anita.

"Well, what are they going to do?" The tone of Mom's voice echoed with questions and unspoken demands: *He was doing so well, how could this have happened? He had the surgery to keep from being obstructed. What did we do wrong? We were so careful, and we've been hurrying to make this trip; this can't be the end. We're not ready. It's not fair! There must be something that can be done!*

I listened to what remained unsaid. My heart ached as my mind raced to formulate an adequate response.

Anita came to my rescue. "Who have you talked to at the hospital? Who are you going to have him see?"

"I've already spoken with Marcel Lagrange, the radiologist, and we talked with him about our options. We think that probably the best next step is to place a catheter into the largest collection of bile within the liver." Under ultrasound guidance and with a local anesthetic, a needle would be inserted below the right ribs into the liver and a catheter threaded into the largest "lake" of bile, allowing it and its tributaries to drain into a removable bag attached to the skin. It could all be done as an outpatient procedure; if all went well, Dad would be home in a matter of hours.

"Dr. Lagrange can do it tomorrow afternoon. And tonight I plan on talking to Dr. Bellows." I looked at my parents. "He's a really good oncologist. I also want to talk to Dr. Catellano, one of my teachers who is a gastroenterologist, and get both their ideas. And before it gets too late tonight, I'll call Joel Shapiro back home, let him know what's going on, and see what he thinks."

"Oh, OK." Mom sounded relieved; at least there was a plan. But I noticed how tired she looked. The illness was my father's, but the ordeal was hers as well. I thought that as emotionally hard as the current crisis was for me, it was relatively easy for me, being inside the medical system. I could only imagine how scary and overwhelming it must be for them, dealing with the various problems and crises in New Jersey.

"Dad, do you understand what I've been talking about? Do you have other questions about the procedure, or other things I can answer, or that I should ask the other doctors?"

"No." It was classic Sy. He knew the score, the problem was straightforward, and we had a game plan. It wasn't pretty and it wasn't fun, but it had to be done.

Complaining was not Sy's style. He didn't even complain the next day during the "percutaneous, transhepatic, biliary pigtail catheter placement," although it ended up taking twice as long as expected and was much harder on him than I had hoped. I knew he was in pain because he wasn't kibitzing with the young radiology technicians who were helping Dr. Lagrange, and there were beads of sweat on his forehead. We started an IV, and I gave him a small amount of morphine, which helped a lot. At the end of the procedure the bile was drained but so was Dad—utterly exhausted from the pain and woozy and queasy from the medicine. We decided that he should be admitted for IV fluids and observation, and I asked Gerritt Smith to be his doctor.

I had my pick of admitting teams and I chose Gerritt, not because of our friendship or his irreverent sense of humor, though I considered both to be assets. Even as a resident, Gerritt was the sort of physician who is sometimes referred to as a doctor's doctor; confident in his knowledge and his craft, he also had a heart and was not ashamed to show it. Dad liked him immediately. I was present while Gerritt took a history and reiterated the plan for Dad to hear. I used the opportunity to discuss Dad's preferences regarding cardiopulmonary resuscitation (CPR). If a patient was in the hospital and had a heart attack, ten people would respond with tubes and chest compressions and electrical shocks to his chest, unless a doctor wrote a "do not resuscitate" order. Dad and I had once before talked about these things, but it had seemed theoretical. Even now it was just a precaution, part of complete planning. As tired and weak as he was, Dad's response to the question of whether he would want CPR was characteristically terse: "Shit, no. If I die, just bury me."

In the early evening Mom, Anita, and Lila came to the hospital to visit. Dad was already feeling better and had been able to eat a little dinner. He was even able to muster enough strength to hold his grandchild for a few minutes. We left at about nine P.M., anticipating that he would be discharged in the middle of the next day.

The next morning Gerritt met me as I walked onto the ward. His somber expression told me something was wrong.

"Ira, your father had a rough night. About one-thirty he spiked a fever and had chills, and about fifteen minutes later dropped his pressure. There were a few minutes when things looked real shaky, but he pulled out of it."

"What happened? Why wasn't I called?!" I looked at Gerritt with annoyance.

"They called me, and I came right in. We cultured him up and I put in a central line. If he hadn't stabilized quickly, I would have called you." As he spoke and I noticed the tiredness in his eyes, I understood. Gerritt was Sy's doctor, and he was doing his job. Part of his job was to allow me to be family here, son to my dad.

"Thanks, Gerritt. Thanks a lot."

As I walked into Dad's room I was struck by how small he looked. Above him an oscilloscope traced the electrical activity of his heart, and chrome IV poles framed the head of his bed. The IV in his left arm was attached to a bottle of saline, and a plastic bag of antibiotic solution was piggy-backed into the tubing at his wrist. Another IV, this one a large-bore catheter that entered the subclavian vein just below the midportion of his right collarbone, was attached to a three-way stopcock valve. Through it saline was flowing at a to-keep-open rate; also attached to the stopcock was a manometer that provided measurement of central venous pressure, a guide to his volume status. The third channel led to a dopamine drip with its own infusion pump that was standing by, just in case that medication was needed to raise his blood pressure. Oxygen tubing ran from his nose. A call button was pinned to his pillow. A urine bottle hung at his bedrail. On his bedside table was a cafeteria tray with his untouched breakfast, a pitcher of water, and a menu of the next day's meals.

"Hi, Dad." I managed a simper. "How are you doing?"

"Oh . . . it was . . . a lousy night." He whispered, not from breathlessness but from sheer lack of energy. His pallid complexion held little more color than the sheets on his bed.

My father was dying. I had become almost accustomed to saying the phrase in conversations with close friends, but now I knew it in a new way. Dad was dying; actively, perhaps *imminently*.

As if to reassure me that he was not dead yet, Dad opened his eyes and whispered, "You know what? That son-of-a-bitch . . . friend of yours . . . Gerritt . . . told me jokes . . . the whole time . . . he was torturing me." He closed his eyes with a wan smile.

I leaned over and kissed his forehead. "I love you, Dad. Get some rest, and I'll be back a little later." As I was leaving, I reached under the sheets and tickled the sole of his foot. "And Sy, no more shenanigans, OK?"

Mom was shaken by the news of Dad's near demise and, at the hospital an hour later, by his appearance. But together she, Anita, and I regrouped. The samples of blood and bile tested grew a coliform bacteria that was sensitive to two of the antibiotics, so after forty-eight hours without a fever he was changed to oral medications, and the next morning we took him home.

He slept the rest of that day but, with some coaxing, was able to sit with us during dinner. He took only sips of juice and chicken broth and spoke very little, as if conserving his strength. Lila was asleep in her Sears wind-up swing, rocking and clicking beside our dining room table. After quietly looking at the baby, Anita, and me, he spoke. His voice was strained, but his determination was clear. "I want to give you a gift. I want you to go out and buy one of those video recorders and cameras. I want her to know who I was."

"Oh, Dad. We'll do it if you want, but I promise you she'll know who you are."

Anita rose and put her arms around him. "I love you, Dad. I promise, too, our daughter will know who you are." She began to cry as she hugged him.

"I love you, too, honey." He patted her arm and recited one of his famous Syisms: "Don't worry, it'll all come out in the wash." This stain, of course, would not come out; his absence would indelibly color our lives.

Despite Anita's training as a physician's assistant and my own expertise, caring for my father was not easy. Yet it did seem natural. If we had had less clinical experience, I'm certain we would have hired visiting nurses or brought in hospice. As it happened, Esperanza, the hospice affiliated with VMC and which I had cofounded, was still rudimentary and offered little we could not do for ourselves.

As I look back it seems ironic, yet fitting, that what I really needed to know about care of the dying I learned not in medical school or my residency training but from the care my parents had given to Leah, my maternal grandmother. I was eight years old when Gramma Leah had her stroke. She nearly died abruptly, but over the first few days she stabilized and slowly improved enough to be discharged to Kessler Institute, a state-of-the-art rehabilitation hospital in northern New Jersey. Months and months of therapy left Nano, as Molly and I called her, able to barely communicate and to minimally assist with her own feeding and toileting. Money and insurance coverage were gone. Nursing home placement was advised, but it was out of the question; my parents took her home. Nano lived with us for the next year. Mom shouldered the heaviest load, but our entire family took part in her care. A nurse and a physical therapist visited weekly and taught us what to do. While my Mom's care for her mother might have been taken for granted, I was struck, even as a boy, by my father's unabashed tenderness toward Leah.

With our love and care, Nano steadily improved and eventually returned home with my grandfather, Harry. With help she could manage her own household. We made the hour's drive north every weekend to visit, take her shopping, and do chores around the house. Twice a month for the next twenty years my Dad also did another thing she could not do for herself. With a stainless-steel basin and special clippers reserved for the task, a ritual developed: she soaked her feet in soapy water, and then while he bantered, relayed gossip, and told her fibs and bawdy stories, he cut her toenails. This ritual continued well after Dad had himself become ill, until she died in September 1980.

Actually, Dad required little care when he was first discharged from VMC. He rested all afternoon, garnering strength, and on his sixty-third birthday we celebrated in the evening with a sumptuous meal and home-baked cake. It was a happy time. Nothing was said about how fleeting and precious it was. As I look back, these two weeks seem an almost idyllic respite from the violence of his illness and inexorable decline. Dad regained some of the ground he had lost. He was able to get around by himself and do all of his self-care, with Mom and me managing his medications and changing the adhesive ostomy bag at his right flank into which the catheter drained. We played in the park with Lila and shopped for a video camera. Mom indulged herself in buying little dresses and tchotchkes for Lila. Dad went along on as many of these ventures as his energy—and patience—would allow. One of us was always with him if he chose to stay home.

Anita and I lived in an older home in the neighborhood of the community college. Over these few weeks our one-bath, two-bedroom, stucco Spanish-style home had gradually acquired a quasi-clinical decor. A front room that doubled as a guest room was now the sickroom. We rented a queen-size bed with a firm mattress and placed our dilapidated sofa bed in storage. The urine bottle became a familiar fixture in the room, and a portable bedside commode had been tucked behind the closet door since Sy's most recent trip to the hospital. In the living room stood an aluminum walker that he refused to use. In the kitchen, cans of Ensure formed a pyramid on the counter. Jars of Metamucil and plastic bottles filled with medicines and vitamins were neatly arranged between the toaster and the windowsill. A three-ring binder containing the current medication log, selected medical records, and a copy of Sy's living will stood upright alongside the cookbooks. We had cleared a vegetable drawer in the refrigerator for other medicines, a liquid morphine solution, and two types of suppositories—one for constipation, another for nausea. Also in that drawer were several vials of injectable pain medicine Gerritt had prescribed.

One morning Mom woke me at around six o'clock; Dad had awakened in a cold sweat and was complaining of his side hurting. Within minutes I pinpointed his liver as the source of pain, undoubtedly due to another infection, and we immediately took him to VMC. Within an hour he was admitted to a semiprivate room.

An announcer called the play-by-play for a baseball game in Spanish from a television in the corner of Sy's room while I started an IV, drew blood, and collected new samples of bile for culture. As soon as the radiology department could take him, I sent him down for a chest X-ray and another ultrasound test. Gerritt, the attending physicians, and I assumed that the collections of bile within the liver had again become infected, but we wanted to make sure he didn't have pneumonia or an abscess that needed draining. Dr. Lagrange repositioned the biliary catheter for better drainage. Dad tolerated all this without complaint, but it sapped his energy and washed him out for the next few days. On the fourth day, I knew he was a little better because his main concern was how for his new roommate, who had been admitted the day before. Dad was worried about the late-night wailing in Spanish that he could not help hearing. I inquired and learned that his roommate, Jorge, an undocumented migrant worker, had been in a serious car accident and had been told the night before that his four-year-old son had died in the crash. Though Jorge spoke almost no English and Dad even less Spanish, by the time of his discharge three days later, Sy and Jorge had somehow become good friends.

Early on a Saturday afternoon, two days after he had come home for the second time, Dad and I sat together on the covered porch in our backyard. I had just returned from weekend rounds, and he had just finished breakfast and come outside to sit in the shade. At first neither of us said much, and I busied myself adjusting the video camera atop a sturdy tripod. While Dad felt self-conscious about his appearance in public, he seemed completely unaffected by the presence of the camera. I focused it and pushed *record*, knowing we were about to have an important discussion, and wanting to capture every fleeting minute of our time.

Mom and Dad had been scheduled to leave two weeks earlier, but when he had gone into the hospital their return had, naturally, been postponed. I'd begun to worry whether he would make it back to New Jersey. We hadn't talked about it for months, but I knew the hospital in New Jersey was where he wanted to die.

Dad sat in a padded wooden armchair I had dragged out onto the porch for my parents' visit. Although it was already seventy-five degrees out, he asked me to help him on with his beige cotton jacket, and he wore his light blue summer fedora. When I watch the video now, it is as if the mental image I carry of my father has been digitally morphed with that of a famine victim. He is all bones, his nose more prominent than ever, and, even seated, his once-heavyset frame seems almost lanky.

"Mom told me you ate well." For weeks the status of his caloric intake had replaced the weather as preferred small talk.

"Yeah, it was good," he responded, without emotion.

"Did Molly call this morning?"

"Yeah, she called, but I told her to stay home." He looked out at the remnants of last year's garden, his chin cradled in his left hand in a pensive pose. Molly had just spent a week with them in New Jersey, and he knew she needed to be back at work in New York City.

"What do you see happening after you get home to Jersey?"

"Dr. Markham will find something to do for me." He referred to his oncologist. After a long pause he added emphatically, "I just want to get stronger so I can move myself!" Another pause. "That's all. I want to lay out in my backyard."

He was somber. Our conversation had an eerie, matter-of-fact tone, despite our mutual acknowledgment of the gravity of the situation.

I pulled aimlessly at the crab grass that had overgrown the flower beds on which I squatted.

"One problem with being at home is going to be the stairs." The small trilevel tract home would be confining for him, even now.

"If I am too weak, I'll go to the hospital." He turned, meeting my gaze for the first time, and, wordlessly, with his eyes and an upward turn of his palm, asked, *What else is there to do?*

"So you still see yourself eventually going to the hospital?"

"I don't know. When I'm at home I might just rest."

"Dad, I think one possibility, if things get to be too much at home, might be getting the hospice team involved. They are really set up to do this sort of thing and they could provide Mom with the support that she'd need. Another possibility might be the hospice unit at Riverside. It's better suited than the hospital to people who are sick but not needing a lot of acute treatment. It's something to keep in mind."

"Yeah." He nodded slightly in reply.

We sat without speaking for a long time. A minor commotion next door, where a garage sale was in progress, provided a momentary distraction.

"Well, shoot, I wish things were different, Dad."

"Me, too." He answered quickly, as if I had spoken his thoughts. There was sorrow in his raspy voice.

"I know it's selfish, but I wish you could stay here," I said, as I pulled weeds. He was absorbed in thought and his expression remained unchanged. But he didn't say no. A month before he would have rejected the idea outright. I was trying not to pressure him, but we needed to be ready to do something. Yet on any given day I don't think any of us knew quite what. Dad's physical condition changed almost daily; at the moment of our conversation he was still too weak to consider traveling, yet he seemed to be getting a bit stronger. But I knew that things could take a turn for the worse in any hour.

Two years ago, the idea of dying at home would have been completely foreign to Sy. During his lifetime, medical care had advanced by leaps and bounds; antibiotics, surgery, and cardiac care were routinely saving people who would have succumbed to their diseases without these miracles of modern medicine. In the culture of his time, being in the hospital provided assurance that "everything possible" would be done for a loved one. Even before he became ill, we had had discussions about the work I was doing with hospice and the advantages of home-centered and family-centered care for people who were dying. When I was in New Jersey, we had talked about it again, though still within the context of my work. He had seemed interested, though he had mentioned that he saw advantages to being in the hospital so that Mom would not suffer.

On Wednesday morning he complained about his side hurting. For Sy to report pain without being asked meant it was serious. When I examined him, the right upper portion of his abdomen around the liver was tender. I gave him an injection of pain medication and he was able to sleep. When he awakened from his nap, he was chilled and had a 101-degree fever.

I immediately started him on an additional oral antibiotic, per the contingency plan that Gerritt, the other doctors, and I had worked out. I knew it was a temporizing measure at best, and Dad needed to know it. He was lying on his bed in the guest room, his head and upper chest propped up on a red corduroy reading pillow. The windows were all open; a gentle breeze made our batik curtains billow into the room. He was awake but very weak. His skin was almost gray and his brow was beaded with sweat. I pulled up a chair to the side of the bed and put my hand on his forearm. "We have a couple of serious things to talk about."

He looked at me briefly and then turned back to facing straight ahead, as if to say "OK, I'm ready." Once again, we would conduct business shoulder to shoulder.

"Dad, the infection has obviously returned. It's pretty clear that the antibiotics pills aren't going to cut it by themselves. If we're going to get you home, we have to move quickly. I know you hate being in the hospital, but if we put you in for a day or two we could pump some more heavy-duty IV antibiotics into your system and, hopefully, get things back in control. I could then fly home with you to make sure that things go all right. We would have to leave as soon as you were discharged, because I think all of it will only buy a fairly small amount of time."

He continued to look ahead, knowing I had not finished.

"You're the boss, and we'll do anything you say. I know you've talked about wanting to get back to New Jersey and wanting to be in the hospital when you die, but it's important for you to know that Anita and I would like to care for you right here, in our home. We've talked with Mom, and she is OK with staying here if you are. We are already set up to care for you; everything we need is right here. More important, we *want to take care of you*. We love you so much, it wouldn't seem right to have strangers taking care of you when we could be doing it."

Dad slowly turned his head and looked into my eyes. My efforts to be matter-of-fact in this exchange had collapsed, and I was no longer bothering to blink back my tears. I tried to smile while I held his gaze, wanting him to know how deeply I meant what I had said. I expected him to ask questions, but he didn't. Instead, after what seemed like minutes, he again turned to stare past the foot of the bed, laid his head back against the pillow, closed his eyes, and nodded.

"You mean you'll stay with us here? You'll let us care for you here until you die?" Once again, he nodded.

"Oh, Dad, thank you! Oh, Dad, I love you so much!" I kissed his forehead. Until that moment I had not realized—had not allowed myself to consider—how important his decision was for me. I knelt at his bedside, gently laid my head in his lap, and openly wept, while he stroked my hair.

I believe my father figured out at that moment that Mom and Anita and I had more at stake than he did in where and by whom he was cared for. He understood this before I did. It might sound selfish, but it really did matter more to us than him. We had more at risk. When I asked him to stay, I was speaking out of my own needs and love, and also out of pain, exhaustion, and confusion. I imagine that Dad's preference even then would have been to be in a hospital; it was less messy, physically and emotionally. He acceded to our request for the sake of Mom and Anita and me. We all needed to care for him—even more than we knew. He no longer really cared where he was, but he knew we did. At that moment he stopped resisting his physical dependence and turned toward it, as if acceptance of his naked, utter vulnerability was the next landmark on his route out of life. His decision to allow himself to be totally cared for—dressed and undressed, toileted and turned—by his family was his final gift to us.

Once he had decided to die in our home, Dad knew there was nothing left undone. His affairs were in order. Love had been expressed. Goodbyes had been said. He took his pain medications and Tylenol for fever, but otherwise he accepted only sips of ice water or juice. He spent his time resting quietly with his eyes closed, but he aroused easily when one of us spoke his name, as if we had interrupted a train of thought. Often we just sat with him, at times placing a cool washcloth on his warm forehead or placing small amounts of water from a straw on his tongue.

He seemed withdrawn, almost as if busy on some inward endeavor. Saying "I love you Dad" might evoke a whispered "I love you, too" before his attention drifted elsewhere. If his eyes opened, it was only briefly.

On Friday, forty-eight hours after his decision to die in our home, Dad slipped beyond responding. We still talked softly to him as we moistened his lips, bathed him, or changed his pajamas. At this point our "I love you, Dad," or Mom's "I love you, Seymour," needed no response. We just needed to say them. At this point the work of dying was physical, like the early labor of childbirth. I thought how appropriate the obstetrical term *labor* was; it looked like hard work. Toward evening Dad's condition changed again, now bringing to mind a late phase of labor, also aptly named: transition. Dad was sweating, his heart raced, and his breathing was rapid. His body was working toward the completion of his dying. There was no way to know what he was feeling. We sat by him and held his hand and adjusted his pillows and kept his lips moist and his forehead cool. And we watched. I continued to give pain medication, by injection, whenever he seemed uncomfortable.

There was little for us to do, and none of us wanted to leave his side. This time felt sacred, but not in the way that scripture, liturgy, or chants are sacred. There was a luminous—or numinous—quality to the moment. A great man was passing. So much was being lost, but oh, what a treasure he was. What a privilege to have known him, to have loved and been loved by him and to have been raised by him.

As we sat around his bed and sipped coffee through the long hours of that last night, Mom and I told old Byock family stories that Anita had never heard. Sleeplessness had left us emotionally defenseless, and our shared sadness contributed to a bleary camaraderie. We cried in sadness but also in joy.

At two-thirty A.M., Anita and I lay down for a nap. Less than twenty minutes later, Mom woke us to report that Dad's breathing had abruptly changed. He appeared suddenly to be relaxed, as if the work, whatever it had been, was over. He was peaceful, no longer sweating, and his breathing was easy and deep, though irregular. Mom stood touching his foot, and Anita and I sat on each side of his bed touching his arms, as he drew his last breath and left. For the next hour we continued our vigil: hugging one another, crying intermittently, grieving openly and together.

At four A.M. we called Molly in New York. Our father was dead. It seemed incomprehensible. It was still dark when I called Gerritt at the hospital to let him know my father had died and to thank him again for all he had done. We called the mortuary, and at eight A.M. they took Dad away. It was so real, yet so unreal. Dad was dead. The world had forever changed, yet it still turned; the sun still came up. The next day Mom and I boarded a plane and took Sy home.

Two

Questioning Assumptions and Dawning Awareness: My Journey

Dad's dying jolted me, and provided me with powerful, if unwanted, lessons about dying and about life. Like anyone who loses someone he loves, I groped to make sense out of the inherent meaninglessness of the event. Losing him, the thought that I would never again see him, caused me so much pain that if someone had asked at the time what I had learned from his death, I might have been offended. Yet I asked myself the same question.

Death was beyond anything I could probe; however, the time of my father's dying, especially the last months and weeks, pervaded my thoughts and permeated my dreams. The memories were full of compelling images and poignant vignettes that connected me with a deep, aching sadness. Something about that time was also, undeniably, precious.

I had grown accustomed to seeing death through medical eyes; my father's cancer forced me to experience terminal illness from the vantage point of a patient's family. Furthermore, through my father's eyes, I glimpsed dying from the point of view of a person living in the shadow of death. Dad's dying was certainly not the happiest time in our family's life, but as a family we had never been more intimate, more open, or more openly loving. His illness allowed us, I could say forced us, to talk about the things that mattered: family, our relationships with one another, our shared past, and the unknown future. We reminisced about good times and bad, we cried, and we laughed. We apologized for a host of transgressions, and we granted, and were granted, forgiveness. Through Dad's illness and in his dying, we all grew individually and together.

After my father's illness I began to question my assumptions about dying and everything I had been taught about the care of the dying. I became acutely aware of how patients dying of cancer or other relentless illness were thought of as undignified, particularly in medical settings. I remembered my fierce, proud father, who died slowly, at the age of sixty-three, being consumed too early in life by his disease. I remembered the courage and personal integrity he had exhibited and the ultimate dignity of love he had demonstrated even as he lay dying. As he had done time and again when I was a little boy, Dad had set an example for me as he met the hardest of life's challenges head-on.

In the teaching hospital, death was always treated as a problem. There were questions to answer, a Death Summary to dictate, inches of forms to fill in, and presentations to be made at Morbidity and Mortality Rounds. And, of course, there were always the painful, awkward discussions to be had with family. A strong presumption throughout my medical education was that all seriously ill people required vigorous life-prolonging treatment, including those who were expected to die, even patients with advanced, chronic illness such as widespread cancer, end-stage congestive heart failure, and kidney or liver failure. It even extended to patients who saw death as a relief from the suffering caused by their illness.

Death in the hospital was a macabre event. I had pronounced more than a few people dead in the ER (emergency room) or in one of the ICUs or on the wards. Almost always the declaration was made only after dramatic attempts, such as heart resuscitation, were made to save the person's life. These were often literally dramatic: The actors knew the efforts were futile and for show.

A very old patient named Faith Carver typified a common dilemma on the wards. When she developed a high fever, Faith was transferred to the VMC emergency room from the nursing home where she had resided for years. Ninety-two years old, she was long widowed and had no relatives in the Fresno area. Because of advanced dementia she had not recognized friends for years and was completely dependent on staff for bathing, toileting, and even feeding. Despite the fact that her health had been declining for several years, the photocopied chart from the nursing home contained no living will or other advanced directive regarding her preferences for care. Contacting her next of kin in a distant city, I learned that choices for care in the event of heart failure, stroke, or serious infection had never even been discussed. Mrs. Carver's family, called in during a crisis situation by a doctor they did not know, were understandably reluctant to withhold life-prolonging treatments. This was especially true because her family had not witnessed the extent of her decline.

The situation was all too familiar. Without clear directions from the patient or family to do otherwise, once the patient was in the hospital, efforts to forestall death were obligatory. Every patient with a pneumonia or fever from bacteria in their blood received intravenous antibiotics. Those who died only did so after an emergency code was called over the loudspeaker and a team was summoned to perform CPR, invading the body with tubes, compressing the chest hard enough to pump blood manually (and sometimes crack ribs), and applying electrical jolts to try shocking the heart back into a rhythm. I wondered what it was permissible to die from.

If death on the wards was macabre, in the ER it was ghastly. In the hands of the medical system, even passings that should have been peaceful turned gruesome. Nursing homes, for instance, routinely sent patients only moments away from death to the hospital by ambulance, lights and sirens blazing. By transferring the almost-dead to the emergency room, nursing homes could claim a mortality rate of nearly zero, while providing evidence to families, and any interested attorneys, that "everything possible" had been done. This bizarre scenario extended not only to sudden deaths but also to people who were unconscious, in the final minutes of dying, and expected to die. Even though the medical people knew that death had arrived and any efforts would be futile, the system and their training compelled them to attempt CPR before they could pronounce someone officially dead.

At the time of my father's dying, hospice was unknown to the general population, and dying at home was very unusual. One busy night in the ER, a black family rushed its ancient grandfather to the hospital by ambulance. As I assessed him, lying on a gurney amid the noise and commotion of the ER, it was clear that he was very nearly gone from this world, beyond discomfort or any need for medical care. In taking a brief history I learned that this tightly knit family had been taking excellent care of him at home. They knew of his widespread prostate cancer and recognized that he was now dying. Gingerly, I asked why they had called the ambulance. The patient's granddaughter, a well-dressed woman of about forty, looked at me and, as the meaning of my question dawned and pained realization widened her eyes, she asked in reply, "Isn't it illegal to have someone die in your house?"

As an intern at VMC I realized that I was unwittingly part of the problem. Working on the hospital wards or in the outpatient clinics, I regularly met patients who were dying from advanced disease but did not even have a doctor to call their own. People with widespread cancer might show up in Surgery C clinic on a Tuesday afternoon and be seen by whichever resident happened to pick their chart from the rack that day. During shifts in the ER, I would occasionally meet patients who probably had only weeks to live, who had waited four or six hours merely to have their medications refilled. Reading the label on the empty pill bottle, I'd see that the prescribing physician was a fellow resident who was now rotating through obstetrics or pediatrics or orthopedics.

The county home health nurses were the glue that held together Fresno's sparse public health system across its vast, rural valley. Yet communication among the hospital, the outpatient clinics, and the home health program was next to nil. Cultural and language barriers added myriad difficulties. Within the Mexican migrant community, it was common for patients to spend intervals with different members of an extended family; thus addresses provided to the visiting nurse agency would often have changed between the time of discharge and the first scheduled home visit.

I tried discharging patients from the ward with appointments to my own clinic and writing specific orders for a nurse to check up on them in their homes. Still, more often than not, I was frustrated by a missed appointment, no report from the nurse, and, a week or two later, the readmission of the patient through the ER. Confusion reigned. It seemed obvious that some planning and coordination would benefit all concerned.

What was to become a hospice program began as a weekly early-morning meeting in the cafeteria, which I initiated over a year before my father became jaundiced and started itching. I was not aware of having any special insight into dying, nor did I have any special interest in terminal care. My involvement came, I think, from a basic sense of justice and a sense of pragmatism.

One day, while on my first-year surgical rotation, I was told to discharge Mr. Waters, a patient who had an open abdominal wound from cancer surgery that found unresectable tumors and from which he would never heal. Mr. Waters was fairly comfortable but would die within a week, two at the most. He didn't really need to be in the hospital, and we needed the bed on his ward. I worked for hours to arrange for the equipment and services needed to adequately care for him at home. In the process of doing so I began talking with a social-work student at the hospital, Kimberly Dougherty, about how things might be different.

Kimberly and I decided to keep a file card on each terminally ill patient who had recently been discharged from the hospital. The card included the names of a resident physician (who agreed to follow the patient in his supervised clinic), the home health nurse assigned, and the primary caregivers in the patient's family, with the patient's address, phone number, and address, with directions. Each Thursday morning Kimberly and I and a number of people representing a discipline or department of the hospital met over coffee and doughnuts and shared updated information about the patients' whereabouts, clinical condition, and functional status. Dr. Larry Stohlberg, a faculty oncologist, attended regularly, as did a social worker supervisor, a nurse from the medical floor, a chaplain, a dietician, a physical therapist, and a pharmacist. The county visiting nurse service also sent a nurse every week as a liaison to the home health staff. They were particularly enthusiastic; nurses now knew which doctor to call for medication refills, and the incidence of wasted long drives through the hot Central Valley had plummeted.

Within a couple of weeks we decided to call the meeting a program and chose the name Esperanza, from the Spanish *esperar*, "to hope" and "to wait." We borrowed two drawers of a file cabinet in the social service office at the medical center and printed half a ream of stationery. The Esperanza Care Cooperative was born.

The administration of VMC was initially wary of this upstart hospice program within its walls. But within months the positive effect Esperanza had on staff and patient satisfaction was indisputable, and the attitude of the administration gradually shifted from tolerance to acceptance. Communication within the hospital improved as the social workers and nurses were better able to exchange critical information with the resident doctor who knew a patient from previous admissions or from her clinic practice. Discharge planning for Esperanza patients was streamlined and some hospital stays were shortened because of improved coordination between the wards, the clinics, and the home health program. In the course of the weekly discussions a number of major crises were averted because problems could be dealt with in a timely manner.

After my father died, my interest in hospice deepened. Most of the discussions at hospice meetings were about pragmatic or medical things: how to get a hospital bed into a trailer; how to coordinate care within a family of five adult children from two generations, some of whom would never admit that the family's matriarch is dying; how best to treat bone pain in metastatic breast or prostate cancer; and what to do when a patient's nausea will not go away.

Every once in a while a family would return after a patient died and say that their loved one's passing had been extraordinary. "When we heard Mama was terminal, it was the worst thing that ever happened to our family, but this last month with her was some of the best time we have ever spent together" was the sort of comment I had occasionally heard before but had always dismissed as a peculiar, if pleasant, phenomenon. Now my ears perked up whenever someone mentioned a case that had gone especially well. A nurse might talk about a patient who reported a sense of well-being or contentment in the midst of their dying. Indeed, I began to notice that every so often a terminally ill patient would smile at me and seem not only comfortable, but also oddly satisfied, while only days from death.

It was a revelation to me that good deaths existed outside the realms of fiction, religious literature, or poetry; they were apparently uncommon, but real. The phenomenon of "good deaths" seemed to provide a window into the core of hospice work and, perhaps, into the heart of the human experience of dying. I began asking patients and families to help me understand how they felt and why.

Several things became apparent early on. The first was that the experience of dying was highly individualized. Some people died much as they had lived, while others changed in dramatic ways. The most positive experiences reported by patients and families involved change that they described as important or even "healthy." I also noticed common, salient features within the rich variations of individual experience. Patients who died most peacefully and families who felt enriched by the passing of a loved one tended to be particularly active in terms of their relationships and discussions of personal and spiritual matters. These families in particular also seemed to be involved in the person's physical care. In the broadest sense, it was as if dying from a progressive illness had provided them with opportunities to resolve and complete their relationships and to get their affairs in order.

This was another revelation—that good deaths were not random events or matters of luck; they could be understood and, perhaps, fostered.

While I was working to understand dying and improve my own care for my dying patients, the clinical work of hospice was working on me, sending roots deep into my psyche and soul. In the years that followed my career took me first to a family practice in rural Montana and then back to emergency medicine in Billings, and then Missoula.

Through the years, the geographic moves, and the practice of family and then emergency medicine, I remained involved in hospice work, compelled by the problems of the dying and fascinated by the phenomenon of the good death. More than once I have witnessed a hospice nurse smile and nod to a colleague in acknowledgment that a case had gone well, as if fulfilling the old adage: "To those who know, no explanation is necessary, to those who don't know, no explanation is sufficient." At conferences and in the medical literature there was surprisingly little, if any, discussion of good deaths. Without a consistent language and conceptual model for the range of human experiences at life's end, a taxonomy to label what we clinically saw, it was as if the phenomena did not actually exist. Out of curiosity, I began asking hospice colleagues to help me define success at life's end. I asked nurses, social workers, pastoral care providers, bereavement coordinators, and doctors. The choice of words used to describe "success" varied widely. A number of hospice caregivers referred to the dying person's having changed in a spiritual manner, but there seemed to be a wide variation in what was meant. At least as often as not, the account of the patient's good death did not sound particularly spiritual. Others talked about the person or family having coped well with the illness and death. Still others spoke of healing that had occurred between the patient and loved ones or within the person dying. And some chose the terminology of growth.

In recent years I have consciously rejected the term *good death* because I have not found it helpful in describing the personal, human experience of decline and demise. Good death connotes a formulaic or prescriptive approach to life's end, as if a good outcome chiefly depended on the right mix of people, place, medications, and services. Furthermore, the phrase *good death* tends to blur the distinction between death—the state of nonliving—and the preceding time of living.

If you ask someone to describe what, for them, would be a good death, they will typically tell you what they want to avoid. "I don't want to die in pain." "I don't want to suffer." "I don't want to be a burden on my family." "I don't want to leave my family with debts or go through our savings." "I don't want to die alone." The image such statements convey of a good death resembles a photographic negative, devoid of tone and texture or real color.

In contrast, the phrase *dying well* seems better suited to describing the end-of-life experience that people desire. It expresses the sense of living, and a sense of process. To my ears it also carries a connotation of courage. Furthermore, dying well expresses what I have witnessed most consistently: that in the very shadow of death one's living experience can yet give rise to accomplishment, within one's own and one's family's system of values.

Over the years I have met a number of people who were emotionally well while their physical body was withering and, for some, literally rotting. Logically, if even the most emotionally robust among us will eventually die, it follows that a certain wellness in dying must be possible. My experience in hospice confirms that this is true. Even as they are dying, most people can accomplish meaningful tasks and grow in ways that are important to them and to their families.

In my clinical hospice work, the conceptual model of lifelong human development has provided me with an orientation and thus has helped me to orient others. Years ago I began keeping notes on the developmental landmarks and "taskwork," as I call it, relevant to the end of life. I hoped that defining the landmarks might provide some light and offer a general sense of direction within this dim, foreboding landscape, and that naming the taskwork might provide paths for a person's individual journey.

This developmental work reliably enhances the quality of living.

The process is intriguingly similar to the stages of pediatric development. To the toddler, the world keeps shifting; her physical and emotional environments change frequently and in unpredictable ways. How she sees herself and how she is seen differ from month to month and, at times, week to week. What others expect of her continually changes. Within her body and her person, new needs regularly arise and must be satisfied. Life for the toddler presents fresh challenges that must be successfully negotiated, or she feels insecure. To the extent she persists in clinging to old strategies of navigating in the world and relating to others, there is distress. For some children, the rate of change proves too fast—the extent of growth and development demanded by circumstances proves too large to compress into a few weeks' time, and, at least transiently, there is suffering.

Someone who is dying, like the developing child, goes through stages of discovery, insight, and adjustment to constantly changing circumstances in his person and in the ways people react to him. People who are dying often feel a sense of constant pressure to adapt to unwanted change. As a person's functioning declines, the physical environment becomes threatening. A trip to the bathroom may become an hour's chore and then, a few weeks later, a major event. On learning of the grave prognosis, family and friends may begin acting differently, becoming serious or even solemn in one's presence. People may avoid one out of their own emotional pain, leaving one feeling awkward and isolated, an innocent pariah. New strategies are urgently needed to forestall a sense of personal annihilation. Mastering the taskwork may involve personal struggle, and even suffering, yet it can lead to growth and dying well. The tasks are not easy. But as a dying person reaches developmental landmarks such as experienced love of self and others, the completion of relationships, the acceptance of the finality of one's life, and the achievement of a new sense of self despite one's impending demise, one's life and the lives of others are enriched.

For the growing child and her family, each developmental landmark is typically accompanied by feelings of mastery, expansion, a sense of wellness, and, at times, exhilaration. The same feelings are expressed in the stories of patients and families who may be said to have died well. Often the challenge for a family, loved ones, and other caregivers is to recognize the opportunities for growth and development and to help the dying person achieve them. This takes courage. It takes a willingness to talk about things usually avoided, like painful memories, hurt and buried feelings, and the pragmatic details of dying and death—including with whom and where, obituaries, cremation or burial, and funerals. The time of dying is a dark, foreboding place—the end of the road, beyond which lies an unknown, terrifying terrain. But identifying the tasks and landmarks to be met can provide a reassuring map through an otherwise dim future. One way to start this journey is by asking "What would be left undone if I died today?" and "How can I live most fully in whatever time is left?" These questions can illuminate the tasks and landmarks ahead.

Over the years our hospice team in Missoula has become increasingly adept at helping people work toward end-of-life goals that have meaning *for them*. And it has become common for people we encounter to achieve a sense of inner well-being even as they die, and for families to express that their loved one's dying was as precious as it was painful. I know of no better way to explain what I have learned than to relate the stories of some of the people I have cared for.

Three

Learning to Die Well: Anne-Marie Wilson

During the time I helped care for my father, I saw his dying through the filters of medical school, where I was taught to focus all efforts on treatment, relief from physical pain, and cure. If cure was impossible, my job—a doctor's job—was to manage symptoms and keep a patient as comfortable as possible. This is how most doctors approach health care today. Medical attention is concentrated on illness and injury, and its goals are cure, longevity, rehabilitation, and the relief of physical distress. In this crucial respect, medical training is not very helpful for understanding the personal, as opposed to the medical, nature of dying.

Modern clinical training, procedures, record-keeping, and economics constrain doctors and force them to approach dying as if it were strictly a set of medical problems to be solved. For someone with an advanced, terminal illness, this approach offers only relief of symptoms. Dying of a progressive illness does, indeed, present a set of medical problems to be identified and dealt with. The terminally ill are, almost by definition, among the sickest people in the health care system and require the most intensive medical care. But dying cannot be reduced to a collection of diagnoses. For the individual and the family, the enormity and depth of this final transition dwarfs the myriad medical problems. For the person, the process of dying—that is to say, living with a terminal illness—cannot be understood as simply a medical event. The purely medical approach serves as a lens through which doctors analyze patients' experiences, but it goes only so far, and at its edges there is distortion. It is two-dimensional, and without the color, tone, or texture of life. It offers no place for the real stuff of human experience.

The idea of dying well is foreign to many people, families and patients as well as medical people, because of this grounding in the factual, impersonal side of dying. Most people cannot conceive of dying well or that dying can encompass more than solely physical pain and tragedy, because accounts of dying rarely go beyond a person's medical records. The case of Anne-Marie Wilson vividly illustrates the limits of a strictly medical perspective and reveals the rich possibilities within dying when the emotional and psychological aspects of the event are told.

A few weeks after Anne-Marie died, I reviewed her extensive medical history. Her medical records documented that in April 1994, after experiencing bloating and cramping after meals for two months, she saw Dr. Osborne. He did biopsies during a colonoscopy and diagnosed colon carcinoma. Standard tests also showed that the tumor had spread to the liver. Initially she resisted Dr. Osborne's recommendation for surgery to remove the tumor in her colon; however, when she developed pain and jaundice two months later, he convinced her to go ahead. The surgeon removed a section of her colon and placed a plastic stent or tube into the common bile duct to ensure the drainage of bile. He also performed a chemical destruction of the celiac plexus, the relay station for nerves carrying sensation from the liver, stomach, pancreas, and first portion of the intestines. According to the records, she was much more comfortable after surgery. For many weeks the only entries are of a brief postoperative visit and notations of routine prescription renewals. In late June, on rising from bed to go to the bathroom, Anne-Marie abruptly collapsed, cutting her head on a table as she fell. She was taken to the hospital by ambulance, stitched up in the emergency room, found to have anemia from slow, ongoing blood loss from her bowels, and admitted for a transfusion.

Within Anne-Marie's hospital chart and records from Dr. Osborne's office, and in her hospice plan of care, there is a mountain of information. The medical chart addressed the problems of colon carcinoma, the liver metastases, and her history of hypertension and diet-controlled diabetes. Dr. Osborne's notes were meticulous. Each entry was organized in the usual "SOAP" format, beginning with the data, Subjective (history) and Objective (examination, lab, and X-ray), leading to a diagnostic Assessment, on which was built the clinical Plan. It was all there: the details of her cancer; her blackout spell; her medical history, family history, and history of habits such as smoking and alcohol; a survey of bodily systems and symptoms, including her digestion and pains; her medication list; records of repeated physical examinations; and reports of laboratory tests, biopsies, and various types of X-ray studies.

As comprehensive as the medical chart was, I was struck as I reread Anne-Marie's medical records by how much they left unsaid. They gave no hint of the richness of her final months and weeks. There were no indications of the intensity with which she lived, her thoughts and feelings, her emotional struggles and successes, and the personal landmarks she achieved. In truth, Anne-Marie's dying was remarkable in its accomplishments. She labored over her relationships with her sister and daughter, grappling with the unspoken resentments and affections that hung between them. Despite the brutal encroachments of an implacable disease, she packed her days with humor and vitality. Toward the end, while it was difficult for her to relinquish a life full of activity and expectation and to accept that her future was limited, she found something of value in each day.

When Anne-Marie learned she had cancer, she was sitting in a tiny exam room in Dr. Osborne's office, across the street from St. Patrick's Hospital. A middle-aged woman with broad shoulders and oversize glasses, she wore a yellow plaid jacket and matching yellow heels, and nervously fidgeted with the cloisonné rings on her fingers.

The diagnosis—adenocarcinoma of the colon—was not a surprise. For a couple of months she had been bothered by bloating, cramping, nausea, and occasional vomiting. She had tried an assortment of antacids but nothing worked. The previous week the doctor had hospitalized her, after an ultrasound examination, for a CT scan and then a colonoscopy and ERCP (endoscopic retrograde cholangiopancreatography), so she knew her aches and pains were more than indigestion. Before discharging her he had said that her liver test pointed to cancer but he wanted to wait for the results of the biopsy to be sure. Now he was sure.

Adding to her sense of foreboding was the belief that misfortune was her fate. Her life had been a series of near misses with happiness. The marriage with her late husband Frank was typical. They had married, had a daughter, who now lived in Missoula, divorced, and fifteen years later got back together. Anne-Marie had never stopped loving him and was joyous at this second chance. But the day after they exchanged vows, Frank had dropped dead from a heart attack.

The same had happened with her father. The son of Italian immigrants, George Romolo was an old-school parent. Argumentative and authoritarian, he fought with his daughter throughout her childhood. But when she had her first daughter, he softened, and they called a truce. The baby proved to be a catalyst for some internal chemistry: Something shifted. In becoming a grandfather George Romolo became far more of a father than he had ever been. He even came for dinner every few weeks, bringing stuffed animals for Cindi and a grudging approval of Anne-Marie's maternal skills. For the first time, warmth began to seep into their relationship. Then, when Cindi was just six months old, he had a massive stroke and died. So now, hearing that she had colon cancer and perhaps a year to live did not frighten Anne-Marie. The aching sadness, all too familiar, left her feeling strangely detached and numb.

Anne-Marie asked only one question after Dr. Osborne had explained the full results of the surgery and biopsy. "Did you see anything that might have been caused by smoking?" The internist said no. "Then I'm going to smoke until my dying day, and I don't want to hear another word about it," she announced.

Anne-Marie left St. Pat's and drove straight to the Target store on the north end of town. She wandered the aisles, fingered the glittery earrings, and debated whether she needed a new scarf. Recognizing her as a regular, the salespeople waved and asked why she was not at work at the cafeteria at the high school. She joked about being promoted to Queen of the Creamed Corn and continued her strolling. This was how Anne-Marie made decisions; while pursuing her favorite pastime, surrounded by colorful distractions and temptations, she mulled over her options. In the display window today, so to speak, was the question of treatment for the cancer.

Dr. Osborne had pushed hard for surgery that could provide more information about the location and stage of the cancer and might make her feel better. The other item in the window was whether to tell her sister, Kathy.

This deliberation had a bitter taste. Eighteen months apart in age and raised as if they were twins, the sisters had once felt like soul mates. Until Frank. Anne-Marie had always suspected that Kathy had designs on him, and the discovery that they had spent a night together ended her marriage. After the divorce Anne-Marie referred to her sister only as "that woman" and avoided the stores and the part of town where Kathy shopped. Marrying Frank again pacified some of Anne-Marie's hostility, but it was Kathy who had made tentative overtures to reestablish their bond. They went on outings to outlet stores outside Spokane, and exchanged small gifts at Christmas. Anne-Marie found it hard to forget the bad blood; it was an emotional remnant of Frank. She had not shared an emotional confidence with her sister since they were girls. Another reason not to tell her sister about the grim prognosis was the memory of their mother, who had taken two years to die miserably of colon cancer. The sisters had both suffered through their mother's demise, and Anne-Marie felt strongly that no one should go through that experience twice. She decided that when the time came and she could not take care of herself anymore, she would go to the hospital. Then would she tell Kathy.

Anne-Marie bought two scarves and a miniature cactus garden at Target. Spring was starting to poke through Montana's deep winter snow. It was April; the days were less gray and more blue, and the thermometer lurched toward fifty degrees. But it would be months until she saw flowers; the red-and-orange bulb cacti were a colorful fill-in. She paid for her purchases and walked to the parking lot. As she fumbled for her keys, she dropped the round terra-cotta dish containing her little garden. Dirt and pottery splattered over the asphalt. At the sight of the ruined plants, Anne-Marie began to weep. As tears wet her cheeks, she found her keys, slid into her car, and sobbed uncontrollably. She pounded the steering wheel in anger. It was so unfair, she wailed. "Why me, why always me?"

She did not keep her unhappy secret from her sister for long. The cancer was spreading, and it altered the careful route she had planned. A boring, achy pain in the pit of her gut could not be ignored. It began to curtail her favorite activities, including Friday night dancing at the Lodge, and even though her weight continued to drop, she often felt bloated. The truth came out while they were shopping at Costco, a warehouse-sized discount store that sells everything from tires to underwear. As they were picking through jackets and sweaters, Kathy confirmed her impression that Annie had lost a lot of weight: Normally a size fourteen, Anne-Marie was edging toward the tens. Kathy admired a fleece-lined jacket Anne-Marie was trying on and asked for her dieting secret.

"Oh, lots of fast living, darling," Anne-Marie joked, as she hurriedly took off the jacket and pushed their cart toward the frozen foods.

Kathy knew something was not right. Not only did her sister seem physically uncomfortable much of the time, walking slowly and shifting constantly as she sat, but she had stopped buying the matching outfits she so loved. Her closet was stuffed with at least a hundred pairs of high heels and dozens of jackets and suits, but Kathy had detected no new purchases lately.

In temperament, they were opposites. While her sister was flamboyant and outgoing, Kathy was quiet and shy, and more so because she suspected that her sister had never forgiven her for Frank. If the tables had been turned, however, Anne-Marie would have confronted her sister long ago.

Kathy agonized over how to broach the subject of her sister's health without appearing critical.

"Annie, have you been feeling OK? You seem to be slowing down a bit," Kathy asked.

Anne-Marie pushed past a woman in a white butcher's jacket who was dishing out samples of sausage.

"Nothing a little rest won't fix. Did I tell you I'm retiring? Yup, time to take some of Frank's money and live it up." Anne-Marie gestured broadly with her hand, then glanced around at the industrial-sized cereal boxes and jars of peanut butter. "Think I can smoke in here?"

"That's real good. I'm glad to hear it. You sure you're OK? You look a little pale." Kathy followed as her sister pushed the cart to a pallet stacked with cases of soft drinks and plopped herself down, her face taut with pain. Anne-Marie dug out a pack of cigarettes, quickly lit one, took three deep puffs, and then stubbed it out.

"That's better. I tell you honey, anyone who says nicotine isn't a drug doesn't know the ecstasy of a Camel." In truth, Anne-Marie's pain was reaching crisis proportions. She was popping Percocets as if they were TicTacs, and she had reluctantly agreed to undergo the "comfort" surgery, as Dr. Osborne called it. He had referred her to Dr. Albano, who was going to perform a bypass around part of her colon (a gastrojejunostomy and a choledochojejunostomy) and inject alcohol into the celiac nerves in the back of the abdomen to block her pain.

Anne-Marie waved her hand to disperse the smoke around her. "Well, honey, to tell you the truth, the shit has hit the fan again." She paused to enjoy the drama of the moment. "Yup, your sister's been dealt another rotten hand. It seems that all this gas and achiness is the big C. I had a bunch of procedures a couple of months ago, and they found colon cancer. But they didn't do much when they were poking around. Didn't take out anything. I guess they couldn't. Anyhow, I'm going back in, this time for surgery they say will make me feel better."

"When?" It was all Kathy could think to ask.

"Next week. St. Pat's. They say I'll be in for about a week."

Kathy was stunned. For a split second, she wondered if her sister was making this story up to test her loyalty. She had assumed that her sister's high blood pressure was acting up. But no, this was too horrible for fabrication. Her next concern was that Anne-Marie lived alone.

"Who's going to take care of you? You're going to need help. Why don't you move in with us? Roger wouldn't mind, and we've got an extra bedroom. Really. Like when we were kids." Although she blurted out the invitation without thinking, it felt right.

Anne-Marie snorted at the idea that they could recapture their childhood. Yet the spontaneity of Kathy's statement and her sincerity were undeniable. "I don't think so." Her voice turned serious. "Remember Mama, how sick she was? This is not going to be pretty. If I can't take care of myself, I'll go to the hospital."

"That's not right," Kathy declared. "Let me take care of you."

"I don't want to be a burden. How could you forget the tubes and the mess and the smell? I *never* want to smell! Please, Kath, don't you ever let me smell," Anne-Marie added.

"If I promise you'll never smell, will you come stay with us?" Kathy pleaded, eager now for the chance to make amends to her sister for the years of hurt.

"Don't you want to talk it over with Roger?" Anne-Marie said.

"Oh, I know what he'd say. Please, Annie, we'd love the company."

"Only if you'll let me help out as much as I can," Anne-Marie insisted. "I still can cook a great leg of lamb, and you know my famous mashed potatoes!"

Many months later, when Kathy related this conversation to me, I marveled at how quickly they had cleared the "burden" hurdle. In the face of a terminal illness, patients and families struggle with assumptions about the physical demands of caring for someone who is dying. People who are ill fear their needs may overwhelm, and families worry whether they have the necessary stamina and skills. Caring for someone who is dying is never easy and can be enormously taxing. Medications must be administered and daily hygiene needs must be met. A caregiver has to administer medications, cook every day, do housekeeping, and, as the person becomes weaker, help with feeding, toileting, and bathing. And all this may happen around the clock. It is no wonder that many people believe that they cannot care for a dying loved one. Yet time and again I have seen families and patients ignore common wisdom and turn the burden of care into an opportunity to express their love, heal old wounds, change flawed ways, and discover hidden strengths. Kathy was desperate to right old wrongs, so the burden of care became, in truth, a gift of care. A dying patient lets family and loved ones express devotion by tending to his or her most vital needs, and the family seizes the chance to be close and loving. Neither Anne-Marie nor Kathy knew how far this gift of care would ultimately stress or stretch them—or maybe they did—but they did not hesitate to share whatever time remained.

Anne-Marie lived in a rented house in an older neighborhood not far from the school where she had worked. Her home was a square, red-brick structure with a screened porch and two bedrooms into which she had crammed the booty of hundreds of shopping trips. Before moving in with her sister, Anne-Marie announced that she was giving away everything. She telephoned Cindi, who had just gotten engaged, and told her she had first pick, and then alerted her friends that her famed shoe collection was up for grabs. She gave her good china to a close friend from work who had lost her home in a fire.

When moving day arrived and Kathy came to pick up her sister, she was taken aback by how little Anne-Marie had kept. Whatever her daughter and friends did not want, she had given to the Salvation Army. Her house looked empty except for the heavy furniture.

"What about your crystal glasses? All those lovely goblets," Kathy asked.

"Not needed," Anne-Marie said dismissively. "All that stuff, don't need it anymore. The doctor said I might have a year. I don't want to waste time worrying about *things*."

While Kathy accepted Anne-Marie's new outlook on the uselessness of possessions, the hospice people were skeptical. Our hospice had been brought in after Anne-Marie's second surgery, with Andi Dreiling assigned as the primary nurse and Vickie Kammerer as the social worker. In addition to performing the colon resection around the tumor and inserting the pain-killing block, the surgeon had biopsied her liver and removed portions of her lymph nodes. In confirming cancer within the biopsy specimens two days later, the pathologist had termed her condition a stage four colon carcinoma, the most advanced and extensive phase of the disease. The referral to hospice was made promptly not only because of the extent of the disease, but also because Anne-Marie had refused any consideration of chemotherapy. "I don't want to spend my last days bald and puking up my guts," she asserted.

Andi visited Anne-Marie at Kathy and Roger's right after she moved in. They lived in a bungalow in a part of Missoula called "the Rattlesnake" because it borders Rattlesnake Creek and a wilderness area of that name. Towering spruce trees shade many of the houses, and pine cones litter the edges of the streets. The front door opened into a living room with a curved, crushed velvet couch and a light brown, velour recliner, where Anne-Marie would spend her days. Across the room was a large-screen television. Anne-Marie was watching a soap opera and muttering wisecracks about the characters' twists of fate. Andi waited until the program was over before going through her routine of checking vital signs and asking about pain and bowels and the like.

With new patients, Andi often appeared tentative. Yet her exceptionally acute antennae were especially alive in new situations. She listened closely as Kathy described the move and all the things Anne-Marie had given away.

Small, almost birdlike, with a pixie haircut and a permanently furrowed brow that revealed her intensity, Andi had been a hospice nurse for six years and had tended to hundreds of dying patients, offering tender medical care and warmhearted attention.

"Oh, dear, that must have been difficult," she exclaimed when Anne-Marie confirmed that she had given away most of her things.

"Yes and no," Anne-Marie replied vaguely.

"Look, dear, I don't mean to doubt you, but that's the kind of thing people do when they're thinking about swallowing an overdose of something and getting it all over with. Is that on your mind?" Andi's voice was stern; she would accept no equivocation.

"Lord, no, honey," Anne-Marie replied, smiling, and looking Andi straight in the face. "I don't believe in that kind of stuff. I'm here until someone else turns off the lights." Her response was so immediate and natural that Andi did not doubt its truthfulness.

It is a rare person dying of a terminal illness who does not think about suicide. Most often, I have found, persistent thoughts of suicide are really a response to unbearable pain. People in pain often start to assume that their symptoms will never end. The fact that they are dying and have been told that "nothing more can be done" is misunderstood as meaning that they must simply endure their pain. Too often and for too long doctors and nurses have referred to dying patients as "hopeless" or "helpless," and that is how people who are dying may feel. The desire to kill oneself usually signals that one's suffering is being inadequately addressed, and often that suffering is physical pain that has been uncontrolled.

I and hospice nurses and social workers are used to asking about suicide. It is commonly on people's minds, and the discussion gives us a powerful opportunity to investigate sources of pain and emotional distress. It also offers us a chance to respond in caring ways and to prove that the symptoms of *any* fatal illness can be eased. By voting with our presence and by doing whatever it takes to provide comfort we demonstrate our conviction that there is no such thing as hopeless or helpless.

When the soaps were not on, Anne-Marie spent her days doing small chores around the house and cooking. She vacuumed and dusted, and especially enjoyed preparing large meals for Kathy and Roger. The menu was usually a roast, homemade mashed potatoes, seasoned vegetables, and baked goods she had made herself. The sisters had not been together so much since they were teenagers. Weather and energy levels permitting, they cruised yard sales and antique junk shops. Frequently, Anne-Marie scrutinized the merchandise from the car, and if she saw something she liked or that she thought Kathy would use and enjoy, she asked her sister to purchase it. Anne-Marie was not just a consumer of things; she consumed life. Big appetites, bold gestures, and bright appearances were her trademarks. While Kathy's temperament was very different, she enjoyed sharing in her sister's exploits. They clashed, however, when Kathy seemed to grovel in her efforts to please, or Anne-Marie, not quite able to forget Frank, bullied her sister out of sheer devilishness. By fall, many of their expeditions were for a mother-of-the-bride dress and accessories. Cindi was getting married in December, and Anne-Marie promised herself that she was going to be there for the whole show—rehearsal dinner, ceremony, reception—and decked out in her finest.

Anne-Marie told Andi all about the wedding and her future son-in-law and her hunt for the perfect outfit, although she denied the suggestion that staying alive for it was a goal. "Maybe I'll make it, maybe I won't," she maintained. Despite her nonchalance, everyone around Anne-Marie suspected that she dearly wanted to share this occasion with her daughter. Ever since Cindi's father had died, the mother-daughter relationship had been strained. With Frank's passing their nuclear family had dissolved and been reduced to an occasional birthday card or holiday gathering. Although they now lived in the same town, Cindi remained emotionally distant. When Anne-Marie had first moved back to Missoula, she had tried to break through Cindi's calcified defenses by arranging dinners and get-togethers and calling to say hello every week or so. In recent years she had given up and let Cindi dictate when and how often they saw each other.

Anne-Marie did not tell her daughter about her illness, even when she moved into Kathy and Roger's, and Cindi never asked why she had emptied her house and moved in with her sister. The mother assumed that the daughter did not want to know. Cindi's distance and denial further complicated Anne-Marie's plans for the wedding day. She was afraid that she would look frail and not only reveal her fatal illness but, worse yet, upstage her daughter by attracting people's attention to her health.

The idea of staying alive, and in Anne-Marie's case, staying visibly healthy, for a specific goal occurs frequently when people are terminally ill. The goal may be a single event, like a wedding, graduation, or encounter with a long-lost loved one, or something intangible, like the expression of forgiveness from an important person. Recognizing such a goal and helping a person achieve it contributes greatly to a person's peace of mind and progress through the process of dying. Reaching a goal gives a person a feeling of completion and completeness—important landmarks at the end of life. Attending Cindi's wedding represented more to Anne-Marie than the celebration of a happy event. The day of the wedding represented an opportunity to fulfill her role as mother, and an opportunity to see a number of relatives and old family friends whom she would never see again. After the wedding, she told herself, there would be fewer loose ends.

Anne-Marie's health deteriorated through the fall. At Dr. Osborne's request, I visited her at home in September to help with her pain regimen and scored a minor therapeutic triumph. During that first visit with Kathy and Anne-Marie, I asked about the quality and pattern of her pain. I also took a dietary history, asking about what she most liked to eat and when. It turned out that she was a "milkaholic," as she termed the condition. "Oh, I gotta have my milk." Her abdominal pain was crampy and generalized and occurred mostly after meals. I had suggested that she and Kathy begin adding Lactaid to her milk to predigest the lactose, or milk sugar. It worked like a charm.

By late October, a dull, persistent pain had shifted from her back to her abdomen to her chest and increasingly kept her pinned to the living-room recliner. When I visited her one morning in November, making sure to arrive before her soaps, she was dozing as Kathy puttered in the kitchen. The house smelled of cigarette ashes and fresh-baked bread. It was noticeably warm inside. The curtains were drawn and the crocheted blankets and pillows scattered about the couch and chairs made the house feel swaddled. Despite her make-up, her polished nails, and the smell of perfume, Anne-Marie looked sickly. She was losing weight, and no amount of foundation could hide the tinge of pastiness in her complexion.

I sat on the end of the couch next to her and took her vital signs, blood pressure, and pulse, while watching her expression and body posture as she sat or shifted slightly in the recliner. She offered me a piece of butterscotch candy; she kept the cut-glass candy bowl full and it had become a recent tradition for visitors to bring sugary offerings.

As I rolled up the blood-pressure cuff, she looked at me. I said, "You're not feeling so hot this morning, are you? You look like you're hurting."

"It gets bad sometimes when I move, and sometimes it's bad in the late afternoons. We went shopping yesterday, out at the mall, but the pain up under my ribs was making me sick. We had to come home. It's better now. Nighttimes can be bad, too." She paused. "Oh, this is such a pain. I don't mean pain pain, but pain in the ass. Cindi's wedding's coming up. I can't be down and out. Can you do something to help, maybe give me something, Dr. Byock?"

"Where exactly is your pain, Anne-Marie?" I scribbled notes on a yellow pad, from which I would dictate an entry into her chart.

"It's everywhere—around my back and my chest—and at night I can't seem to lie on my left side." She gestured vaguely with one hand; it jangled.

"Is that a charm bracelet?" I asked of the shiny bangle.

"Sure is. I've been adding to it for almost twenty years, every time I take a trip. I think I'm out of links, no more room." She held out her manicured hand for me to inspect it.

"It's lovely. I'll bet there's a lot of miles in that bracelet." I continued to take a medical history of her pain, such as whether it was better or worse after eating. I also asked about related symptoms. "Have you been having any nausea? How's your appetite been?"

Kathy had been in the kitchen, apparently waiting to bring Anne-Marie her breakfast. She came out carrying a tray with two bowls and a glass of orange juice and put it on the television table next to Anne-Marie. "Here you go, Annie," she said. Then, looking over at me, Kathy winked, and teased her sister: "I never know whether to say 'Enjoy it' or 'Good luck!' "

The family resemblance between the sisters was growing as Anne-Marie was shrinking. They were now about the same size and they obviously shared features, especially a puckered mouth.

"Thanks, honey. This looks perfect," she crooned to her sister. One bowl contained white rice and the other a glob of reddish, leafy stuff. "My favorite breakfast: kimchee and rice," she declared.

I raised my eyebrows in surprise and mock disgust. "Well, it's definitely original. I guess your appetite's been OK, huh?"

"Thanks to Kathy and Roger. They're always getting my favorite foods. Last night we had barbecued ribs, and the night before that Roger picked up Chinese from the Mustard Seed." Anne-Marie stirred some rice into the pickled cabbage mixture and took small bites.

"Any nausea or vomiting?"

"Nope, no nausea and no throwing up. Just the pain. And the weakness. And I'm always so sleepy."

Kathy reappeared wearing a blue car coat and carrying her purse. "I got to run down to Buttrey's. We need mayonnaise and juice. You want me to get anything for you?" she asked. "Jelly beans?"

Anne-Marie shook her head and Kathy left.

"I'm going to give you something that will help," I said. "It should make a big difference. It's called Ritalin. It's an upper, the sort of thing that truck drivers used to use to drive across country and college students use to stay up for days and cram for tests or write term papers. But it's very safe if used carefully. And it works. We'll start with a low dose. I want you to take one pill in the morning and the other around noon. It will perk you up. Just don't take it after around two P.M., because it will interfere with your sleep. If this is helping with your daytime drowsiness, on the day of the wedding we'll make an exception and give you an extra dose around four P.M. to give you a boost. Sort of like an afternoon double latte. I'm also going to increase your long-acting morphine and the dose of the Roxanol drops for breakthrough pain. That should help a lot." I added, "If that doesn't do it, Anne-Marie, we'll try something else. OK?"

With Kathy gone, Anne-Marie became somber, her bright, cheery voice slower and deeper. "I'm afraid, Dr. Byock. Not of dying but of dying here, in this house. Kathy and Roger have been so wonderful, and if I die here, I'll poison it for them. I'm afraid they won't be able to go into my room without thinking of death. Maybe I shouldn't have moved in." She seemed so sad and innocent as she looked at me for an answer. I put my hand on her arm.

"Anne-Marie," I began, then paused. "Can I call you Annie?"

"My best friends call me Annie." She smiled at me. I melted.

"Annie, the idea of poisoning the house is something people worry about, but in the years I've been doing hospice work, I've really never heard of it being a problem. When you think about it, there's nothing embarrassing or bizarre about dying at home. People have been doing it ever since there were beds. It's not like a room in which someone was murdered. And I promise you that you will not be suffering in pain, or screaming or smelling bad. For most families the room where a loved one died becomes a place of honor and loving memory.

"From what I have seen, your sister and brother-in-law love you very much, and wouldn't want you to be anywhere else. It seems to me that you and Kathy—I understand you haven't always been close—are really enjoying your time together."

"Oh, yes, most of the time," she said. Her eyes welled up with tears as she continued, "But how long will it go on? You know what's the worst, Dr. Byock? Not having a future. Not being able to daydream about a trip next year or look forward to the spring fashions. I don't even know if I can make it to Cindi's wedding. I hate that!" she blubbered. "Oh, I'm so sorry for getting so teary. It's not like me! I never cry, I'm so sorry. I'm such a wimp!"

"Oh, Annie. I want to tell you two things that are the exact opposites of each other. First, it's OK to cry. This is the saddest of times. How could it be otherwise? Second, give yourself a break! You're only human—and a good one at that—and you're just dying. That's bad enough, don't beat yourself up for being mortal; it comes with the territory."

I held her hand and had the inane thought that her tears were going to smear her make-up and she would not like that. Anne-Marie had her standards, and always looking polished was one of them.

She sniffled and smiled slightly. "I'm really sorry, I'm normally not a crier. Would you like a piece of butterscotch?"

"Yes to the butterscotch, but Anne-Marie, *please* don't apologize for crying." I handed her a tissue. "Your grief is legit, so important. I can only imagine how sad you must feel. Far from being a wimp, I think you are handling things remarkably well, making the best of your time." I nodded toward the kimchee, chuckled to myself and admitted, "Actually, I'm in awe. Seeing your breakfast reminds me of a favorite quote from Helen Keller: 'Protection in the long run is no safer than outright exposure. Life is either a daring adventure or nothing at all.' "

"I'll smoke to that!" she exclaimed. She reached up from the recliner and gave me a hug.

Anne-Marie's bath aide arrived. I gave her an extra dose of Roxanol and departed. I hoped she'd be feeling better by the time *Days of Our Lives* began. As I drove away, I was thinking about her wonderfully quirky meals and how she was squeezing the best out of every day.

Anne-Marie's pain was intermittent at this point, so Andi did not visit her daily. In truth, Anne-Marie and Kathy had initially resisted calling us, not wanting "to be a bother." Early on, Andi or Vickie often had to fabricate excuses to visit, even though we had rapidly become family.

After Anne-Marie attended Cindi's wedding, Vickie stopped by the house to hear about the ceremony and reception and see how her spirits were. Vickie visited around noon and brought a bag of Jelly Bellies.

A social worker for many years, Vickie exuded warmth and concern, and listened intently to the most labored recitations. Yet there was nothing softheaded about her. She extracted the salient clues to a person's deepest fears and hopes from even the most torturous ramblings. She intuitively knew what mattered.

Anne-Marie was in her recliner, her hair in curlers, and Kathy was giving her a manicure. Each was flanked by an ashtray and burning cigarette, and the house was hazy with smoke. Something about their silence when she walked in made Vickie think she had interrupted a tense conversation.

"Oh, if I had only known you were running a salon, I would have made an appointment!" Vickie exclaimed. "My nails are a mess!"

Kathy smiled tentatively as she pushed and clipped Anne-Marie's cuticles. "You look lovely, as always, honey. Take a load off, come have a seat." Vickie wore an ankle-length brown corduroy jumper with a beige turtleneck underneath. Her long, straight brown hair and the straight bangs across her forehead framed a soft face and a distinctive pug nose.

"Why aren't you visiting the truly sick? Surely there are people who need you more," Anne-Marie said.

"Well, I had to come by to hear about the wedding," Vickie declared. "I hope I'm not interrupting anything." She looked at Kathy, who was intent on her sister's nails. She noticed that Kathy's nails were short and brownish yellow.

"Just reliving old times. The good, the bad, and the ugly. You know how it is with family, dear, lots of water under the bridge. And lots of surprises." She paused, as if debating whether to continue in the same vein. "Years ago, we had our hearts set on the same man. He married me, but Kathy managed to snag him for a bit. Now, she tells me he was two-timing both of us. Doesn't that beat all!" She patted her sister's hand with her freshly done hand. Kathy looked up with a grateful expression.

"Wow! Now I understand why you guys love the soaps!" With this they all just roared. The laughter continued for several minutes. Vickie sensed that a gray cloud had finally moved off. "So tell me all about Cindi's wedding," she insisted heartily.

Anne-Marie wore a royal purple dress, matching shoes, and jacket, made small talk with the groom's parents at the rehearsal dinner, alternately stood and sat in the reception line greeting guests, and managed to dance for a few moments with Roger. It sounded to Vickie like she had been the belle of the ball, and she silently thanked the wonders of Ritalin. Vickie also learned, however, that after the wedding, Anne-Marie had all but collapsed. She went to bed and, according to Kathy, barely rose, even for meals, for three days. Kathy had wanted to call hospice, but Anne-Marie would not let her. She insisted on toughing it out until the scheduled hospice visit on Thursday.

Anne-Marie still looked exhausted and weak to Vickie. Loose skin hung from her neck, and her hands were bony and had a small tremor. She worried about Anne-Marie's will to live, now that she had seen her daughter married.

Vickie sensed that they had accomplished what they could for the day. She found that it worked best with Anne-Marie to deal with pragmatic things while staying alert for opportunities to talk about more intimate concerns. She rose to leave. "Do you need anything, Anne-Marie? You know, it's real easy for me to pop down to Target or wherever if you need something."

"As a matter of fact—this may sound peculiar, but I'd like a book of poetry. I've been making my funeral plans, and I've got the music and flowers all picked out, and I'd like some poems." Kathy looked horror-stricken. "I didn't want to trouble you, honey. I just hate sounding so morbid," Anne-Marie told her sister.

Anne-Marie marked the first anniversary of her diagnosis and survival with a festive meal. She'd beaten the odds, and that was enough reason to celebrate. Although she had lost much of her interest in eating, she felt that Kathy and Roger enjoyed feeding her, even when she only took a few bites of this or that. They liked to concoct favorite menus and assemble odd assortments of food. On the celebration table were egg rolls, sweet and sour pork, pickled garlic, banana bread, broccoli au gratin, and sherbet sundaes with Cool Whip. By this time, Anne-Marie moved very little from her recliner, and each time Andi or I visited, pain was the first topic of conversation. I increased the doses, although sometimes Anne-Marie told Andi more about her pain than me.

During one of Andi's visits, when Kathy and Roger were doing errands, Anne-Marie said, "I want you to tell me exactly how I'll die. I want to know how it'll go."

Not much ruffles Andi, and she methodically explained what would probably happen. "As the days go by, you will feel weaker and weaker, and a day may come when you will not want to move around. You'll want to be in bed and not get up. You'll be alert but weak and gradually you'll feel sleepier and sleepier. You may spend several days sleeping. And one day you'll not want to wake up, and you will drift off peacefully."

Anne-Marie listened as if following a complicated recipe, then said, "You didn't say anything about pain. Andi, I don't want to have pain. And I don't want to smell!"

"I promise you," Andi insisted forcefully. "We will *not* let you suffer in pain. My word of honor. Whenever you tell us you're in pain, or whenever we sense that you are, we'll take care of it. I promise, Annie, we won't let you die in pain."

It wasn't long before sleep consumed much of Anne-Marie's days. One morning in June, while rising from bed to go to the bathroom, she became lightheaded, felt herself beginning to swoon, and passed out, hitting her head against the sink as she fell. When Kathy found her sister unconscious, sprawled across the hallway, and bleeding profusely from a gash on her scalp, she thought she was dead. Roger called an ambulance while Kathy sat with Anne-Marie's bleeding head in her lap, sobbing. Anne-Marie was hospitalized overnight at St. Patrick's; in addition to the acute loss of blood from her cut, she was found to be anemic from slow, ongoing bleeding from her bowels. It was not enough to cause urgent problems, but enough to gradually cause anemia, worsen her weakness, and make her finally pass out. Because of her advanced cancer, there was not much in the way of curative measures that could be done. Of course, there was still much to do in the way of care. Anne-Marie's laceration was sutured in the emergency department and she was admitted overnight—to receive a transfusion and to make sure her blood pressure responded and that she had tolerated this latest ordeal.

While the event had scared the wits out of Kathy, Anne-Marie experienced only mild discomfort while she was being sewn up. The transfusion left her feeling significantly more spry. When I asked her about her misadventure, she rolled her eyes and let out an exasperated, "What a mess!" But I suspected she enjoyed the excitement, and, despite the bruising and bandages, she looked better than she had in weeks.

The episode did accomplish something positive for Anne-Marie's family. Sensing the end was near, her daughter inched closer. Cindi, who, according to Kathy, refused to believe her mother was dying, came by the house to share the wedding photos and ask if her mother needed help, like a ride to the doctor's.

When you ask most Americans how they want to die, the response usually is in the form of dark humor. I've collected these flippant quips for years: "I want to be hit by a truck." "I want to be struck by lightening after sinking a birdie on the eighteenth hole." "I want to live to be a hundred and be shot in the back by a jealous husband." While sudden deaths are attractive among the healthy, in reality they leave many things undone, and they are often the hardest deaths for families to accept. In contrast to an abrupt, easy death, dying of a progressive illness offers precious opportunities to complete the most important of life's relationships. This includes the chance to reconcile strained relationships, perhaps between previous spouses, or between a parent and an estranged adult child. When the story of two people ends well, a warm light is shone on all that has preceded. Even at the very end of life, healing a relationship can transform the history of a family. A relationship that is complete need not end; in this context, complete means there is nothing left unsaid or undone. When a dying person and a loved one come to feel complete between themselves, time together tends to be as full of joy and loving affection as sadness.

Some people are very methodical about expressing specific things to every important person in their life. Others, like Anne-Marie and her family, communicate more indirectly with a word, a look, a touch. As long as the style is mutual and understood, the effect is the same.

I last saw Anne-Marie one morning in early August. She was bed-bound and actively dying. I stopped by just after the bath aide had left. I gathered that asking for help with bathing had been a major acquiescence for Anne-Marie. Always fastidious and well-groomed, she usually devoted hours each day to washing, primping, and powdering. When she could not do these things anymore, Kathy offered to help her. Natural modesty and fear of being a bother stopped her from accepting. The ensuing clash lasted for a day and a half, until Andi negotiated the compromise of a bath aide.

Anne-Marie was propped up in a hospital bed, her hair in curlers, but in full mascara and smelling of Shalimar. A slight breeze ruffled the curtains; she insisted on always having a window open—Kathy believed it was so her spirit would have a way out. I pulled a chair up beside her bed and held her hand.

She was drowsy and appeared weak, but she had been primped and now she forced herself alert. I could tell by the look in her eyes and the half-smile with which she greeted me that her spirit and sense of humor remained. "How are you feeling this morning, Ms. Wilson?" I inquired, with exaggerated formality.

"Well, I'll tell you, Dr. Byock," she answered, in the same measured, polite tone. "I feel like I just won the chili-eating contest at the county fair and got run over on the way home. And how are you?"

We laughed together at the image. I said, "You may feel like hell, but in all honesty, I want you to know you're still as cute as a button!"

"You ought to see the fellow I'm going out with—he looks worse than I do!" she retorted in a whispery voice.

For a moment we said nothing and smiled into each other's eyes. "How are you feeling, really? Any pain?"

"No, it's under control. Just sleepy and tired. Andi said that would happen."

"How about other discomfort—is your breathing OK? Have you been sick to your stomach?"

"No, I get some rumbling in my belly late in the afternoons, and I've had to cut out my milkshakes because they were giving me gas, but I'm really doing pretty well."

"And how are you within yourself? Do you have any concerns or things that feel unfinished that you want to talk about?" I asked.

"The only thing that worries me is money. All this nursing care and medicine, I know, is expensive. Maybe Frank's nest egg is gone. I don't want Kathy and Roger to pay anything." Her voice was dreamy but her logic clear.

"You've no need to worry about that, Anne-Marie. Don't you remember, we filled out those Medicaid forms a while back? They'll take care of everything," Kathy reassured her.

Tears slowly dribbled down Anne-Marie's cheeks, mingled with flecks of black makeup. She pursed her lips in resignation. "I'm a little nervous, afraid of the pain. Can you give me another shot? Just in case?" She was receiving a continuous infusion of morphine as well as extra bolus doses whenever she needed them.

"No problem." I administered a bolus dose of the medication through the subcutaneous infusion line.

"Do you think I'm ever going to get up again?" she asked.

I took her hand again. "I don't know, but you do seem weaker and more sleepy. What do you think?"

"I think I'm dying," she replied.

"Annie, whenever you do die, I am going to miss you. We all are. You are really a privilege to know. It's a helluva way to do it, but I'm really glad I have had the chance to know you and help care for you. Is there anything else that you need or want? Anything you can think of that I can do for you?"

She smiled with a faraway look. "Call that nice chaplain, Tom King."

Two days later Anne-Marie slipped into a coma, and people from our hospice team were with her every afternoon and evening to make sure she was comfortable and that the family was getting the help they required. Around nine on the last morning, Kathy frantically telephoned Andi. "They haven't come, the bath aide hasn't come to take care of Anne-Marie!" she cried. "I don't know what to do. She's lying in urine, just dripping wet! And I think something's wrong with the catheter."

Kathy's distress immediately became Andi's. Anne-Marie—this

wonderful woman, this friend whom she had promised would never smell—lay helpless in a pool of urine.

Andi telephoned the private duty service, and when she was told everyone was in a staff meeting, angrily demanded to speak with the director. "Do you realize that this is a woman whose dignity means more to her than anything else! And not only is she my patient, she is my beloved friend! I want Dana to call me immediately!" Andi could always forgive human failings; she could not tolerate indifference and bureaucratic foul-ups.

Andi was not going to wait for the aide or for a call back from the director with useless excuses or explanations. She rushed to the house to bathe Anne-Marie herself. Kathy, Cindi, and Meg met her at the door, wrought up over what to do. Anne-Marie's catheter had become kinked, and Andi found her friend lying in a small pond of urine. It was seeping into her hair and beginning to soak through the protective mattress pads. Andi gasped in dismay; she knew her friend would be horrified to be found in such a state.

"Come on, you guys, help me out," she said to the women hovering in the doorway as she literally rolled up her sleeves and got to work.

They gathered dozens of towels and washcloths, washbasins with warm water, soaps, shampoo, and perfume, and began a transformation. At first they worked tentatively, gently rolling Anne-Marie over to remove the wet sheets and pad. No one spoke. They touched her gingerly, afraid of causing pain or waking her. Her body was emaciated and gray, skin sagging from bones. The warm August sun spread across the room. The sound of water squeezed from washcloths and tinkling into the metal basins played a syncopated music. Quietly, almost to herself, Kathy said, "When we were little Mom used to bathe us in this old claw-foot tub," and she spun out a chain of childhood memories. Cindi was at the head of the bed, sniffling as she lovingly shampooed and combed her mother's hair. Meg was at the other end, gently applying lotion to her feet and legs, massaging, stroking, powdering between her toes. They touched and caressed the body of their mother and sister as if it were consecrated.

"When she was little, she followed me everywhere." Kathy laughed lightly and looked at her sister. "And you were always asking 'Why Kathy? Why?' I got so tired of that. Why, why, why!"

At that moment Anne-Marie opened her eyes and looked up at Kathy as if to answer. Then her eyes closed, and Kathy began to weep. "It's hard to love so much and lose."

When they finished, Anne-Marie was gorgeous, at least in the eyes of the assembled entourage. She lay in fresh sheets, smelling of her favorite perfume, her hair soft and curly, her make-up smooth, her complexion rouged. The phone rang. It was Kathy's daughter, Mary, calling from the Colorado hospital where she had just given birth to a baby girl, the family's first girl in a generation of many grandsons. Kathy took the cordless phone in to Anne-Marie and put the receiver to her ear. While Mary described her new grandniece, a tear rolled from each of Anne-Marie's eyes and her eyebrows lifted slightly. As the phone call ended there was a wonderful, though peculiar, sense of solemnity and celebration in the room. Everyone began telling Anne-Marie how much they loved her and how much they would miss her and to journey on knowing that she would always be loved. Andi remembers feeling as if she were at a shrine. As the women stood around her bedside, tears of sorrow and joy in their eyes, Anne-Marie sighed deeply and breathed no more.

The story of Anne-Marie's passage from life demonstrates that the actual experience of dying is not captured by a purely medical perspective that sees only problems. The profoundly personal experience of dying ranges from agony to bliss; for most of us it will fall somewhere in between. Without adequate medical care, dying can be horrible. With skillful medical care and attention to the personal experience of the patient and the person's family, dying can be made bearable. When the human dimension of dying is nurtured, for many the transition from life can become as profound, intimate, and precious as the miracle of birth.

Four

SUFFERING AND BEYOND: DOUGLAS KEARNEY

Suffering commonly goes hand in hand with an incurable illness as people struggle with discomfort, disability, and their inevitable demise. They may suffer from the physical pain of their disease, and they may suffer as well from the emotional and psychological pain that comes with losing all they have been and all they have imagined they will be. While these two kinds of suffering are almost universal among the dying, they are not untouchable. Suffering persists when a person's physical pain is ignored or declared uncontrollable or when a person's emotional pain is not understood or is dismissed as inevitable. In my experience the personal, internal suffering can be far more intense and require even more skillful intervention.

Ironically, the pain most people associate with dying, the physical hurt of a terminal illness, can usually be straightforwardly contained. What my profession drily calls "symptom management" involves not only a pharmacopeia of medications (palliative care has advanced far beyond the old morphine-based Brompton cocktail), but also a collection of aggressive symptom-relieving techniques. Within the hospice pharmacopeia, a large array of medications (from glucocorticoids to anticonvulsants, antidepressants, and even psychostimulants) are remarkably useful when applied to specific pain syndromes. Modern medical technology and advanced pharmaceuticals have given doctors the ability to reliably ease the physical discomfort of terminal illness.

The fact that many doctors and medical centers do not treat pain aggressively does not mean that physical pain is uncontrollable. Physical pain among the terminally ill exists because doctors lack the will, not the way. Deterred by opioid phobia or ambivalence about medications, doctors, patients, and families may step back from the firm commitment that is needed for assertive pain management. The current state of medical education, which does not train its practitioners to adequately evaluate or aggressively treat pain, further hampers such efforts. In the minds of too many people today, the answer to unbearable pain among the dying has become assisted suicide or euthanasia, as if effective pain treatment did not exist. Physical pain must be understood in its proper perspective, that is, as a single, readily manageable component of suffering. With strong resolve from patient and doctor, relief of *physical* suffering is *always* possible.

I have found that suffering from personal, mental pain is a much more complex and thornier problem. The mental anguish of impending personal annihilation and the emotional despair of losing all that one has, and *one is*, can be far more intractable. Personal suffering hinges on what gives a person purpose or meaning, or what Dr. Eric Cassell, author of *The Nature of Suffering and the Goals of Medicine*, calls "personhood." By personhood he means dimensions of the self that extend beyond the body and encompass personality traits such as temperament, distinctive characteristics, and personal habits. They include a person's cultural background, life as a social being, and relationships with others. A person's past and future, as well as beliefs, moral values, and unconscious or interior life, are a critical part of personhood. Possessing a future—not only hopes and dreams but also immediate plans and expectations—is also vital to feeling whole. People act out the essence of their personhood every day in the routine activities that give daily living shape and texture. When terminal illness alters or amputates these activities, one's sense of self and personhood are under assault, and suffering follows. For someone who is dying, this problem is often the crux of personal suffering. When one is debilitated by illness and frequently confined to bed, one's very sense of *who I am* is in jeopardy.

Douglas Kearney was a forty-six-year-old father of three who developed lung cancer. By the time it had begun causing symptoms, the disease had spread to his brain and was progressing rapidly within his chest. With the support of his wife, Barbara, he sought out the most aggressive surgeries and treatments, and for more than a year waged war against this dreadful foe. Suffering was daily fare for Douglas during much of this time, and his physical pain was frequently immense. Yet Douglas's distress extended far beyond what was happening to his body.

The particular suffering that Douglas experienced gnawed at his emotional well-being and personal identity; it affected his relationship with himself and with others. Douglas stubbornly refused to face the sadness caused by losses within his dying, and he ultimately reached the deepest depths of personal despair. In denying the enormity of the sadness around him, he distanced himself from his family and was unable to grieve with his shattered wife and children. Instead he became angry at the world, and his anger threatened to consume him and obliterate any opportunity for loving interaction with his family. I cannot remember a patient whose anger, as well as the emotional suffering it caused, was more excruciating.

Douglas's suffering demanded extraordinary measures, and I struggled to help him. In striving to help Douglas find a way to ease his suffering, my capabilities and those of our hospice team were sorely stretched. I did not know what, if anything, would work. But we were committed to keep trying.

On a warm, gray Saturday morning in January, Douglas Kearney was driving his pickup down the hill from his home in south Missoula when his world changed forever. Beside him sat his older son, Peter. As the truck neared a red light, Douglas barked at Peter to step on the brake, because he could not move his leg. His dad often kidded, so the disbelieving fifteen-year-old sat still. Fortunately, the light turned green just in time; unfortunately, this time Douglas wasn't kidding.

After struggling with the pedals, the frightened pair pulled into a parking lot, and the forty-six-year-old husband of Barbara and father of Peter, Darlene, and Sean went into a full grand mal seizure. Peter yelled for help; within minutes an emergency vehicle rushed Douglas to St. Patrick's Hospital in downtown Missoula. His vital signs were stable. The doctor examined him and ordered a battery of tests. Peter telephoned his mother. "Something's wrong with Dad," he told her.

It took Barbara Kearney an hour and a quarter to drop off her younger son and arrive at St. Pat's. Douglas had already had a series of laboratory tests and X-rays, including a CT scan of his brain, and had been transferred to a room. He sat awake and comfortable in his hospital bed, gazing aimlessly at the snow-laced Loco Peak and worrying about what he would say to Barbara when she arrived. On her way to his room, Barbara was stopped by Douglas's physician, Dr. Foster. He said that Douglas was feeling better and was in no immediate danger, but that he was still very concerned. He hinted at a problem with Douglas's brain, then cut off the conversation. "I don't like to talk about a patient away from the patient. Let's go see him," he said.

Barbara is tall and slender, with long, dark brown hair and a permanently furrowed brow; her face relaxed when she saw Douglas sitting up. She hugged and kissed her husband, who kept muttering, "I'm OK, I'm OK." They turned expectantly toward Dr. Foster, who was leaning against a wall near the door. "Tell me about cancer in your family." Then, as if to fill the gaping silence, he added, "You've got a lesion in your brain; a tumor in your left frontal lobe."

Barbara bowed her head in numbed disbelief, but Douglas blurted out, "You're shitting me! How can it be a brain tumor? I'm supposed to get a lung cancer, for Christ's sake!" In fact, it was. As Dr. Foster went on to explain, although Douglas's seizure had been triggered by a brain tumor, the growth was the offshoot of lung cancer, small but visible on his chest X-ray, that had almost certainly metastasized and spread.

A grim realist, Barbara had always half-assumed that her husband would succumb to cancer. The family tree, she had learned early in their marriage, "was just loaded with it." Moreover, Douglas's lifelong smoking habit provided fertile ground for the disease; over the years she and Douglas had often argued about his smoking. Now that she was right, she felt no satisfaction but instead a sense of numb unreality. She heard the diagnosis with no doubt that it was true. Yet her sadness mingled with a hot anger she felt toward Douglas for bringing this on. His bullheadedness was now going to not only rob her of a husband but destroy her children's father.

Barbara Kearney is the kind of person whose world is orderly and under control. Whether confronted by a broken kitchen appliance or a broken brain, Barbara needs to understand why and how it happened, know what is required to fix it, and do whatever is necessary to get the job done. When she heard the details of Douglas's diagnosis, she immediately telephoned the National Cancer Institute, a government research and information agency, and asked for everything even vaguely related to Douglas's illness. She pored over stacks of studies and journal articles, learning the science and vocabulary of cancer and the "prognosis and protocol of nonsmall cell adenocarcinoma of the lung." She memorized the statistics and drug interactions, delved into the complexities of cellular biology, and carefully read about every available treatment option. Barbara was doubly motivated: She was going to do everything possible to take care of Douglas, and she hoped that this knowledge would lessen her terrible fears and ease some of her anger.

Douglas had a different temperament. He was an ex–army sergeant, a former fire jumper, and a construction worker who possessed a rigid "can do" optimism about his life and his abilities. Defeat was not in his vocabulary. He believed in traditional values: He belonged to the Loyal Order of Moose and regularly attended services at St. Francis Xavier's. And he believed in playing by the rules. If he did everything asked of him, he would be rewarded; if he fought the good fight, he would win. So, while he suspected that this cancer might eventually prove insurmountable, he chose to believe he could beat it. His life, so far, had justified this determined optimism. He and Barbara had been through difficult times before. They had not only survived, they had thrived.

Above all else, Douglas Kearney prized family life. Raised in a strong Catholic family, he carried into adulthood an almost old-fashioned belief in family roles. His most cherished duties were those of traditional breadwinner, devoted husband, and loving father.

The goal of fatherhood had been threatened early in their marriage when he and Barbara had tried unsuccessfully to have children. Rather than accept what seemed to be fated, he had applied his determination to creating a family. Through Catholic social services the couple adopted an infant boy and, within fifteen months, an infant girl. Then, as so often seems to happen, a few years later Barbara became pregnant and gave birth to their son, Sean. Their joy was tempered, but not extinguished, when he developed the first signs of autism.

Sean was a blessing in disguise for Douglas. As a role model for Peter, Douglas was either quiet and unemotive or brusque and commanding. But with his younger son he showed a softer side. With Sean, Douglas's tough, macho exterior gave way to tender emotions evidenced by warm words and easy touching. The clash between Douglas's cold, uncompromising reason and his gentle, loving soul would become the hallmark of the struggle that defined the final months of his life.

Perseverance had always paid dividends for Douglas, certainly in forging a family. He was now going to apply his steely determination to beating his illness. After a lung biopsy that sealed the diagnosis, he charged ahead with a raft of treatments. In January, Barbara accompanied him to Seattle for surgery to remove some of the tumor in his brain; in February, surgeons cut away parts of one lung. This is very aggressive therapy. Even with surgery to remove every sign of disease, when lung cancer has already metastasized to the brain at the time of diagnosis, it is a rare person who survives for long, and damn little really helps.

As soon as Douglas regained his strength after the surgeries, he signed on for extensive radiation and chemotherapy. Crippling headaches and growing weakness on his left side signaled that he was losing ground. He spent the summer resting and gathering strength. In the fall, new tests showed that the cancer had spread to his liver.

Douglas and Barbara functioned like a general and aide-de-camp. Douglas pinpointed the targets, and Barbara assembled and mobilized all the necessary weapons. He asked the big-picture questions, and she studied and absorbed the medical literature. When it became painfully clear that the cancer was spreading, Douglas demanded that Barbara tell him what the medical studies reported about his odds of survival. She resisted, knowing that the "cure" rate—living beyond five years—for a stage IV lesion of a certain size in someone his age was only 2 percent. She had seen signs in her husband of discouragement, watching him "go through all the stuff that Kübler-Ross talks about: the bargaining with God, the denial, and the anger, a lot of anger," and she did not want him to become discouraged any further. But Douglas was demanding, and Barbara usually acquiesced, and she finally told him. To her surprise, Douglas was buoyed by the news.

"He figured somebody was in that 2 percent, and he was going to be in it too," she told me. "His attitude was based on five points: because of his youth (he wasn't some eighty-nine-year-old), and our kids were so young. He had a lot of insurance and good medical care. And his fighting spirit—he was going to try anything and everything." As Douglas plunged into treatments, Barbara bravely soldiered on beside him and only once gave in to the enormity of their struggle. Back home after the second surgery, Douglas lay in bed resting, and Barbara sat beside him. Her once handsome husband had lost all his thick, black hair, which had been replaced by ugly scars, and the muscles on his six-foot-plus frame had withered. Seeing him this way, she erupted into hysterical crying, wailing over their fate. Douglas opened his eyes and grasped her hand. "Stop!" he commanded. "You have to stop this right now!" His voice turned plaintive. "Can't you see this is taking all the guts I have to fight it? I don't have strength enough for both of us."

In December they returned to Seattle for still more brain surgery. The new year brought more radiation and chemotherapy to stem the growth of a recurrent tumor in his chest, which pushed on his breastbone and produced a visible lump.

Normally a little testy and curt, Douglas over the months became even more temperamental. Sarcasm and flippant remarks had always been his style, but now his amusing comments were mean and cutting, particularly with family and medical people. When sweet, demure Barbara couldn't answer his questions about a drug's side-effects, he'd ridicule her intelligence. When Peter took all morning to cut the small square lawn in front of the house, Douglas accused him of being lazy. He lashed out at the doctors and medicine that were not helping him. When Dr. Foster had no cures for his crushing headaches or paralyzing seizures, Douglas ranted about useless medical technology. Everyone and everything was failing him, and he struck back.

His temper and anger grew as virulently as the tumors. Barbara recalls, "It was as if no matter what we'd done to any part of his body, after every procedure he was a little less Douglas. There was no way he could suffer the insults that he did and not change—not only the physical trauma of cutting into the brain but also the chemical assault, the chemotherapy, other medications, even the anticonvulsants. And there was the psychological pressure of knowing that unlike the other men in his family, he wouldn't see his children grow up or even live into his sixties."

Anger consumed Douglas. That is what I remember most from our first meeting. We met in June at his house, about a year and a half after his seizure in the pickup. The Kearneys lived in a split-level ranch house in a neighborhood pulsing with young families. The sidewalks were speckled with bicycles, and many of the fenced yards harbored a barking dog, bright plastic toys, and a barbeque grill. I talked with Douglas and Barbara in the living room, which was decorated with a perfectly matching couch, easy chair, and broadloom carpet. The only odd piece of furniture was a round, individual-sized exercise trampoline in front of the television. This was for the constantly moving Sean. I was introduced to all the children as they wandered in and out, but clearly they were under instructions to keep quiet and play elsewhere.

Given the barrage of treatments and surgeries, Douglas looked remarkably good. Dressed in sport shirt and slacks, he was thin but not wasted, pale but not sallow. The telltale signs of his ordeal were on the left side of his body—his face and eyes drooped, and he could barely move his left leg or arm. His head was largely hairless, with new growth just beginning to cover the surgery scars.

The hospice nurse, Bonnie Brown, and his oncologist had both asked me to visit him. Douglas's temper was frightening people. Bonnie thought that maybe I could help him get beyond whatever was feeding his anger. Dr. Foster was at his wits' end trying to help Barbara deal with Douglas's outbursts and would be grateful for any help I might give. I knew that it would not be easy. I was familiar with his story from my routine chart reviews and our weekly marathon hospice meetings. At one meeting Sister Vivian, who ran the cancer support group that Douglas and Barbara attended, had delivered a sobering opinion. "Douglas will die with his anger. It is the cause of his suffering, but he knows no other way." She spoke slowly, her voice echoing the sadness in her eyes.

I very much wanted to connect with this tortured man and his distraught wife. His anger was causing suffering far beyond what I usually encounter in dying patients. Like a raging inferno, it was sucking the air out of his relationships with his wife and children. The blaze left no room for expressing the sadness and loss they were feeling. Unless he somehow allowed himself to admit that he was dying and grieve the losses that death meant, his suffering would become unbearable.

I had read Douglas's chart and I knew about his surgeries, therapies, and medications. I also knew that he had recently decided to stop treatment, admitting, at least on an intellectual level, that a cure was impossible. Emotionally, however, he was tightly controlled, searching for a way to apply his take-charge determination.

It took only a few minutes to discover that Douglas and I had both grown up in New Jersey, and we talked about the things we missed about the East, like good Italian food and the boardwalk. It was small talk, but I was getting a sense of him and Barbara as people. In medical parlance, it is called "taking a family history." Eventually we got down to the medical business. After some general questions about his condition, I asked him if he was in pain. "Nope, I feel pretty good, Doc. Oh, I get some aches and pains, but just little stuff, nothing major," he stated. Barbara sat by his side holding his hand, which he seemed to tolerate, not invite.

"I see you're taking Tegretol, Dilantin, and Imipramine." I scanned his medication list. "And that you've stopped Methadone. That's a little unusual. Were you having problems with it?"

"Well, the pain is nothing I can't deal with. I'd take it if I needed to. Actually, Doc, I'm doing pretty well. I know I'm dying, but I can't fix that. And apparently none of these damn doctors can—or will—do anything to fix it. No sense griping about something you can't change," he declared defiantly. Barbara opened her mouth to speak, but a quick glare from him stopped her. I nodded, but his admission was unconvincing.

I asked about the cancer support group. He continued, "The cancer support group's helping a lot. Sister Vivian's real good at getting people to come to grips with their situation. Barbara likes it a lot, don't you?" The look she gave Douglas contained an exasperated "Oh, Douglas!" Her mouth formed an obedient smile, but her eyes revealed a mixture of sadness, bitterness, and disappointment. And I remembered Sister Viv saying that Barbara had to twist Douglas's arm to get him to attend the support group. It was he, not she, who was fleeing the emotions of his illness.

"I'll tell you though, there are people there in a lot worse shape and a lot more screwed up than I am. There's this one woman there, who's got lung cancer and is still smoking. Holy Mother, Doc, can you believe it? I get so angry when I see her outside the meeting, puffing away, I could shake her. Smoking's the reason I've got this thing." He glanced at Barbara, checking to make sure he had preempted her response.

"You know, Douglas, as I read your medical history and listen to your story, anger is a theme that runs through the last few years of your life. It is evident in our conversation today." I probed to see how he would explain his anger.

"Maybe," he agreed, "but I've got a right to be angry. Look at me! I didn't used to be this ugly, you know!" he chortled. "Between the chemotherapy and the Decadron, I look like a bald Pillsbury Dough Boy. I've done all the treatments, seen all the doctors, even took those experimental drugs." He turned to Barbara. "What's that called?"

"Clinical trials."

"Yeah, clinical trials. I did it all. I jumped through everybody's hoops, and where'd it get me? You doctors don't know jackshit about what I'm going through." He was yelling and now glared at me. I was glad I was out of fist range. His flaring temper seemed to have a life of its own, and it was not hard to imagine it erupting into violence.

"You've been through a lot, that's for sure. You've put up with more than most people could ever imagine. I think you still are. You know, people who are sick—especially when the illness keeps progressing, despite everything they do—often suffer from more than physical pain. Serious illness can nibble away at parts of a person until eventually it feels like you're falling apart."

My words were interrupted by Sean coming into the room, followed by Darlene trying to contain him. "We're going to the Dairy Queen, Mom," she announced cheerfully. "Can I have some money?"

"In my purse, there's lots of change in the bottom." Barbara pointed to the bag on the desk in the hallway. While Darlene fished through Barbara's purse, Sean wandered over, in his rocking gait, to the vicinity of his father. Douglas reached out and stroked his arm, and Sean mimicked the motion, then returned to his sister's side. For a moment, Douglas's face relaxed. The children disappeared out the front door, and I continued.

"This is an extraordinarily hard time for you and your family, a sad time for you all. The loss for all of you is enormous, and I can only imagine the pain you must be feeling."

"Yeah," Douglas responded. "Think of how it feels, not being able to go hunting with your kid. And not being able to teach your daughter how to drive." His voice trailed off, then snapped back. "What really worries me, Dr. Byock, is the money. I want to be able to leave them something, but there's not much left." He added sarcastically, "Good thing I've stopped the surgeries. They drain all the money you have. Maybe that's when they stop!" He looked over at me to see if the jab had landed.

Barbara's eyes teared up. I wondered if Douglas had ever cried during these long months of illness. Probably not.

I addressed both of them. "Have you talked to your children about what's happening? Have you told them how sick you are? Although they may not show it, they may be more afraid than you are. Being this ill—dying—is especially terrifying when people don't talk about it." I would not have used the word *dying* if Douglas had not used it himself. I chose it now because it allowed me to test how comfortable or threatened Douglas and Barbara were with discussing these issues. "Your kids are losing a parent, and I can't think of anything more frightening for a child. Perhaps, during whatever time you have left, Douglas, there are things you can do for your children, with each of your children, to let them know how much you love them, simple things, but things that may be very important to them in the years ahead."

Douglas sat motionless, his face frozen. Barbara bowed her head, as if in deep thought. They both looked tired; it was time for me to leave. I gathered up my briefcase, stuffed my notes into it, and rose to leave. "I'd like to come back," I offered. "To see how you're doing, make sure your pain medications are helping, and talk some more about what you're going through."

Barbara lifted her head, and her slight nod was enough permission for me.

"Sure," said Douglas, "I'm around, I'm not going anywhere. At least not for another few months, they say," he added, with no humor at all.

A week later, I visited the Kearneys again, hoping to break through Douglas's steely denial and nudge him toward working on issues of life closure and his relationships with his family. Barbara looked exhausted as she greeted me at the door. Her face was drawn and she slumped.

"Please come in, Dr. Byock," she said. "Forgive the mess. Doug's brothers have been visiting and his niece is coming tomorrow." Except for a sweatshirt dropped in front of the television, the home looked spotless and tidy. Compulsively straightening and cleaning helps distract the mind from larger, uglier concerns.

"How's he doing?" I asked, glancing down the hall toward the bedroom.

"Not so good. It's been a bad morning. Ever since he woke up tangled in the sheets, he's been yelling at me and the kids."

"I thought he and I could drive down to Break Espresso for coffee and pie. It may be easier for him to talk there," I suggested. Douglas seemed indifferent, and offered no resistance. We bundled him into a warm jacket and helped him into my old Isuzu Trooper.

One of the beauties of living in Missoula is how easy it is to get around. No errand takes more than a fifteen-minute drive, and metered parking spaces always open up just where you want them. Break Espresso is one of my favorite haunts. Its espresso and coffee are as good as anywhere in town, and its large round oak tables are spread out, perfect for quiet, solitary paperwork or private conversations.

During the drive, and as we picked up our coffee, Douglas told me about his seizures, which were gaining in intensity and frequency. They usually attacked his left side and lasted a few seconds or many minutes. Although he did not lose consciousness, they were virtually paralyzing.

"I can't believe they're coming back like this," he said. "It's only been a couple of months since the last surgery. Jesus, give me a break! This is so unfair. I've done everything," he spat out.

"Yes, it is unfair, Douglas."

"I'm going in for another MRI tomorrow," he said. "You know, they're discovering new things all the time. I saw something on TV last week about, I think it's called interferon, and all the success they're having with it."

I looked skeptically at him.

"I know, I know," he said. "You don't have to tell me. I got Barbara for that," he added angrily. "She knows it all, the jargon, the statistics, everything but the time and date."

"You know what else is not fair?" I said. "Barbara gets a lot of your anger. She's suffering too, you know. Both of you are suffering and hurting and grieving."

"She knows I love her, Doc. You don't have to worry about that."

"Good, Douglas, because she needs to know that. Your children need to know you love them, too. As parents, we assume our kids know how much we love them and are proud of them, but we don't ever actually say so. We work long hours for their sake. We worry and plan, scrimp and save, and all the time we assume they know we are doing it for them. But what our kids see is that we are usually preoccupied and don't have much time for them. I only found out that my dad was proud of me by what the customers in his business would tell me he said to them.

"Even if it seems obvious, I think it's important for us parents—especially fathers—to tell our children how much we love them. So Douglas, even if you think Peter, Darlene, and Sean know you love them, it's worth saying. It's especially important now. And knowing that at times your anger seems to get away from you, I think it's important that they hear you say you love them and how proud you are of them. Don't leave them with a memory of an angry, bitter man."

Douglas stirred his coffee and the metal spoon clanked against the porcelain cup. "I hear you, Doc."

I asked if there was anything I could do for him. He responded quickly. "Yeah, make sure I don't suffer, Doc." He locked my gaze. "And don't let me make a fool of myself as I die."

"I hear you, Douglas. That's a promise." With the pie finished and the coffee cold, we headed for home.

Initially, during the next few weeks, Douglas did better. His medications were adjusted, and his anger seemed to lessen just a bit. But only for a while. The next time I saw Douglas, things had again gotten worse.

I was working a Friday night shift in the Community Hospital emergency room when Barbara telephoned around nine P.M. Her voice quivered as she told me that Douglas had been ranting in the backyard, wearing only boxer shorts—yelling at the neighbor's dog, shaking his cane menacingly, and urinating into the bushes. I asked her if she felt she was in any immediate danger, and she said that Douglas was sleeping now. We hung up, agreeing that I would come over first thing in the morning after getting off shift.

The ER was relatively quiet that night—a couple of car accidents with whiplash injuries, a few lacerations, and one sick infant. Around four A.M., when I was dozing in the call room, a nurse told me that a tearful Barbara Kearney was in the ER and needed to see me.

Under the hospital's fluorescent lights, Barbara looked pallid. She wore a lightweight jacket and wrapped her arms tightly around herself to stop shivering.

"Dr. Byock, I'm so sorry to bother you, but Douglas's gone crazy. Before he finally fell asleep, he was yelling at the children, telling Peter he's going to sell all his things and saying he's going to put Sean in a home. He was waving his cane in anger. I'm afraid, and the kids are so confused and afraid. I don't know what he's going to do next." She stopped to catch her breath. "Oh, this isn't right," she wailed. "I promised him that I wouldn't let it happen this way, losing all his dignity, dying like some madman, not the Douglas I know. I promised him."

I folded my arms around her and held her as her body shook and tears rolled down her face. Dignity is important to everyone, but especially to someone who is dying and has already begun losing control over much of his life. And while many people think of dignity in terms of appearance, independence, and personal embarrassment, people close to a dying patient seem to know intuitively that their loved one's dignity does not depend on these. Dying is not inherently undignified, it is simply part of being human. With supportive family and friends, even needing help with basic bodily functions need not diminish dignity. But Barbara knew—and I agreed—that Douglas's bizarre behavior in the backyard was undignified.

"I know, you're right," I comforted. "We're going to have to do something. But our options aren't many. Douglas has to face his sadness. Anger is familiar to him, almost comfortable, and sadness is unknown and terrifying. I think for Douglas, acknowledging the sadness that lies on the flip side of his anger may be the only way through his suffering. I'm certain that when he finally faces it, it won't be nearly as frightening." I paused, waiting for Barbara to absorb this. "But to do this, he needs a safe place. I wish we had an inpatient hospice facility in Missoula, and some day we will, but for now I think we will have to use the psychiatric unit at St. Pat's." For a moment Barbara looked frightened again.

"I know, I've been thinking the same thing." She paused. "Will they put him in a straitjacket?"

"No, certainly not. But he will be on a locked ward for the first few days. I don't think that'll be necessary for long, but it depends on Douglas," I told her. "I know it sounds scary, but he'll be safe. And he'll be with people who can help him talk about his fears and sadness. His anger's gotten so out of control it's making him sick." I told Barbara that I would come to the house to talk to Douglas and take him to the hospital after I finished my shift. I warned her that it might not be easy and that we would have to stick with our decision and take him against his will if necessary. I explained that the law allows a doctor to hold a patient for seventy-two hours for psychiatric evaluation and treatment if the patient is an imminent danger to himself or others.

The ER traffic picked up considerably after Barbara left. An elderly woman with pneumonia and two more sick children kept me moving, so when I finally left, around nine A.M., I was jangly from lack of sleep, too much coffee, and nervous exhaustion. And I was worried about Douglas, not knowing how he would react to being approached about a stay in the psych unit. His outbursts verged on being psychotic, and I was afraid for Barbara, and for him. In his state of mind, he might indeed hurt someone, or himself.

As I drove up I could see Barbara standing over the kitchen sink, watching the street outside for me to arrive. I recognized Bonnie Brown's red Ford Bronco parked across the street. I had paged Bonnie around seven-thirty and asked her to meet me at the Kearneys' house. Barbara opened the front door, I took her hand, and we just looked at one another for a moment, as if to confirm our resolve. I told her that everything would turn out all right; I needed to hear those words, too, feeling the uneasiness of fatigue and apprehension. I went in to speak with Douglas.

He was in his pajamas, leaning on his cane in front of the bedroom closet, ripping clothes from hangers.

"What the hell are you doing here, Doc?" he demanded.

"Barbara's worried about you, Douglas," I said, keeping my voice calm and not getting too close to him. "And I'm worried about you, too. You must be in great pain. I can only begin to imagine how bad you feel. I'd like to help, but at the moment that means going to the hospital."

"The hospital? I don't need to be in the hospital, Doc, I'm not that sick, and besides, they've told me there's nothing they can do for me."

"Douglas, you need to be in the mental health unit, the psych hospital. At least until things cool down a bit."

"The psych hospital!!! Now I know what's happening. She's got you believing I'm going crazy. She's been talking about me behind my back. I've heard her whispering on the phone, she thinks I can't hear. Oh, sure, I get angry at times, who wouldn't with their wife pulling this kind of shit! Well, get the hell out of my house. You're not welcome here. Get out before I throw you out! *I'm not dead yet!* She wants my money, that's all she's ever wanted!" He spat out the words.

"Douglas, that's not true. Barbara loves you very much, and she's very worried about your safety. You can get angry with me if you want, but for your own safety and the safety of your family, you really need to be in the hospital. Remember when you made me promise that I wouldn't let you embarrass yourself as you died? Well, that's what it's come to." I stayed by the door. The bedroom was a shambles, with clothes strewn about and torn magazine pages littering the bed and floor.

"No way, I'm not going back to that fucking hospital. I'm finished with those assholes! And you can't make me," he growled.

"I'm afraid I can, Douglas." I paused, hoping he'd calm down. "If it comes to that, I can and I will. I can have you held for seventy-two hours. Please, Douglas. Let's go to the hospital. I'll drive you or Barbara can drive you down."

"You're going to put me in the loony bin! No way! I'll shoot myself first. I've got a gun, I'll shoot myself!" Douglas began to wobble, so he slowly backed up and plopped down on the edge of the bed.

Although Douglas was weak, he wasn't resting. I took some solace in knowing that Barbara had given Douglas's rifle to a friend to keep for him. This wasn't going the way I'd hoped.

"No, Douglas, you're not going to hurt anyone. You're going to the hospital, but if you won't go voluntarily, I'm going to call the police to help me get you there. It's up to you, Douglas. You can go with me or go with the police. Either way, you're going to the hospital."

Neither of us moved. Douglas glared at me as if I were Satan. I held his gaze for a few moments, waiting for the fire to subside. The sagging left side of his bony, angular face made him look fearsome.

"Barbara, get my gun, damn it!" he commanded. She responded only by coming to his side and saying, with remarkable composure, "No, Douglas, remember, I gave your gun to Ed. Dr. Byock's right. You need to be in the hospital."

I had called the city police shift commander before I left the ER to let them know what was going on. Now I needed them to come by. I used the kitchen phone while Barbara and Bonnie stayed with Douglas; then I returned to the bedroom.

I sat on the floor by the door while Douglas lay back on the bed, staring at the ceiling, rhythmically slapping the sheets with his cane. The morning sun filled the room, and I thought how nice it would be to fall asleep in the soft yellow light. Barbara sat down beside me, and I held her hand as we waited for the police to arrive.

The two deputies looked young, but they were probably in their late twenties and were both physically large men, imposing in their dark uniforms and huge leather utility belts. Barbara led them down the hall to the bedroom. As we huddled in the doorway talking, Douglas lay motionless on the bed. He had stopped slapping the cane.

"Douglas, this is where we're at: You can either drive to the hospital with Barbara or me now, or these two gentlemen will escort you there. It's your call, voluntary or involuntary."

The deputies knew that the situation called for slow, deliberate calm, not heavy-handedness. "He's right, sir. If the doctor says you need to go, we'll help him get you there. We'd rather not have to restrain you and take you in, but . . ." As young as they looked, these guys were clearly pros.

Douglas changed strategies. He looked pleadingly at Barbara. "Oh, I'm so sorry, honey. I don't know what gets into me. Please, it won't happen again. Please, please. I want to stay here with you and the kids. You know I'd never hurt you. I don't have much time left. Please." He was sitting up, his pajama top so large it seemed almost empty, his face ravaged by scars, scraggly hair, and thick beard stubble. He didn't like what he saw in Barbara's face. Her eyes showed pained sadness backed by determination.

"It's really come to that, huh? Boy, I really must be fucked up." He stared at the floor. "OK, well, let's get on with it, then. Barbara, where's my coat?"

We left Douglas and Barbara in their bedroom. She helped him dress, and they spoke. I heard him say, "I just can't believe you'd do this to me." But when they emerged, Barbara said that Douglas had agreed to let her drive him to the hospital. The officers and I would follow in our own cars.

The locked psychiatric unit of St. Patrick's Hospital is a place of dimmed lights and muffled noises. Its soft lighting, dense tweed carpeting, and pale earth-tone colors make it feel like a modern monastic retreat. Douglas's room contained only a hospital bed and opened onto the nurses' station. Like a public aquarium holding exotic fish, the room had a glass wall (with a privacy curtain that could be pulled from outside the room), so Douglas was constantly under observation.

The nurses' detailed notes about Douglas's time on the unit, plus what I gleaned from daily visits with him, confirmed the level of his despair. Douglas spent the early days in his room sleeping or staring out the window toward the Conoco station overlooking the interstate. He was irritable and short-tempered with nurses and visitors. He asked a nurse, "What would happen if I didn't take the seizure medication? Could a seizure kill me?" When she told him that it probably would not, he launched into a diatribe over Barbara's treachery. "She's going to pay for this!" he declared.

Barbara agonized for an entire day before visiting Douglas in the hospital. Since his first seizure, she had always been with him or close by, and all her instincts told her to go to him immediately. She reined in her heart and listened to her head. "He needs space from me," she decided.

When I visited Douglas the next morning he was in bed and had cleaned off his breakfast tray.

"Good morning, Doc. Checking up on the prisoner?" he asked, without rancor.

"Morning, Douglas. I see the food agrees with you," I replied.

"Oatmeal. Even a hospital can't ruin oatmeal. All you got to do is add hot water," he said evenly, and then scowled. "So when the fuck do I get out of here?"

I sat on the edge of his bed. "That depends on you, Douglas. Right now, you need to be here. You have to realize that all your anger and venom is a very destructive way to avoid admitting how much you're losing."

"I'm not angry anymore," he hastily interjected. "That was yesterday. I'm over all that. It's under control. I'm much better now."

"Like hell you are," I snapped, choosing a tone that matched his own. "You've been feeding me that line, basically bullshitting me and yourself, since we first talked in your living room. I'm not buying it. The fact is that your anger has gotten out of control. You're not here because I'm mad at you or because Barbara is mad at you. You're here because we're both worried about you. It's pretty damn obvious how much you're hurting. She loves you, Douglas and, although you may not be able to hear it, I care about you, too."

I paused. He remained quiet, gazing toward a far corner of his bare room. "I think you're still keeping your real feelings at bay. You say things like 'I'm doing OK, Doc.' And 'Oh, there's nothing any of us can do about dying,' as if that diminishes the pain. But you're also a smart and honest guy, and you know what the fact of your dying really means. You're losing your family and your family is losing you. As long as you can't admit to the sadness, they really can't either. They have to pretend to be strong, like you. So a lot of important things go unsaid.

"You asked how long you have to be here, and I don't know yet. You're not nuts, Douglas. Not yet. But knowing you're dying and dealing with it by denying the pain is slowly making you crazy. Your anger has become a real threat to Barbara and the kids. Behind it, I can feel your sadness. What is most important now is to share your sadness."

I waited. After a moment he looked up. "How would I do that?"

"Begin by telling the kids how much you love them."

"They know I love them, Doc." he retorted.

"They probably do, but hearing it from you aloud may be really important. We parents tend to assume our children know we love them and are proud of them. Your kids will have a lifetime to think back on these days. You will always be their dad, Douglas. The fact that you didn't die suddenly gives you an opportunity to make sure they know how proud you are to be their father and how much you're going to miss them. Until you can own up to the emotions that come with that knowledge and share your grief with your family, and listen to theirs, your anger will make it impossible for you to go home."

Dry-eyed, he declared, "You can't keep me here forever."

"Pretty close to it. The law says I've got seventy-two hours now, and after that I put your case before a judge. You may think that you can b.s. a judge and convince him that you're ready to go home, but I'm telling you, no way. I can make strong arguments for holding you indefinitely." I sounded hard, maybe even heartless, but I had to deliver the cold truth: Squirm as he might, there was no way out.

Over the next two days, Douglas changed, physically and emotionally. He looked haggard and beaten, and the tumor that was pushing on his breastbone seemed to be growing by the hour, intensifying his physical pain. I think the pain scared him; it was the alarm that would not stop ringing, wearing him down, forcing him to face his vulnerability. The psych nurse reported that Barbara visited daily, bringing letters from home, and that for the first time, the evening of his second day on the unit, they cried in each others' arms.

On the third day I noticed a change in Douglas as soon as I saw him. There was no anger in his greeting or posture. His calm was almost unnerving. I didn't know what to think. He spoke softly, but was eager see me. "I'm glad you're here. I had a nightmare last night." In his dream, he told me, he had visited his mother's grave and unearthed her body. He could not recall many details, but the dream was clearly an emotional watershed. Somehow in the dream, in the shadow of mortality, he had confronted his identity as a son—and, perhaps, as a father—more deeply than ever before. We were alone in the windowless, dimly lit patient lounge, and he was in a wheelchair parked in front of the television.

"You probably think I'm crazy," he despaired. He spoke slowly and softly, but his tone was urgent. "I don't know what I'm thinking, but this thing in my chest is growing. Oh, God, I'm so scared. I know I'm dying, I could die tomorrow." He paused and clutched my arm, adding emphasis to what came next. "I don't want to die in here. Please don't let me die here!" he implored.

I did not say anything for a moment, and just listened to his fears. *At last*, I thought, with poignant relief. The wall of denial between his anger and sadness had been breached. Within the dream he had experienced sadness and found that it was not overwhelming, as he had feared, nor as uncomfortable as the isolation he was feeling. His work was not done, but could now begin in earnest. The taskwork of accepting the finality of life and his changed sense of self and completing his relationships lay ahead.

"It's always been up to you, Douglas. Your time here offers you an opportunity to look behind your anger and frustration, and to explore your fears. Once you do that, I think you'll feel less afraid."

Two days later, I met Barbara and Douglas together in a conference room on the ward to make plans for his discharge and to talk about caring for him at home and involving the children. They were waiting for me in a tiny conference room situated at the end of the psych unit, away from the general traffic. With Douglas's wheelchair edged into a corner and Barbara standing beside him, our knees almost touched as I sat on the couch. He looked like a different man: Despite the bony angles of his jaw and brow, which had become accentuated as he lost weight, his eyes radiated peacefulness. I had never seen him look so at ease with himself. I had become used to being on guard in Douglas's presence. This change in him, if it was real, would take getting used to. Barbara's hand was on his shoulders, and his hand rested comfortably over it. Her bitterness seemed to have faded with Douglas's anger; now that he had accepted his fate, she could forgive him.

At first I did not say anything; I just smiled, reflecting this welcome warmth.

"We were wondering if Douglas could be discharged on Monday," Barbara said. "He wants to be home, and Peter and Darlene want to help take care of him."

"I can't think of any better care," I said.

"You know, Sean hasn't been able to visit his Dad," Barbara explained. "The lights and sounds here would be too stimulating."

"I miss him," Douglas softly interjected.

"But I think we're going to need more help, you know, a real nurse," Barbara said.

"Yeah, someone who can change a catheter without spilling," Douglas's irritation passed over him like a brief cloud. He would probably always have that jagged edge to his personality, I thought.

"We can set up a schedule for a hospice nurse to be there daily, or whenever you like," I offered.

"Yeah, that's good. Give Barbara a rest," Douglas said. His voice softened as he looked into the distance. "I have to apologize, Doc. I know you put up with a lot of shit from me. I got to tell you that being in here—even for these few days—being forced to work things out, well, someone should have done this to me twenty years ago. This has been the best experience of my life." At a loss for words, I could only manage a smile. That was the last thing I had expected to hear from Douglas Kearney.

In accepting his sadness, Douglas reconnected with parts of himself that were threatened by his impending demise. He was no longer husband or father in the old way, but he still was Barbara's husband and his children's father. By acknowledging his losses, he had, paradoxically, become more whole. The exhilaration he expressed typifies the experience of personal growth, the sense of renewed mastery in a changed life situation. With this new strength and sense of wholeness, Douglas could deal with whatever the future held.

Douglas's acceptance of what was happening to him and his new sense of self altered him in more ways than one. When he returned home after his time in the psych unit, he started smoking again. He had thought it all through and decided that smoking was one pleasure he no longer had to deprive himself of. Having entered a new phase of life in which the priorities and rules were different, he was determined to live fully and enjoy whatever time was left. Barbara saw it differently. She pulled me aside when I came to the house the day after he was discharged.

"Could you please talk to Douglas?" she implored. "It's so upsetting. It's like he's trying to hurry up his death with his chain-smoking. It's so unlike him. When he stopped treatment in April, after going through all those surgeries and drugs and pain, he asked the doctor, 'Would you think me chicken-shit if I quit?' And you know what the doctor said? 'Douglas, you've fought harder that any cancer patient I've seen.' And now"—her voice quivered—"he says it's the only thing left that gives him pleasure. But it's like he's trying to kill himself." When Barbara was discouraged, her shoulders sagged and her head bent.

"What am I going to do?" I said softly, commiserating with her. "Tell him smoking's bad for his health?"

Douglas asked me to push his wheelchair to the back patio so he could smoke outside as we talked. It was a sunny, warm day, and the neighbor's dog yapped at us, but Douglas did not seem to notice. He held a cane to help with maneuvering, and while I was talking, he kept pushing the tip across a crack in the cement as if it were a piece of rope he was trying to move. He said little as he puffed on the cigarette and hypnotically poked at the crack. I realized that he was hallucinating, seeing something on the patio. I could think of six things that might cause it, but at this stage these medical musings were of little practical value.

"My dad's coming this weekend," he told me. "He lives in Connecticut. We've sure had our tough times. It'll be nice to see him now. I got rid of a lot of real old baggage in the hospital. Childhood stuff. I think we can be friends. You know," he smirked. "I think I've grown up. Better late than never!" He chuckled wryly.

Peter came outside while we were talking. He seemed a little stiff and tentative with Douglas, as if waiting for the fiery father to resurface.

"Mom said to ask you if you want a cup of coffee."

"No thanks, son. Dr. Byock?"

I shook my head, and watched Douglas reach out to touch Peter. As Peter looked at his dad, I saw the warmth in both their faces, and as the boy disappeared back into the house I noticed how relaxed his posture had become.

Even with the change within himself, Douglas did not die an easy death. As the tumor in his head grew, he had difficulty swallowing. So he stopped taking his dexamethasone tablets, a steroid that was helping control swelling around the tumors, and developed a constant twitch and restlessness. His days shortened as he lapsed into unconsciousness, broken only by brief periods of wakefulness. And the hallucinations worsened. One afternoon as Barbara brought him back inside from the patio, he looked at their house and, apparently mystified, asked, "Who lives here?"

But when he was lucid, Douglas could not love his family enough. He would not let Barbara out of his sight, and they relived happier times and humorous adventures as newlyweds and new parents. During these glorious moments, sitting on the end of his bed like devoted followers, Pete and Darlene hung on every word and laughed at every joke.

Somehow Douglas sensed when death was very near. The morning he died, he told his children that he probably had only a few hours left. He said goodbye to each, one by one, and then instructed them to go to their grandmother's house. When they left, Barbara lay down beside her husband and put her arms around him.

I made my last visit to Douglas around nine that morning. Bonnie had been there since six, and we reviewed the recent adjustments in the medication he was receiving to prevent seizures and control his pain. He was comfortable but beyond responding. I touched his brow to let him know I was there. I gave Barbara a hug and told her I'd keep checking in.

Douglas Kearney died around eleven o'clock. Barbara was at his side. For over half an hour she sat holding his hand and intermittently stroking his head and tenderly speaking to him. She then asked Bonnie to call the mortician. Despite her emotional and physical exhaustion, she felt at peace. Reflecting on that time, she later told me: "For all the agony, it was unbelievable. There were so many good things, it was overwhelming." She had almost lost Douglas in the course of his illness, but paradoxically, in the process of his dying, he had reached out and reunited with her.

Douglas Kearney's dying, at the outset, was a very messy struggle with little hope for a gentle end. When he was referred to hospice, two people told me that it was probably useless. One cited the tumor in his brain, which was affecting his personality, the other the fact that his anger was so ingrained. There were times, before and during his psych ward hospitalization, when I doubted whether he would ever change. Admittedly, his personality had always contained anger, and his brain tumor certainly fueled his uncontrollable outbursts. The gradual loss of his precious role of father and provider surely fanned the fire. He got angrier as the disease progressed, and he felt increasingly helpless. Because of his denial and his image of himself as strong and goal-oriented, he could not bring his relationship with his children to closure. He needed sadness to say goodbye, to say how proud he was of them and how proud he was to be their dad.

All his life, anger had been his reaction to disappointment and frustration; this emotion was familiar territory to him. He had no training in sadness, no experience with it. Sadness was an absolute unknown and thus terrifying. When he was forced to confront his sadness in the psych unit, he finally took that first step off the diving board and realized, as frightening as it was, that he could enter the darkness and survive. Once he was able to cry and to acknowledge the depth of his own sadness, it lost its power. He was changed by the experience, but somehow more whole.

Personal distress or suffering of some extent is universal among people who are dying, even those who have no physical discomfort. It may range from an almost subtle loss of interest in life and a pervasive sense of uneasiness to terrifying, agonizing torment. While easy passages from life do occur, for most people the months and weeks that precede the moment of their death involve effort and inner struggle as they confront the gradual loss of their abilities, roles, and relationships and as they work to achieve some equilibrium in the face of inexorable decline.

Yet I have seen that there is a way around—or through—such suffering. Much of my thinking has been shaped not only by personal experiences but by cultural and spiritual beliefs. I do not work within a specific religious context, but I find more than a little truth in the spiritual philosophies of Christianity, Buddhism, and Judaism. In the traditional Christian world view, suffering is an inevitable component of human life. Release from suffering exists not in this world but in heaven. From a Christian perspective, the purpose of human suffering has less to do with one's own enlightenment than with alleviating the suffering of others. Buddhism holds that suffering is part of the human experience; it is nature itself, the stuff of existence. It arises from a person's attachments to the world—possessions, physical pleasures, personal accomplishments, relationships, and, ultimately, one's very identity. Only by severing these attachments can one transcend suffering and experience liberation and enlightenment. Suffering also forms a strong, recurring theme within Judaism. Judaism teaches that God chose the Jews for certain roles and responsibilities within a cosmic plan. Inevitably, some human suffering will occur and must be accepted, for the sake of others, or the community as a whole, or in congruence with God's eternal plan.

Another philosophical source of remarkable insights into personal suffering is exemplified in Victor Frankl's account of his internment in a Nazi concentration camp, *Man's Search for Meaning*. Frankl, a psychiatrist, maintains that physical discomfort and deprivation, no matter how extreme or brutal, do not cause suffering. The true root of suffering is loss of meaning and purpose in life, he says. Being free of physical suffering, he believes, is not enough to sustain a person, and he quotes the philosopher Friedrich Nietzsche to explain the power of meaning to triumph over physical suffering: "He who has a *why* to live, can bear almost any *how*." Pain and privation can be endured if it is for a purpose. Although each person's meaning is different, existence that is merely a burden and lacks a future with any direction or point produces the worst kind of suffering.

Douglas's sense of self was most severely assailed in his family life, especially in relation to his role as father and provider. Parts of himself were tumbling away in a frightening cascade. Everything that had given him meaning was under attack. From the moment when he awoke from his seizure in the ER, he was no longer a construction worker and a productive member of society; he no longer worked at all. Douglas also suffered mightily as his ability to function as a father and parent diminished. He was no longer the breadwinner for his family. Nor could he hunt or fish or play ball with his kids. He wasn't even able to watch them play or go to their schools. Instead he consumed the family's attention, and its money. The battering to his sense of self was severe.

In fact, as his illness progressed, his role in the family reversed, and his needs were increasingly like those of a child. Pride had always been a prominent part of Douglas's character. With illness, he became the dependent one requiring constant care, feeding, and nurturing. He hated how self-absorbed he had become, yet he felt so needy.

By ignoring, dismissing, or minimizing facets of a person's identity, doctors or family members add to a patient's suffering. This suffering will persist in someone actively dying until the integrity of the person can be restored some other way. Even with seemingly limitless, endless suffering, I have found that transformation is possible. Often, in retrospect, it is as if there had been a thin vein or membrane that divided the sufferer from relief and release. With Douglas Kearney, the curtain between his suffering from the threat of self-annihilation and his relief was thick and heavy. Yet he not only got beyond his suffering, he embraced it, and that gave him the strength to share his pain and sadness with his family. By finally allowing himself to be immersed in sadness, he *moved through* his suffering, emerging beyond it into the arms of his family. In so doing, he achieved a paradoxical wellness in his dying. In the end, his suffering became a catalyst for dying well.

Five

Finding Dignity amid Disease and Disintegration: Wallace Burke, Julia Rosauer, Hap Visscher

For many people there is no worse pain, no greater suffering, than when they feel that they have lost their dignity. "I feel so undignified" is a constant refrain among terminally ill people whose personhood is being assaulted from all directions. A dying person may not be able to dress and feed himself or evacuate his bowels and bladder. One may be totally dependent on loved ones, even strangers, for daily care. One may slowly lose those pieces of one's identity that stemmed from one's reputation and self-image as a doer, an organizer, an achiever, or a nurturer. In dying, a person's sense of worth may wane as he or she can no longer fulfill roles and responsibilities as coworker, community member, or parent. Not only does one not contribute anymore, but one has become a burden to the very people one wants to serve. All that gave one's life meaning and dignity is being lost.

When I hear people refer to the indignity of dying as illness dissolves pieces of who the person was, I think of my father's passing and I become sad, and then annoyed. My father taught me that "you play the cards you've been dealt." My dad would rather have died quickly, even suddenly, yet that was not what God or fate had in store. Was my father undignified in his slow decline and dying? For me the answer is a loud *no*. Sy accepted dependency as an unpleasant but inescapable fact of his condition. He accepted the care he needed with grace and dignity.

Unfortunately, society reinforces the belief that the loss of normal capability and independence renders a person undignified. Our society reserves its highest accolades for youth, vigor, and self-control and accords them dignity, while their absence is thought to be undignified. The physical signs of disease or advanced age are considered personally degrading, and the body's deterioration, rather than being regarded as an unavoidable human process, becomes a source of embarrassment.

While dignity and personhood may be abstract notions, there is nothing abstract about what makes us feel personally valued and worthwhile. When we are active and healthy, we derive dignity from the things we do well and the qualities about ourselves that we value most. And regardless of where we find it, dignity is accompanied by respect for oneself and respect in the eyes of others. Can there be dignity when we can do little for ourselves and nothing for others? When all that we were has passed? It is a fact of the human condition that as we die we need care—is this inherently undignified? I think the answers lie in exploring our attitudes and assumptions about individual behavior and worth. Dignity needs to be accorded the remarkable achievements in personal growth that can occur while someone is dying. The waning phase of a person's life deserves to be a time of satisfaction and to stir feelings of self-esteem and self-worth.

Most people who are dying grapple with the question of how to maintain their dignity. While each person in the next three stories suffered a loss of dignity, each derived dignity from a different source and eventually reclaimed it in different ways. These stories are about people who were afflicted with progressive neurological diseases, because the twin extremes of indignity, from the perspective of both patient and family, are vividly reflected by advanced neuromuscular disease and by advanced dementia. When we think of family members or ourselves becoming ill, we tend to think that dementia or feeblemindedness would be the ultimate loss of dignity. However, for the person dying, the assault may be more acute when functional decline and dependence advances while intellect is preserved. A person with a disease such as amyotrophic lateral sclerosis or multiple sclerosis may feel undignified as the disease inexorably robs him of physical abilities and the capacity to care for himself, while leaving the awareness of his diminution intact. In contrast, by the time dementia, such as Alzheimer's disease, is far advanced, dignity no longer has meaning for the patient. Indignity is suffered vicariously by the person's relatives when their loved one is no longer the person they knew and when her behavior becomes at first childlike and, later, infantile.

For Wallace Burke, dying of ALS, dignity returned when he recognized that, despite the disease leaving him as helpless as a baby, he was contributing to his family and his community. Julia Rosauer, who had multiple sclerosis and a tenuous hold on self-respect throughout much of her life, found dignity when her sisters, children, and boyfriend recognized and expressed their love and respect for her, and thanked her for her years of selfless devotion. Hap Visscher's dignity arose from a strong, singular sense of self: he was a man who could make things work. When Hap felt incompetent and incapable, he felt undignified. His sense of worth and self-esteem were restored by taking on a task that added meaning to the final stage of his life. Even as Alzheimer's was erasing his memory, he could feel that his life had been worthwhile and that he was valued by his family and caregivers.

WALLACE BURKE

When I met Wallace Burke, he was petrified, in terror of a plate of scrambled eggs and toast. Although only sixty, he looked much older. He was pale and thin, and the skin around his jaw sagged. He was sitting up in bed, wearing blue striped pajamas, and trembling, with a fork in his hand. I do not think he heard me come in.

"Mr. Burke? Are you all right?" He was frozen, riveted on his breakfast. Almost reflexively I took his wrist and checked his pulse. He looked up and seemed relieved to have company; the distraction temporarily broke the spell of fear.

"Oh, hello," he said apologetically. His words were choppy and breathy. "Are you the doctor? I'm having a difficult time. Swallowing. I'm worried about choking. I don't want to choke to death," he said.

"Yes, Mr. Burke. I'm Dr. Byock. I understand that you have been having problems with choking. It's one of the things I want to talk with you about." I tried to reassure him that I would address his concern, but I felt we needed to get acquainted first.

Beset by rapidly developing amyotrophic lateral sclerosis (ALS), also known as Lou Gehrig's disease, Wallace was being robbed of all muscle strength, even the power to eat and clear his throat and protect his airway. Someone with advanced ALS can choke on anything, even soft foods or tiny bites. Eating for Mr. Burke was not the unconscious, pleasurable activity it used to be. By the time I met him, it probably felt more like tightrope walking.

Wallace Burke had been admitted into Missoula's new hospice house two days earlier. He had been transferred from a nursing home in Lewistown, four hours east of Missoula, and referred to hospice because he was steadily losing control over his bodily functions and would ultimately die from complications related to his disease. He had come to Missoula because his only son, Eric, his daughter-in-law, Jenny, and his grandchildren lived there. While they were unable to care for him in their small home, they were devoted to him and wanted him to be nearby.

I had met Eric Burke years ago when we had served together on the board of the local food bank. Though I had never met his father, I knew of him. Wallace Burke had been mayor of a small town and then a state legislator. He was known throughout Montana as a politician who fought hard to preserve funding for rural health care and education. Years earlier he had run for governor and been defeated in the primary. He had earned a reputation for being that rare politician, a public servant who was both tireless and quiet-spoken. When he retired, the *Missoulian* referred to him as "The Gentleman of the Front Range."

Just a year earlier, after he had retired from politics and was, as he put it, "perfecting my short game," he had developed an uncomfortable tingling in his hands. He was having trouble climbing stairs, reaching plates from the top shelf of the cupboard, and even turning the car ignition key. He felt a weakness in his legs that was spreading to his arms. His general health had always been good, although fifteen years earlier his doctor had told him that he had coronary artery disease and atrial fibrillation and had given him nitroglycerin to stem chest pain and Digoxin to control his heart rate. Initially, the tests in Lewistown were inconclusive, and his doctor had referred him to a neurologist in Great Falls. The ALS was definitively diagnosed by an electromyogram, which tests muscle contractions, just seven months before he came to hospice.

This disease usually does not move quite so fast, and its precipitous progress stunned Wallace Burke. In less than a month, he had lost control of his "golf hands" and found that he was too clumsy to write a letter or even sign a check. Long widowed and living alone in a house surrounded by wheat fields, he was soon forced by the disease to make changes. He researched his illness, contacted the ALS Society, and quizzed his doctor. Some of his questions were unanswerable: "How did I get this illness?" "How long have I had it?" "How long do I have?" He learned that his weakness would get worse and eventually render him immobile, and that he could do nothing to stem the tide. He asked his doctor in Lewistown how he would die and was told that people with ALS usually just "waste away" or die when they can no longer breathe on their own.

"I've looked forward to meeting you since Eric and Jenny told me you were coming. I know of your work in state government. For what it's worth, I have a lot of respect for what you've stood for and gotten done. It's nice to finally meet you, and it's a real privilege to have you here with us."

"Well, that's kind of you to say, Doctor. The people here have been so nice, and they seem to understand what I'm going through." All signs of his panic had vanished. I moved a chair from the corner of the room to his bedside, unobtrusively moving aside the stand with the offending plate of eggs. He continued, "Eric and Jen have been telling me about this place and I'm intrigued. I'd never heard about a hospice residence. They tell me it's the first one in Montana. Do other places have them?" The inflection of his voice told me that his curiosity was genuine. It also confirmed that his mind remained clear and he was still interested in social welfare.

"Yes, that's right. This is the first hospice facility in the state, and we're pretty proud of it. There are similar places in a number of larger cities around the country. In general, however, hospice in America is focused on helping people to stay at home and live out their days in familiar surroundings. Over the years we've found that it really isn't possible for some people to stay in their own homes. Sometimes they live alone and can't manage by themselves, and there's no family close by to help out. Other times a person's husband or wife is too sick or frail to provide the care needed, or the care is too complicated or physically demanding. Sometimes the family house or trailer is simply too small to accommodate a hospital bed or the equipment needed for home care. And, as you might imagine, in some families there is too much discord and dysfunction to make care at home work."

"Do most of your patients still manage to stay at home?"

"Oh, sure, most of our patients do well at home. At any given time, however, there has always been a small percentage of folks, maybe 10 or 15 percent, who are just unable to make it at home and have had to choose between a nursing home or, for some, even the hospital. We've needed a homelike alternative, and, thankfully, now we finally have one."

"How did you folks pay for this place?" I was struck again by his lucidity and his obvious continued fascination with social systems.

"Actually, the community paid for it, Mr. Burke. Like most hospice programs, ours is just getting by. Medicare, Medicaid, and most insurance companies pay for hospice care, but barely enough to meet expenses and not nearly enough to pay a mortgage. For us to operate a residence we knew it would have to be fully paid for before we moved in."

"How'd you do it?" he asked.

"Well, I might bore you with the details, or maybe not. You and I have some things in common. I've been a community organizer for years, mostly around hospice-related projects, though I've had the good sense never to run for office." I paused long enough for him to see my sidelong glance and to witness his smile in reaction to my friendly barb. "I've helped start several hospice programs in the places I've lived. This project—finding, purchasing and remodeling this house—took over a year and endless meetings and a formal capital campaign to accomplish. It wasn't easy, but it was fairly straightforward. Basically, we defined the problem and our need, presented a proposal to the community, and asked for help. The response has been very gratifying."

"Well, I am impressed, Dr. Byock."

This interaction set the tone of our friendship over the months to come. Despite all the tragedy that had befallen him and that lay ahead, he remained delightful and engaging. The formality of his use of my title seemed to extend from a lifelong habit; his manner was not at all starchy; instead, it was warm and already somehow familiar. I was always aware of his stature, and I often addressed him as Mayor Burke. The formality was feigned, but the respect was real. In return he often called me, with a sense of humor and in a gesture of professional respect, Dr. Byock.

A nurse's aide came in to remove his breakfast tray, and we repositioned Wallace in his bed and straightened his sheets. When she left, I returned to the questions of his declining health. Though I told him that I had reviewed his medical records and had spoken with his family, I asked him to relate the events of the last year from his perspective, and I listened as he detailed the personal effects of his illness and galloping disability.

"Can you imagine, me, a baseball fan all my life, now dying of Lou Gehrig's disease? It doesn't seem fair, does it?" he asked.

"No, it certainly doesn't seem fair. As I listen to your story, I can only begin to conceive how frightening it must be. When I came in today, you looked terrified."

"I was. Doctor, I am so afraid of choking to death."

"I can understand your concern, but I want you to know that we're aware and will do everything we can to prevent that from happening. For what it's worth, hospice patients I have known with ALS or similar conditions do not die by choking. It's far more common for people to die quite peacefully," I said.

"But what am I going to do? Some days I can hardly eat a bite without gagging."

"Does the choking happen only when you are eating?" I inquired.

"Yup, pretty much. It's like the food doesn't want to go down the right pipe."

As I pondered how to explore this subject with him, I glanced around the room. In the corner was an oxygen tank and a muted television tuned to ESPN. The dresser was crammed with framed photos of Eric, Jenny, and their children; an ornately framed wedding portrait of his wife radiantly posed atop steps draped with the train of her gown; and a yellowing picture of Mr. Burke in a uniform standing beside a tank. Well-thumbed sections of the *Missoulian*, the *Great Falls Tribune* and *The New York Times Magazine* were draped across a nightstand and chair. A couple of plaques with state seals hung on the walls alongside a child's crayon drawing.

Normally the option of consciously choosing not to eat is too delicate a subject to discuss on a first visit with a patient, but Wallace's candid fear invited an equally honest response. "Well, this may seem out of line, but I'm going to ask you a naive question. Why are you still eating?"

An impish grin came over his face. "I guess it's just become somewhat of a habit."

I laughed. "Yes, I'm pretty fond of eating myself!" I paused. "But seriously, do you find that you are hungry and look forward to eating during the day?"

"No, hell." He spoke slowly. "I haven't really been hungry for months. I've been eating because everyone encourages me to. I've been losing so much weight, I hoped I could get a little stronger. You know, Doctor, I have thought of refusing my medications. I talked about it with Eric—did he mention it? He said I should ask you."

"Yes, he did, and I've reviewed your medicine list. I don't think there's anything you're currently taking that is prolonging your life."

Before I could continue, he interjected, "What would happen if I stopped eating? Is it a painful way to go?"

"No, you don't have to eat. At some point in diseases like ALS, people find that it's impossible to eat normally. For a time they may be fed, but eventually even that may not suffice. Often people have feeding tubes inserted into their stomach and continue to be nourished that way. That's a legitimate option; not eating is, too. Whatever you choose to do should fit your goals. Really, only you can make this sort of decision. It's obviously a very serious, intimate decision. I don't want to encourage you one way or the other, but I think you need to know it's one place you still have control."

"I already told them, I mean the doctors at home, that I would never want to be fed by a tube. If I stopped eating, how long would it take? How long would I live?" he wondered. "Would it be painful?"

"No, it would not be painful. Over the years I have routinely asked people who stopped eating whether they were hungry, and the answer is always no. Hunger is almost never a problem for the patients we serve. Sometimes when we ask people if they're thirsty, they'll say yes, but when we moisten their mouth and throat and ask again, they say no. It's always hard to say how long someone is going to live, even in this situation. I don't think it would be long, perhaps two or three weeks. Probably less if you stop taking in fluids," I told him. "People usually become increasingly sleepy and gradually drift away peacefully, without any pain or other discomfort. Sometimes people develop a fever, probably from an infection, but we can usually bring the temperature down with medications and cool baths.

"Mr. Burke, whatever you decide about this, as long as you are here with us, we can help with any discomfort. I can't promise you exactly how or when you will die, but especially with you being here at the Hospice House, I can promise that we will not let you suffer."

He nodded solemnly, and we sat together quietly for a minute or two before I spoke again. "It's a lot to think about."

"Oh, that it is, Doctor. But I so appreciate you stopping by. This has helped me a great deal. Will you be coming back?"

"Absolutely. I'll look forward to it," I replied, adding, "I'm a regular around here."

I visited with Wallace for over an hour that first meeting. We agreed to let our conversation sit for a few days. In the weeks that followed I often dropped by to see him. Our visits might begin with small talk, discussing state or national news or the Montana Grizzlies' winning football season. Whenever it fit, I would ask him about his earlier days, eliciting stories about dry land ranching or Montana politics.

The Hospice House sits in the middle of an area west of Missoula that the settlers called Grass Valley. The fifteen-minute drive out of town always gives me a quiet, thoughtful time in the middle of the day. The rural road leading to Grass Valley passes hay fields, small cattle ranches, and an occasional cluster of tract homes. The house is a rambling ranch-style home with six bedrooms, a large living room, and an equally large family-style kitchen. My favorite feature is an expansive wooden deck that wraps around the back of the house and faces a split-rail fence, beyond which miles of open fields roll on in the distance. A favorite pastime for residents is sitting on the deck, even on the coldest days, bundled in blankets and watching hawks soar and hunt. Every now and then deer graze in the field and foxes appear.

One day Wallace was sitting in a wheelchair on the deck when I arrived. It was around four P.M.; charcoal-gray clouds were backlit by the bright setting sun. Beside him sat Eric, his son. He looked like a mountain man, with a full beard, thick brown hair, and his boots and a red-and-black lumber jacket; he shared his father's hairline and square face. We shook hands. Shortly after I greeted them, he announced that he was leaving and promised his father he would be back the next day. I walked Eric to his car, and asked how he thought his father was doing.

"I think he's comfortable. He's weaker, though. I can see a change, even in the last ten days. It's good to have him here and be able to spend time with him. Emotionally, I think he's still having a hard time. He doesn't show it, though. He is still very much my dad, trying to figure it all out and come up with a rational solution. I left because I know he has some things he wants to talk with you about alone." As he drove off, I returned to the deck.

"Glad you stopped by," Wallace said, in a halting, strangled voice. He looked downcast, slumped in his chair, with a plaid wool blanket wrapped around his legs and torso; he was unable to sit up straight. I knew his lack of breath made it hard for him to string together long sentences.

"How are you doing today, Mr. Burke? Are you hurting anywhere?"

He thought for a moment. "No, it's not that." He hesitated.

"Shortness of breath?" He shook his head. "Tell me what's happening, if you can. Are you hurting inside?" I said, holding my hand to my chest. "Are you suffering?" His eyes grew heavier still, and he gazed toward the mountains.

"It's just that—I feel awful, such a burden. It all seems so undignified. So awful. The nurses, they have to, you know." I leaned closer as he looked at me to see if I understood what he was referring to. The disease had affected his bladder and his bowel function, and he was continually constipated. Although he had sensation, he had no diaphragm power to open the sphincter and push out a stool. So every couple of days the nurses had to manually disimpact him.

"I know it's hard for you—it would be really hard for me to accept, too. But to those of us who are caring for you, it's just part of what we do. I've disimpacted lots of people over the years, and it's just no big deal. Yet I know that when my time comes and I need to be disimpacted or otherwise cared for, it's going to feel lousy. I wish there was a way of making it easier for you." I was standing beside him; I now moved to the rail of the deck and faced him. "But I don't agree with you about one important thing. I do not think that you are the least bit undignified.

Years ago when my father was dying, he told me that he felt embarrassed by his appearance and by being ill. It's something I've thought about a lot during my practice. So I think I understand how you feel, but from my point of view, you are just being human. You have this lousy disease and, unfortunately, you're dying, but you're just human. There is absolutely nothing in any of that to be embarrassed about." I paused to give him a chance to respond.

When he didn't, I kept going. "Most of the time I'm careful to speak only for myself, Mr. Burke, but I know the people I work with and can tell you that we all feel this way. You are no more of a burden to us than an infant or toddler is for their parents and caregivers. At the end of life, it sometimes just turns out that we need care like we did when we were very young.

"Think of it, Mr. Burke. An infant isn't undignified needing to be changed, and neither are you. You need help with eating and with your bowel movements. No big deal. You may think we are all a little loony, but we do this work because we want to. In fact, we consider it a genuine privilege to care for people at the end of their lives. You could not be undignified in my eyes or in the eyes of any of the people around here. People are inherently dignified, and they are only made undignified if they are placed in situations that are demeaning."

His eyes were slightly teary, but his expression was relaxed, and his mood seemed to have lifted. I tucked in around his legs a corner of the blanket that the wind had pulled loose. I sat down next to him again, watching starlings swoop after invisible insects in the early evening sky. Five minutes passed before he said anything. "Once again, you have given me a great deal to think about, Doctor. I sure do appreciate your visits."

For the time being, we left it at that. He asked me how I thought Eric was doing. I said, "Other than being understandably sad and worried about you, I think he is doing OK."

"I'm very proud of my son, you know. He's a great boy. He married a wonderful woman, and he's a good father to those kids. They tell me he's also a good geologist." Although speaking took effort, he continued to reminisce and told a story of Eric's earliest interest in rocks; when he was nine years old and the two of them were hunting upland birds, Eric had found a geode.

I suspect that Wallace Burke's feelings of being a burden were magnified by his life of public service. It was especially hard for him not to be contributing in some way. For most of his adult years he had been the helper, the caregiver. He had raised his son, managed the family ranch, and served the people of his city and state. Now the tables were turned, and it was a novel experience.

When I visited Wallace a few days later, he was in bed watching sports on television, but he pushed the *off* button on the remote control as soon as I walked in. Although he seemed weak and had his oxygen on, he was bright-eyed and eager to chat. I asked if he was comfortable.

"No, nothing is hurting." His voice was a coarse whisper. "I've decided. I want to get this over with. Nothing to extend my life. No more medication. Nothing to prolong my life." I gave him a quizzical look. His primary medication was digoxin to regulate the rhythm of his heart. According to his chart, he had gone off it once before and had experienced tachycardia—a racing heart, breathlessness, and chest pains.

"The only thing you're really taking, other than a small amount of pain medication, is the digoxin. As we've discussed, I don't think it's prolonging your life. It's for your comfort."

"Well, Dr. Byock, I've also decided to stop eating. Not right away. I've still got a few things to do. But it's time for me to get out of the way. These resources can be used better elsewhere."

"Mr. Burke, unfortunately, it seems to me that you've been dealt some bad cards, and I can only imagine how hard it must be lying here and having things done for you and to you," I said.

"Yeah, it's horrible. Every day I feel a little bit more like a lame duck."

I chuckled to myself, wondering whether he was referring to his life on a ranch or in politics. "You know, the social responsibility that you have so well exemplified is not limited to doing things for others. Interactions just like this, caring and being cared for, are the way in which community is created. I believe that community, like the word *family*, is really more of a verb than a noun. Community comes about in the process of caring for those in need among us. It's unfortunate now that you're getting to see that side of it, but in allowing yourself to be cared for, and being a willing recipient of care, you're contributing in a remarkably valuable way to the community. In a real sense, we need to care for you. Not just those of us in hospice, but the community we represent, the community that funds us and supports us." I was sitting on the edge of his bed, aware of the oxygen tube in his nose and his labored breathing. His eyes were clear, and he studied me.

"Community, huh?" he repeated.

I straightened a crimp in his oxygen tube. "Yeah, community, Mr. Burke. Just like you have been all your life, you're still at the heart of it."

Wallace Burke was a philosopher-politician through and through; someone who, I hoped, could be reached through reason. By my reframing the issue of dependency and arguing convincingly for the existence of responsibility and value at life's end, it was just possible that his suffering could be soothed. He was also a proper gentleman through and through. He tipped his head in a half-nod, and in the sad, soulful expression of his eyes I saw the wisdom of his years. "Doctor, you know how much I hate all this, but what you have said does make sense to me. I guess it's time to be on the receiving end." His words, very much in character, let me know I was on the right track.

"I hope it doesn't sound too syrupy or sentimental, but I'm going to say again what I really feel. It's a privilege and a pleasure to know you and to care for you, Mayor Burke," I rejoined. Nodding, he let me know he was, at last, able to accept this feeling and acknowledge the truth in it.

People who pride themselves on being doers and givers find illness and dependency something they are utterly unprepared for and, typically, they resist and protest. Surprisingly, however, with time and what I call "skilled listening," their resistance fades. For someone confined to bed with a rapidly deteriorating physical condition and increasing dependency, conversations about being a burden and the meaning of dignity can have an immediate impact. To the person dying these are not idle philosophical musings. The conversation often picks up a stream of thought that is constantly on his mind and about which he has been thinking on a moment-to-moment, hourly basis, turning it over in an almost obsessive fashion. When he hears a fresh insight or perspective, he tends to be immediately receptive.

This was the case with Wallace Burke. Our civics discussions proved to be exactly what he needed, or so he said. His mood continued to be bright, despite the racing pace of his illness. From his bed over the next two weeks he was busy. At my suggestion and with the hospice staff and volunteer's encouragement, he recorded stories of his boyhood years. He attended his grandson Josh's eighth birthday celebration in the Hospice House living room and gave him a pocket watch his grandfather had given him. He even watched the World Series and was satisfied with the outcome.

A few weeks later, Wallace began leaving his meal tray untouched and limiting his fluids to chips of ice. The hospice nurses asked him if he wanted to eat, and when he slightly shook his head they took the tray away. Although he was offered food every day, he declined it, accepting only a spoonful of pudding from time to time. Eric and Jenny visited daily, sometimes accompanied by the kids, who, when he had the strength, regaled him with stories of school and their activities. Through it all he seemed content. He said he had no discomfort and was delighted that there were no more bowel movements to deal with. Gradually, over several days, he became lethargic and slipped into a coma. Eric was by his side much of the time, cooling his father's brow with a washcloth and moistening his lips with a swab. Mr. Burke never awoke; he died two and a half months after coming to the Hospice House.

I believe Wallace Burke gained a renewed sense of dignity in his passing when he shed his previous notion of dignity, which had been wrapped around physical independence and helping others. He came to understand that care for the frail and the dying is a vital part of the life of the community. By accepting his new role and acknowledging his continuing contributions to his family and community, Wallace Burke achieved a renewed sense of self-worth. Despite his physical dependence—and, in a sense, because of it—he retained his dignity.

Julia Rosauer

Dignity for Julia Rosauer centered less on her physical ordeal than on her self-image, which had been battered throughout her life, first by her parents, then by a husband and boyfriend. In most of her relationships she had been the caretaker, and her self-effacing, obedient nature had allowed her to be exploited and ignored. Until she asserted herself and recognized her own accomplishments, Julia could never achieve a sense of dignity.

When she was admitted to the Sky View Nursing Home, a year before I met her, all she wanted was to die. Suffering from multiple sclerosis, she had been told by a neurologist that her nonfunctioning, neurogenic bladder could not be fixed and that her pain from chaotic, misfiring nerves might prove "uncontrollable." She was becoming increasingly crippled and needed full-time nursing care. When her body became so twisted that simple nodding was almost impossible, the nursing home asked our hospice to help; Stella Pomeroy, a hospice social worker, and I both visited her regularly.

Julia was in bed, her legs braced so she could lie on her back, a pillow propped between her knees to prevent pressure sores, when I first stopped by on a sunny April morning. She shared a room with a much older woman who was sleeping in the next bed. Julia was bony thin with prominent cheekbones and long, thick brown hair, which was lustrous and clean and pulled off her face with a barrette. She looked older than the sixty-two years noted on her chart.

I had barely introduced myself or asked about her pain when she grabbed the conversation. Because of her disease, the pace and volume of her speech jumped wildly as if a mischievous child was playing with the controls of a stereo. Nevertheless, she clearly was a chatterbox.

"Oh, it's too bad you weren't here earlier. You missed Eddie. He's my boyfriend—well, really, the man I live with. We've been together for years," she explained. But I knew that he visited only rarely. "He's really a sweetheart, and feels awful that he can't take care of me, but I understand. Heck, I wouldn't even take care of me if I had a choice! I mean, look. What a mess." She could not gesture with her hands or move her head more than an inch or so, but she could screw up her eyes to express disgust.

"I don't see such a mess, Julia, though I can certainly tell that your illness has taken a toll on your poor body. One thing it hasn't affected is your gorgeous hair," I retorted.

"Pffftt." She let out a noise of dismissal, which I would get to know well. "Believe me, this bag of bones doesn't deserve the time of day. Anyhow, Dennis—he's my boy—is coming later. He visits all the time. But I worry about him. I don't think that wife of his is feeding him right. He looks thin; I think he's hitting the schnapps again." She sounded skilled at deflecting attention to herself and worrying about others.

Multiple sclerosis is not usually fatal, and many of its victims live nearly normal life spans, though their mobility is severely curtailed and many are eventually confined to wheelchairs. In Julia's case, however, the illness would clearly be lethal, probably from the combined effects of malnutrition, recurrent infections of her urinary tract, or the bedsores that would never fully heal. Pain was another constant problem: spasms in her contorted muscles, achy pain in her joints, sharp jolts of electrical pain from her diseased nerves, and insistent urges to evacuate her renegade bowels and bladder.

Julia would have continued to chatter if I had not broken in. I asked her about the pain.

"Of course I have pain. Everywhere. It's a three. But when that hot wire hits, Jesus, that's off the chart. But you can't do anything about that." She used a one-to-ten pain scale to pinpoint her discomforts.

"Perhaps we can. I have reviewed your chart, and Dr. Blanchard asked me to manage your medications. Those electrical pains are awful and can be hard to treat. But we're going to try. With your permission I want to start you on a small dose of medication at night called amitriptyline. When we see how you are tolerating that, within a week or so, I would also like to prescribe an epilepsy medication. It'll take time to find out what's going to work best for you, but we'll keep at it."

"Damn, it sounds good to me that you're not giving up. Oh, and while you're at it, I was thinking, you know, I've got sores on my butt. Those aren't a three, they're getting over five. My butt hurts! And my heel hurts. And I hurt in my legs whenever they move me." As if to soften her complaining, she quickly added, "But I love my bath aide. She keeps me clean and smelling good. I wish she came more often." I wondered if the bath aide had also done her hair.

She let me examine her: The right heel clearly needed to be cleaned of infected tissue and dressed. The ulcer extended deep into fatty tissue and was getting larger, according to the notes in her chart, and would probably need repeated treatments. Julia did not seem to notice much pain as I probed, but she reacted to the rotten smell. "God, do I stink!" she declared.

I chuckled. "No worse than most people taking off their shoes!" She insisted that her the odor was most foul.

The next time I visited Julia, she and her son Dennis were watching a movie in the television lounge. It was around five in the afternoon, and half a dozen other residents also sat in the lounge, waiting for dinner. Julia sat in a wheelchair, but her arms and legs jutted and twisted, making her perch look precarious. She cheerfully greeted me and introduced me to Dennis as "Dr. Ira" before launching into an explanation of how busy he had been lately with his carpentry work. Tall, beefy, and sullen, he appeared to be in his early thirties, though his behavior and posture were that of an arrogant teenager. He grunted when Julia introduced us and stayed riveted to the television.

Stella, who had made several social-work visits to Julia during the preceding weeks, thought she might be clinically depressed and had asked me to consider medication. I asked Julia if she would mind talking somewhere more quiet. She agreed, and I pushed her toward the sun room while Dennis stayed put, showing neither offense at being left nor curiosity about our conversation. We parked by a window and a rubber plant struggling to thrive in the institutional environment. The weather was rainy and gray, but the hills in the distance had a faint cast of green that signaled the coming of spring.

Many people assume that a terminal illness and depression are natural compatriots. They reason that depression is only logical, given the prognosis. This is not necessarily true. As a hospice physician, I frequently need to distinguish between normal grief reactions and clinical depression. While a person's sadness and depressed mood at the impending loss of all the things and people in her life may be intense, it usually can be treated with nonmedical, supportive care and counseling. Clinical depression is not normal, and simple support will not suffice. There is nothing logical about clinical depression. Of course, while disability, discomfort, and a dismal prognosis can contribute to clinical depression, a person's susceptibility may have less to do with the immediate situation than with biology, heredity, temperament, and lifelong self-image and ways of relating to others.

For a few minutes Julia and I made small talk about the length of the gray Missoula winters and the elk she occasionally saw from the sun room as they grazed on the hills across the river from the nursing home.

"I don't know if you can separate what I am going to ask from your pain, but I'd like to get a sense of how you are feeling within yourself." The question *How are you feeling within yourself?* is something I learned during a hospice fellowship in England. Time after time, after a person's physical discomfort had been assessed and "the bowels and bladder dealt with," I saw physicians and hospice nurses cut through layers of polite formality and awkwardness with the phrase. At times, the inquiry provoked open grieving and tears; at other times the response was a solemn and genuine reassurance that, despite the sadness, the patient was well within herself. I had never heard quite so succinct a way of getting to what seemed to be the heart of the matter, and I was impressed with how consistently the interaction resulted in feelings of deepened understanding and satisfaction for both patients and clinicians. I remember Julia's response well.

"It's like I'm being squeezed by giant hands. When I was a little girl, I used to think that big storms were really giants or God cleaning house and running the vacuum cleaner, and now these hands are twisting my body. I can't move. My back and gut ache so much, all the time, that I feel like a lump of sticky mud." She bobbed her head forward and whispered, as if to confide in me, "Actually, I feel like a lump of shit!"

I said nothing, knowing she intended to continue. "You saw on my chart that I don't want any antibiotics if I get an infection. You know, this life ain't worth living, that's for sure," she declared.

"I don't know you well, Julia. Only what I have learned in the last little while and what I can glean from your medical chart. I can't begin to imagine all the losses in your life. I noticed in your chart, for instance, that you were divorced and later widowed. Those are two very big losses in anyone's life."

"One loss, in my case," she retorted. "Well, two losses, one husband."

"Huh?" I was confused. "I thought you were married twice."

"Nope, just once. When Frederick left me, I divorced him. It was no big deal by that time. I mean, being married to him was the difficult part. He could be like a pit bull—sweet enough when he wasn't drinking, but when he was, pfftt, look out. He really did love me. But he was hard on me and hard on the kids. He had no patience for kids, anybody's kids. He'd snap and swat at them. Sometimes I got in the way and got swatted, too. I tried to make sure the kids all did what they were told, but he had a temper. Anyhow, when he got sick, I went to be with him. No one else was going to take care of him. And I was with him in the hospital when he died. Though we weren't married anymore, I sort of felt widowed."

The family history in Julia's chart was sketchy and misleading, as with most other hospice patients, and the real story had to be fleshed out. The process was not strictly information-gathering, however. Conversation often builds a natural friendship and alliance. Listening is sometimes the most powerful therapy.

"When was this?"

"Years ago," she said vaguely, as if the event had been almost forgotten. "Conrad, the older one, was, let's see, in high school, probably around fourteen, and Dennis was still a boy, ten. The hard part was keeping on with Custom Log Cabins while raising the kids, trying to give them everything. I had to work weekends, at the hospital, an aide, cleaning and stuff."

Julia recited the details of her tragic story as if talking about someone else, having probably separated herself from the pain years ago. She described growing up in Darby, a small Montana logging town south of Missoula, the oldest daughter in a family of four. Their father worked as a lumberjack before he left the family, and their alcoholic mother drifted in and out. Julia had virtually raised her younger brother and sisters while her mother worked in a local bar. She sounded disembodied as she revealed the litany of losses: her brother, George, whom she loved dearly, had been killed by a land mine in Vietnam, and Conrad, despondent over a fractured love affair and in the throes of alcohol, had shot himself at twenty-six. When her ex-husband Frederick became ill with emphysema and miner's lung, she stretched herself even thinner, juggling a job, parenting, and nursing until his dying day.

In the same monotone she described her boyfriend, Eddie, who sounded to me so much like Frederick that at times I lost track of the sequence of the story. Eddie was a long-haul truck driver who drank too much, constantly philandered, and had been abusive. After living together for eight years, when her disease began to flare and every bout left her less able to care for him, he had begun complaining that he could not take responsibility for her and had finally insisted that she needed to be institutionalized.

At the time I met her, Julia had not been sleeping well for months. She was disturbed by intense dreams, almost hallucinations, of people complaining. The images in the dreams were grotesque, and her nights were often restless. Her feelings of paranoia sometimes lasted into daylight hours. A medical workup had showed no obvious physiological or metabolic reason for her agitation. As we tried to pinpoint the exact nature of her fears, she realized that these dreams frequently involved people from her past.

We talked about her stormy relationships. I found it painful to listen to the account of her life and contemplate her dismal situation, and I was secretly glad when the smell of macaroni and cheese from the dining room, followed by the arrival of nursing aides to take Julia to dinner, interrupted our visit. I asked the aides for a few more minutes with Julia and they promised to return soon. I was not quite done. Though I knew I was pressing Julia and that my questions made her uncomfortable, I was struck by her suffering, and I sensed that there might well be a way through it. If she was to find peace, she needed to resolve and complete old relationships.

I said, "It sounds to me that although Frederick and Conrad have died, your love for them, and sadness, and even anger, are still alive." She grew quiet and thoughtful. "Even though you understand Eddie and forgive him for placing you here, I suspect it still hurts. You've had more than your share of hardship and grief in your life. It seems that through it all, you've been the one to care for others, always the one who gave.

"Before I go, I want to give you an assignment that I want you to practice every day. It may seem silly, but give it a try. In a quiet time of the day, when you're alone, or at night when you're relaxed, lying in bed before sleep, close your eyes and say to yourself 'I am not a bad person.' Imagine these words written on the rim of a large wheel that is slowly turning in front of you, and repeat them every time it goes round. I want you to do this for at least ten or fifteen minutes every day. OK?"

She rolled her eyes in playful agreement.

"As you're saying this, think about how the words make you feel. Just notice what thoughts come up as you repeat the sentence—the conversation it provokes inside you. Let it all just come and go and keep returning to the sentence 'I am not a bad person.' Notice whether there's any change in your reactions over the week." I shook my finger in mock warning, imitating a stern music teacher. "I will be back next week to make sure you've been practicing!"

She gave me an embarrassed smile and cried in mock distress, "Help, he's torturing me!"

"And I should warn you, once you've finished this assignment, there's going to be another even tougher one. After you've mastered 'I am not a bad person,' you graduate to 'I am a good person.' "

"Oh, Dr. Ira! You're so demanding. I can't say that!" The drama was feigned, but the protests were real. I decided to maintain the good-natured banter while persisting in my efforts.

"Why not? Are you a bad person, after all? Really? Who have you killed this week?"

"No one, yet." She laughed as she delivered her warning.

"Listen, I know it feels funny. If it feels self-centered to say these things, even to yourself, well, that's the point. The fact is that you really are a good person, in fact an exceptionally loving, caring person. But, even though it's the truth, it's hard for you to accept, or more precisely, it's hard for you *to feel.* Like most of us, you weren't raised to feel good about yourself just for being who you are. One of the nurses I work with says that we were raised as human 'doings' rather than human beings. So feeling good about yourself is going to take some time, and some practice. So I want you to try, even if it feels silly. OK?"

"For you, Dr. Ira, I'll give it a try."

"Thanks, Julia." I rose as the aides returned to take her to dinner. I helped them transfer her to the oversized adjustable wheelchair and arranged her hair over her shoulders. "I'll look forward to seeing you again, Julia. Thanks for your patience with me today and for your good work."

A week later I returned and was delighted when Julia reported that she had been practicing the drill and was feeling better "within myself." She rolled her eyes yet again when I told her I had another exercise for her to try, and she joshed, "Why am I not surprised?"

"This time, Julia, after taking a few moments to relax, perhaps by thinking about a time when you felt warm and loved and not squeezed, I want you to imagine someone who you have been close to in your life sitting in a chair across from you. It might be your father or mother, or your brother George, or Frederick, or Conrad, but only one person at a time. Imagine that you both know that this is your last chance to speak to each other. Really picture the person sitting there. Imagine how they look, what they are wearing, and the sound of their voice. This is a chance to say the things that matter most. If you are still angry at them, this is a safe time to tell them so; let them have it with both barrels. To the extent that you can, and want to, tell each person you forgive them for the hardship and pain that they caused you. You can also ask forgiveness whenever it fits. This is also a chance to say 'I love you' and 'goodbye.' "

This time she did not protest. I had the sense that she knew this was something she needed to do. I was drawing, here, on the strength of our relationship and her growing faith in me as a doctor. The work we were doing together was allowing her to begin feeling more whole and at peace within herself. We spent the next twenty minutes practicing the exercise. I asked her to imagine that I was Frederick and invited her to tell me whatever she felt needed to be said. Without a hint of awkwardness she told him about the pain he had caused her and, rather graphically, spit out her anger at him. Then she was able to express love for him and tenderly say goodbye once again. As we brought the session to an end, Julia was excited by the feeling of being unburdened and of satisfaction she felt and said she was eager to continue.

Although I only saw Julia for brief visits during the next month, I heard about her progress every week from Mary McCall, her nurse case manager, and Stella at the hospice team meeting. With their encouragement, she continued to express her feelings in a series of conversations with departed loved ones, and she found the experience liberating.

Julia's bad dreams ceased. She was physically comfortable as we gradually controlled her various pains with a combination of drugs. The meditative "I am not a bad person" training in self-worth and the "empty chair" imaginary conversations helped quiet Julia's critical inner voice and lighten her spirits. Most days she was cheerful, though she still had dark days when she repeated her wish to "just check out."

Over the months, Julia's multiple sclerosis invaded her eyes and slowly stole her vision. No longer able to watch television or play solitaire, she had only the radio and visits to occupy her days and her thoughts. Her general health continued to worsen from the effects of a perennial crop of bedsores and recurrent bladder infections, which she agreed to let us treat with antibiotics, to lessen the discomfort of the bladder spasms. Her crumpled body and contorted arms and legs would no longer permit her to sit in a wheelchair, and she became confined to bed. And she was wasting away, weighing probably less than a hundred pounds, even though she still loved the taste of vanilla milkshakes.

On one of my visits I met her sisters. They had made themselves comfortable on the edge of Julia's bed and in a side chair. Their ease with Julia suggested that they were regular visitors. But from their tones of voice, it sounded like I had walked into a bit of an argument. The youngest, Ingrid, a stout woman with rosy cheeks, was scolding her older sister.

"Nonsense. I don't know how you can talk that way, Jul. Look what you did for us. Isn't that right, Lindy?" Ingrid was looking to her other sister, Linda, a thinner version of herself with the same Scandinavian look and dyed blond hair, who was sitting in an armchair in the corner.

"Don't you remember the time we all thought we had polio, and we had to stay home for weeks? And every two hours you'd come and take our temperature. You were probably sicker than the rest of us, but you did all the cooking and doctoring." Linda explained for me, "It wasn't really polio. Just the flu, but no matter. Jul mothered us day and night. And wouldn't let us out of bed for anything!" The women guffawed.

"Pfftt. I don't know what you're talking about. I didn't do much. No one else was going to take care of you. I really didn't do much. I could hardly read the thermometer," she laughed. "I'd shake it before sticking it in your mouths, but I never knew why. I had just seen nurses do it."

"Jul, that's not true!" Ingrid exclaimed. "If it weren't for you, we'd . . ." she looked to her sister to finish.

"We'd never graduated from high school! We'd never gotten out of Darby! We'd be skinny, broken-down cashiers with bad teeth and rotten husbands!" Linda testily spat out this testimonial, then smiled broadly. Her vehemence momentarily silenced everyone. Paged to attend to another problem at a patient's home across town, I excused myself and told Julia I would come back later.

When I returned late in the day, she filled in for me a little more of the family dynamics. As the oldest and most forbearing sister, Julia had virtually raised her siblings, making sure they were fed, clean, in school every day, and home every night. I gathered that she was a strict surrogate parent and as a result always thought of herself as the witchy, bossy sister rather than the fierce mother hen she probably was. Her disagreement with Ingrid and

Linda was not the first; for months they had been chipping away at her denial of her sacrifice and importance in their young lives. She was a hard woman to thank. Her chattering self-deprecation was a powerful shield against positive emotions as well as pain.

In the last months and weeks of Julia's life, her sisters became her daily companions. We did not have to teach them about reminiscence; it just happened. Dennis, however, remained uncommunicative, visiting his mother infrequently and only as an obligation. Realizing that time was running short, I took an assertive tack and left a note for Dennis at the nursing home asking him to meet with me to discuss his mom. Although he had been ducking family meetings that Mary and Stella had had with Linda and Ingrid, this time he showed up.

Dennis was a young man who had never grown up. With Julia's unwitting help, he had become a self-absorbed man-child. She had doted on him throughout his life until she became physically unable to do so. Instead of appreciating all that she had done for him, he resented her for becoming disabled. When he had lived at home, Julia, along with her two jobs and constant household work, had ironed and mended his clothes and kept him looking crisp. With little effort on his part, he had enjoyed a middle-class lifestyle. Since he had been living on his own, his standard of living had fallen, despite a string of girlfriends, each of whom took care of him for awhile but were inevitably burned out by his lack of gratitude and irritable moods.

When Dennis arrived at Sky View for our meeting, I thanked him for taking the time to come and invited him to meet with me, Mary, and Stella in the conference room. Our preference would have been for Dennis to realize what needed to be done on his own, but sometimes a more direct approach is required. We did not intend to sit in judgement of his recent behavior toward her. Julia was the focus of this session, not her self-centered son, and we would do everything we could to ensure that she felt honored and complete before she died.

The multipurpose conference room was decorated in institutional calico and had a table large enough for fifteen people; it seemed cavernous and cold for our present purpose. We asked Dennis to tell us about his mom before she became ill. He described their home and said that his friends would always come to his house after school or on weekends. All his friends loved Julia. When one of his buddy's parents had divorced, he had moved in with them for two months. In revisiting their earlier years, Dennis grudgingly acknowledged his appreciation for all his mother had done.

Mary asked him if he knew that his mother was dying and that she would be gone very soon. He tried to hide the tears that collected in the corners of his eyes. "If you love her, Dennis, this is the time to tell her so," I said. "Your mom loves you so much. Her whole life has been built around others—you especially, and your welfare. Before she dies, it would be wonderful if you could tell her how much you love her and that she is appreciated."

Dennis studied his sneakers, but nodded in agreement. I felt like a middle-school principal having a stern talk with the school bully whom no one had confronted before. For most of his life, Dennis had been allowed to get away with his selfish, thoughtless behavior. I hoped that by acknowledging that he knew he'd been behaving badly, he could take a big step toward growing up. The meeting lasted about an hour. Before it ended, we helped Dennis rehearse what he would say to his mom. I told him that I appreciated his willingness to meet with us and respected the courage it took to say these sad things. In return, he thanked me for the help I had given his mom. Knowing that his "conversion" was shaky at best, Mary offered to accompany him to his mom's bedside to say all that he had rehearsed.

Mary colorfully described the scene for Sheila and me: "He said hi, and Julia answered with her typically bubbly 'Oh, hi, Denny.' From her tone you'd have thought it was Christmas. Anyhow, he just stood there for a minute a bit stiffly but after a look from me launched the things he decided he most wanted to say. As I'd suggested, he started by naming his feelings.

" 'Mom, it scares me to think that you're dying.' She just looked back at him with her big brown eyes, and he melted and started to cry. They ended up hugging each other, at least as much as Julia's arms allowed her to. The rest of his spiel came right from his heart—though I think he appreciated the rehearsal. He called her 'Mommy' and told her she was the best mother in the world. And he told her he loved her—and if he ever had a little girl he was going to name her Julia." From that day until the day she died, Dennis came by more often and he stayed for longer periods of time.

A similar strategy with Eddie yielded more paltry results. During the months after hospice became involved in Julia's care, Eddie became increasingly scarce. Busy with his job and a new girlfriend, he rarely came by. Several times he arrived drunk and was loud and out of line with Julia, and the nursing home staff escorted him out the door. To Julia, of course, the idea of Eddie was more tangible than the reality of Eddie; to her, he was still the boyfriend she loved.

I decided to take a direct approach, as we had with Dennis. One afternoon I arranged to bump into Eddie at the Union Club, where, between his long-haul trips, he could often be found drinking beer and playing pool. The café in the rear of the Union Club, which makes some of the best sandwiches in town, provided the excuse for our "chance encounter." I told him that Julia was more comfortable physically than she had been months earlier, but that I expected her to die very soon. I added, "You know, Eddie, she still loves you a great deal. I think it would mean a lot to her to hear from you, one last time, that you care for her. Why don't you go by one morning and tell her you love her and will miss her." The only way I could have been more blunt would have been to specify "a morning, while you're still sober." He knew what I meant.

A few days later the nursing home staff reported that Eddie did show up in the morning, before leaving in his tractor-trailer for a cross-country trip. None of the hospice team was present, but Julia told Stella, "It was the best visit we had in years. He has his problems, but he really loves me, you know. And I'll always love him."

Julia died surrounded by Ingrid, Linda, Dennis, and two of her favorite nurses' aides. Family and staff had been paying homage to her for days. The sisters and, at times, Dennis, had continued to thank her for the sacrifices she had made for them over the years.

Two days after Julia Rosauer died, the nursing home staff had a memorial service for her, and the room was packed. People recounted stories from the nearly two years that Julia had lived there, and more than one staff member openly shed tears. When Julia died she was dearly loved by many people. Perhaps most importantly, she knew it.

Hap Visscher

No single diagnosis prompted Hapgood Visscher's referral to hospice. He was eighty-six years old and, despite the effects of early Alzheimer's disease, had been living with his wife, Hilda, until a heart attack had landed him in the hospital. Things had gone steadily downhill since then. He had become confused and frightened while in the ICU and required tranquilizers. After his heart attack he had frequent chest pain, made worse by any exertion. A coronary angiogram showed "extensive, diffuse three-vessel disease," which meant that, particularly in light of his age and dementia, he was not a candidate for bypass surgery. With medication he improved enough over two weeks to be transferred to Heatherfield Nursing Home—to continue his cardiac rehabilitation, and because Hilda was too frail herself to care for him.

One day he suddenly complained of pain in his left leg, and a physical examination could not pick up a pulse in his left ankle or foot, which indicated a blood clot. Despite being given blood thinners, his circulation did not improve. His internist and a consulting surgeon felt that his heart might not withstand general anesthesia, but they explained to the couple that without a surgical amputation, he would eventually die of gangrene. He seemed to understand what was being said. With only a moment's discussion between them, he and Hilda decided not to have his leg removed, and he was referred to hospice.

When I heard about Hap, he had become a "management problem," in the language of nursing homes. He frequently became agitated, especially during the night and in the early morning hours, and had threatened nurses and attendants, yelling in German and shaking his fist. I was asked to help and possibly adjust his medications.

A tall, rangy man with a weathered complexion, large, hairy ears, and thick bushy eyebrows, Hap was a farmer and handyman who had led a robust, independent life. The son of hearty Austrian immigrants, he had grown up on a wheat farm in the Dakotas and acquired his own fields when he came to Montana more than fifty years ago. Dignity was as real to him as a claw hammer and came with the confidence of competence. He could perform any job around a farm or ranch and fix virtually anything that could break.

On the morning I met Hap, he was surprisingly clearheaded. Normally, according to his chart, he was pleasantly confused, at times thinking it was 1956 and he was still on the plains of eastern Montana. We were in the room he shared with an elderly stroke victim; just outside, finches and canaries fluttered and chirped in a closet-sized aviary. He had just had a bath, and his misbuttoned shirt, unshaven jaw, and remarkably full head of long gray hair gave him a truculent appearance. Instead of administering a formal mental status examination, I asked him about his life and times. While his thick accent made him hard to understand at first, he talked readily and lucidly about his daily routine in the nursing home and reminisced about the cold Dakota winters. He knew the names of all his children and seven grandchildren, and he remembered some of the toys he had made for them.

After we had become generally acquainted, I ventured a more serious question. "Mr. Visscher, may I call you Hap?" I asked, knowing that that was what the nursing home staff called him.

"Sure." He nodded.

"Hap, some of the staff has been frightened by your behavior lately. They say you get very angry. Can you tell me what that's all about?"

"Oh, that's nothing," he chuckled, waving his hand to brush away my concern. "I like to kid with them. I joke with them all the time."

"They don't always know you're joking, Hap. At times they are frightened by you."

His face darkened and he grew quiet, as if he'd been scolded. "Ya, sure. I'm sorry, Doctor. I would never hurt nobody." He paused and then looked up at me soulfully from beneath his gnarled brow. "Well, things are not good, here. Everything here is broken! Look at this thing," he said, shaking his bedside tray with his powerful hands. It was designed to move up and down, adjusting to the height of the bed, but it was stuck at its highest setting, making it impossible for him to use. "And that thing, too," he said, pointing to the wheelchair in the corner of his room that the attendants used to transport him to and from his bath and meals. "That wheel in the front there is no good. It's not good like that." He paused to see if I was as outraged as he. "If I was well, I could fix that!" he declared.

I nodded sympathetically. "It must be very frustrating. It's hard to see something that is broken and know that if you were well and had your tools you could fix it. Feeling helpless is awful. Knowing how really talented you are at repairing things, it must be especially frustrating for you."

"You bet! Hilda's friends would bring me their busted lamps and things and I could fix them like that." He snapped his fingers. "Back home, they would all send for me to fix their big equipment, you know, like the threshers and the tractors. They paid me good, too. An old farmer friend of my dad's would say, 'If Hap can't get it to work it's time to get a new one.' " He stopped speaking for the moment, and we listened to the whistles and chirps of the birds.

"You know, there is one important job you can still do." My words retrieved his attention. "I'll bet you have wonderful stories about growing up on a farm and your Austrian heritage. You need to share these stories with your children and grandchildren. You need to record them, so that when you're gone, years from now, they will know who you were and all the wonderful things you could do. No one else in the world can do this, Hap. Only you can tell these stories. This could be a wonderful gift for Visscher children for many generations to come. It is very important."

"I don't think so," he said morosely. "There is nothing left for me to do. I have no stories to tell. The kids don't want to hear them. It was different when I was a boy." He laughed, and then a look that I can only describe as mischief came into his eyes. "Sometimes when my folks and the relatives were telling stories we would sneak out, you know, and have a smoke in the fields. It was a different time, Doctor."

On a hunch, I asked him if he had ever gotten in trouble when he was a young man. This time he giggled, and he spoke so rapidly that his accent made me struggle to understand. "I remember when it was Halloween and my cousin Gus and I dressed up as scarecrows with just corn cobs. What a sight! When my father, he find out, we couldn't sit down for days!"

"And you say you have no stories to tell!" I exclaimed. "These stories may seem ordinary to you, Mr. Visscher, but they are treasures, and it would be an incredible gift to your family to preserve them. It's a job only you can do. If it's OK with you, I want to come back in a few days and help you start." He grunted agreeably and I left.

People of Hap's age and era are often reluctant to make tape recordings. I think it is the supposed formality of the process; they worry that they need to somehow prepare or dress up for it. I have learned to help them past the awkwardness rather than become discouraged too soon. Before leaving Heatherfield I called Mrs. Visscher, introduced myself by phone, and arranged to meet with her and Hap two days later.

Hap did not recognize me right away, but when I began to recount for his wife what he and I had talked about and mentioned details from the stories he had told, he brightened and called me "Doctor." She was a heavyset woman with a round face, totally white hair, and a warm manner. She seemed to instinctively understand the value of these stories and the task I was suggesting. I set up a cassette recorder and showed Hap that I was turning it on and that we were going to record our visit today. He grumbled once again, "I've got no stories to tell." But as soon as I asked, "Can you remember how you two met?" the tape recorder was forgotten and he chuckled and bubbled, telling me that Hilda "was the prettiest girl in the county. And I was the strongest young man." Another contagious chuckle, really a rumbling giggle. "Her father didn't like me too good, until I fixed his plow. Then he tell Hilda to have me come around."

"And I made him a pie." Mrs. Visscher joined in, only partially stifling a coquettish laugh.

A few minutes were still left on the cassette when our session ended. I labeled it, popped the plastic tab to protect it from being rerecorded, and explained to them what I was doing. "You have really created something of lasting value for all your family today. I'm going to ask Jim Parker, your hospice volunteer, to come by this week and help you make some more of these tapes." Hap didn't speak but he looked at me, smiled, and gave me a single nod of his head.

I knew that Hap and Jim had a budding friendship and that Jim had been helping with driving Mrs. Visscher to and from the nursing home several times a week, so coordinating their efforts would be no problem. Mrs. Visscher was delighted by the suggestion and thanked me repeatedly for spending time with them.

In the two visits I had with Hap, I developed the impression that the quality of his daily life still made his life worth preserving. While he was not the man he had been in his prime, he still enjoyed his days. Though his recent memory had succumbed to dementia, his long-term memory was unscathed. And the storytelling sessions accomplished what I had hoped. Reviewing his life seemed to help him achieve a sense of meaning and value about who he was. His agitation dissolved. He was not only peaceful, but once again good-humored and engaging. Within a week, when I asked the head nurse of his wing at Heatherfield how Hap was doing, she replied, "He seems much happier these days. I've not heard of any recent tantrums or agitation. Is he on a new antidepressant?" She added, "He's really such a sweet man."

In the weeks that passed, Hap's physical condition stabilized. His chest pains abated, and his left foot, having responded to routine dressings and modest doses of analgesic medication, withered and came to look almost mummified. I talked about it with Hap's internist, Alice Gregory; after consulting with a surgeon, we reasoned that he would probably survive an amputation below the knee if it was done under spinal anesthesia. Without the operation, it was only a matter of time before he developed a lethal infection in his lower leg. The amputation would make him more comfortable for whatever time he had left. Dr. Gregory and the surgeon met with Mrs. Visscher. The three of them spoke with Hap, though it is hard to know how much he comprehended. Hilda told me that when they asked him what he wanted, he said, "Do what you gotta do," and she felt he understood that he could die in surgery. "My Hap has never been afraid in his life. He is not afraid to die."

The surgery went well. After a single night in the hospital, Hap was back in his own room at Heatherfield. The wound where his left leg had been removed at the upper calf healed without problems, and within days of the surgery we began decreasing his pain medication.

Our hospice team stayed involved in Hap's care for the next month. Most of our attention was directed to Mrs. Visscher and their oldest daughter, Gretchen, who lived within an hour of Missoula. Mrs. Visscher could not manage Hap at home; since he had adjusted to the nursing home, they decided it was best for him to continue to live there. Though he was no longer dying, his future decline from Alzheimer's disease was inevitable, and we posed several questions for them to consider. "What would be his wishes, and your wishes, regarding treatment if he developed a pneumonia? Should antibiotic pills be given? If he didn't respond to those, should he be hospitalized? What would be his wishes regarding tube feedings if he became unable to eat normally?" They agreed that he would not want to be hospitalized or given antibiotic shots for pneumonia and they would not approve it. Although Mrs. Visscher knew that Hap would hate to be fed by a tube, she was uncomfortable with the thought of him "starving to death"; it brought up images from the depression that were hard for her to reconcile.

We also helped Mrs. Visscher and Gretchen relax their attempts to orient Hap to the present reality: person, place, and time. Explaining that his strengths now lay in the past, we encouraged them to visit with him in that context from time to time.

Over the next year and a half I visited Hap occasionally when I was seeing other patients at Heatherfield. One day I found him in his new, high-tech wheelchair in front of an open drawer of his low dresser, arranging and rearranging his socks, underwear, comb, and brush. He certainly looked better than before; he was shaved, his hair was combed, and he wore a clean shirt. When I asked him how he was doing, he answered that he was getting things together before the winter set in. "I'm gonna have to go, you know." When I asked him where he was going, he became annoyed, as if I should have known or had not been paying attention.

As his dementia progressed he was transferred to the Horizon Unit, which specializes in the care of confused patients. I saw Mrs. Visscher from time to time; while she was sad about the deterioration and then loss of the man she had lived with for sixty-two years, she felt strongly that he was being cared for in the best possible way. Jim Parker continued to visit with Hap and help with Mrs. Visscher's transportation. Hap's increasingly childlike demeanor and even the occasional outbursts of frustration were anticipated and provided for, in a unit accustomed to absorbing the strange and sometimes disruptive behavior of people afflicted with Alzheimer's and related dementias.

In early summer, Dr. Gregory again asked hospice to become formally involved; Hap was ignoring his food and had lost twelve pounds over the previous eight weeks. This time when we spoke with Mrs. Visscher about the various options, she listened carefully and asked questions that showed she had been thinking about the issues we had raised many months earlier. She was satisfied that he was comfortable, and she knew we would make certain he didn't suffer. Her decisions were clear. The nurses and attendants were to help him to eat but not force-feed him, and there would be no tubes and no antibiotics. "No, it is his time," she concluded.

Just before Labor Day, Hap developed a cough, followed by a high fever. Mrs. Visscher reiterated her instructions, no antibiotics, and the nurses administered Tylenol around the clock and bathed him as needed, keeping his mouth moist. As he died his wife and daughter were with him, and the lilting voices of the singers from the Chalice of Repose warmed the room. In a renewal of ancient traditions, the music and presence of the Chalice workers are offered to ease the passage of the person through this liminal state. Although dementia had stolen his mind, neither I nor anyone else who knew him believed that he ever lost his dignity.

Living, and dying, with a terminal illness frequently involves making critical decisions about life-prolonging therapy and medications. Patients and families often must decide about eating, taking fluids, receiving antibiotics, or being put on a ventilator or respirator. These decisions cannot be avoided. People can choose to ignore the issues, but in doing so they are making other decisions about the course of a terminal illness. Not infrequently, as in the following story of Janelle Haldeman, the decisions of dying may involve more than the family and the patient and may encompass a wide circle of friends, even an entire community. In the process of confronting these hard decisions, if the right questions are asked, surprising opportunities can be revealed.

Six

The Hardest Decisions and the Greatest Opportunities: Janelle Haldeman

I remember the day I learned that Janelle Haldeman had been referred to hospice. I was reviewing a pile of patient records in preparation for the weekly hospice meeting when I saw her name and list of diagnoses. Seventeen years old, Huntington's chorea, seizure disorder. Two thoughts flashed through my mind: *Oh, God, Janelle is dying* and *Thank goodness, someone referred her. Thank goodness we'll get to take care of Janelle.*

I knew Janelle and her mother, Carla, from my position as an emergency physician at Community Hospital. Every so often, Carla brought Janelle in with minor injuries after she had a seizure, or a minor cut from a fall, or when she was ill with a chest cold or stomach flu. The ER nurses and I would patch her up and send her home, but I always knew I would see her again. Janelle had a rare, juvenile onset form of Huntington's chorea, a hereditary disease that attacks the nervous system and brain, causing uncontrollable muscle spasms, progressive mental deterioration, and ultimately death. The adult form is sometimes referred to as Woody Guthrie's disease, because the famous folk singer died from it. Normally, children do not show signs of this familial illness, but Janelle was one of the few exceptions. Her first twitches had begun around age eleven, and the disease had advanced steadily. The fact that Janelle was being referred to hospice meant, of course, that she was now dying.

While feeling that Janelle's dying was tragic, I also hoped that it could open her and Carla to acknowledging, and savoring, the achievements in her young life. Each, in her own way, had spent her life fighting. Well before I met her, Carla had been constantly battling one bureaucracy or another—the school system, the county or state health system, the hospitals and clinics—always pushing for a little extra, some special service or better handicap device for Janelle. Janelle's battles were more directly with her illness, which was an unprincipled, vicious enemy. She also had regular clashes of wills with her mother and other members of her family.

The family was a stew of emotions: Carla's guilt over Janelle's disease; anxiety over conflicting demands for attention from Tommy, Janelle's brother, and Joe, Carla's live-in boyfriend; Janelle's teenage temperament, exacerbated by the irritability and depression brought on by the disease. The family was in constant turmoil. This final chapter in Janelle's life could be more of the same, but it also represented one last opportunity for them to pull together—for her sake, and for all their sakes.

In talking with family members about the decisions they can make and opportunities they can provide for a dying loved one, I occasionally ask them to imagine a time months after the person has died when, perhaps in the intimate quiet of early morning, they might ask themselves *Did we do the right thing? Did we make the right decisions? Did we give up too soon or hang on too long? Was there anything else we should have done? Did we seize every opportunity, take every action, for a loving, peaceful end?* I want them to be able to review what happened and confidently conclude: *Yes, we did it right.* My hope is that, without reservation, they will be certain of this.

Progressive terminal illness, in contrast to sudden death, offers a chance to reconcile strained relationships or to complete relationships. Completion does not require ending interaction or severing a relationship; rather, it means that there is nothing left unsaid or undone. When a dying person and a loved one feel complete between themselves, their time together is marked as much by the joy of being together and by mutual affection as by the sadness of impending departure. And the history of a relationship and family is transformed when the story of two persons ends well.

Immediate events or goals also take on special significance for someone who is dying. Meaning and purpose for the dying person is frequently anchored in individual events, achievements, and expectations, or in long-term goals that have become immediate. Often the goals are simple, such as yearning for rich interactions with family and friends. People say things like "I want to rest today so that I have the strength to visit when my sister/son/daughter comes this weekend."

For children who may not have the life experiences or capacity for abstraction to imagine distant, intangible goals, events such as birthdays, holidays, and celebrations are especially important. Although it was not noted anywhere in the pounds of Janelle's medical records, it became clear early on that she had a critical goal to accomplish before she died: Janelle needed to graduate from high school. Completing her education and experiencing the reward of the ritual and ceremony of graduation became the driving force in her final months and weeks. It was also clear that for her to participate in her graduation, Carla and the health care system had not only to make peace, but actually to work closely and creatively together. A friendly, funny, likeable kid, Janelle also needed to complete her relationships with school friends and the small rural community where she grew up, or almost grew up. Finally, she needed to feel closeness and achieve a sense of completion in her relationship with her mother. At the time of her hospice referral it all seemed like a real long shot, but, for Janelle, it was worth a try.

No one was happy about Janelle being moved to Heatherfield Nursing Home, a sprawling facility surrounded by shopping centers on the outskirts of Missoula. The medical professionals and the county child protective services staff had concluded that Carla could no longer adequately take care of Janelle. They probably disapproved of her rather chaotic living situation, including Carla's live-in boyfriend, Joe, an admitted alcoholic and ex-convict. Several incidents in which bystanders reported Carla yelling at and at least once shaking Janelle had led to a family hearing and a court-appointed guardian for Janelle. Janelle's natural father, who had developed symptoms of Huntington's when she was a toddler and was now also dying, had left the family years earlier. They lived in a trailer in the woods near the town of Jefferson, about sixty minutes outside Missoula, and this distance undoubtedly also fed the decision to send Janelle to Heatherfield.

Indeed, Janelle needed the medical care Heatherfield offered. She required twenty-four-hour attention, not only for daily living activities such as eating, bathing, toileting, and grooming, but also because of recurring episodes of choking and seizures. Eating had become difficult, food would not stay down, and she had become dangerously thin. Three times within the last eight months she had developed pneumonia from aspirating particles of food. About five feet, four inches tall, with curly blond hair that had once flowed to her waist but was now short, making it easier to wash and maintain, Janelle had an impish grin and flashing, mischievous eyes. From my first contact with her in the ER, five or so years earlier, I remembered her as a preteen on the skinny side. When she went into the nursing home she was almost eighteen years old, and she weighed just seventy-nine pounds.

Carla Haldeman, having battled authority figures all her life, regarded Heatherfield as an extension of an insensitive, stingy health care system. On the receiving end of low-paying jobs and government assistance, she had always seen the proverbial glass to be half empty and believed that help had to be forced. Quiet and serious, she trudged through life with a chip on her shoulder. When it came to Janelle's illness, however, her scrappiness had proven an asset. For years she had insisted on the best treatment for her daughter, refusing to accept second-class fare. It was inevitable that she would butt heads with the nurses and administrators of Heatherfield.

A modern facility, Heatherfield is designed with a functional layout; specialized residential wings radiate from a central living unit. It has a wing for patients requiring skilled nursing care, a wing for more stable long-term care, and a wing just for Alzheimer's patients. With more than ninety residents, there are always people shuffling to and from the dining hall and recreation areas, or staff in green or white scrubs hovering over medical carts, conversing in clusters or tending to residents. It is clean, brightly lit, and thoroughly sterile. For residents, it must feel like living in a Holiday Inn.

Janelle disliked being at Heatherfield even more than her mother disliked having her there. She was lonely and, at times, uncomfortable. Her double room was furnished with the usual hospital furniture, a VCR, which I think she never used, and a boombox so she could listen to her idol, Garth Brooks. While she had the basic creature comforts there, what Janelle craved was people who would talk to her, read to her, and touch her. Given the nature of nursing homes, it was inevitable that Janelle's demands for attention or needs for care were ignored at times.

One of the first times Carla and Joe visited Janelle at Heatherfield, they found her twisted in knots, both literally and figuratively. Locating Janelle's room was complicated enough, a matter of turning left, right, left, left, and right after the reception area. Her room was in the middle of a long wing at the rear of the building; as soon as Carla turned the corner at the nurses' station, she heard her daughter's distinctive howl. Months earlier the disease had robbed Janelle of articulate speech, so she expressed herself with sounds or by slowly, painfully enunciating individual words. Her speech was now similar to that of a person with severe cerebral palsy.

Joe entered the room first, frantically glancing over the bed and the corners of the room for Janelle. He quickly spied her caught under the bed, twisted around the lowered guard rails.

"Baby, baby!" he exclaimed and scrambled to extract her. Over six feet tall, with long, wavy gray hair and weathered skin from outdoor work, Joe looked like a mountain man. Yet his tough exterior disguised a soft, sentimental core. When Janelle needed attention and patience, Joe was there.

Carla hung back as Joe untangled Janelle's limbs from the cold chrome bed. She scowled as she surveyed the room and silently criticized the makeshift mat on the floor that had been provided for her daughter. The middle of the floor was the safest place for Janelle, because there she could not fall or flail and bang herself. Joe cradled and rocked Janelle as she vented her frustration with staccato outbursts of "Help" and "No one."

"Janelle, calm down, you're not hurt," Carla stated flatly. "Don't you have something around here to push for help?" Not seeing a call button, Carla wandered into the hall looking for a nurse. She returned a few minutes later with a young woman in tow who looked just a little older than Janelle and seemed flustered at being collared by this irate mother. Joe had pulled the mattress from the bed to the floor, where he sat beside Janelle, stroking her arm with a slow, soothing motion.

"I . . . I . . . get . . . so . . . mad," Janelle said, her voice wavering like a tape player being shaken, her head rigidly cocked to one side.

"Take your time, baby," he said.

"She needs a better floor mat," Carla scolded the nurses' aide. "And a blanket. Look how thin she is, she gets cold very easily."

"Don't blame us," the young woman snapped. "She keeps pulling off her covers and yelling if someone's not here right away. We've got lots of other residents to take care of."

"I know she's not easy to take care of. God knows, I know," Carla conceded. "She could've even got caught under the bed on purpose." She nervously cast her eyes about the room, avoiding looking at the aide or Janelle. "She'll do that, you know. If she's angry and wants attention, she'll do that. She's bullheaded that way, like me. But she needs a blanket, and a real mattress on the floor."

"I'll see what I can do," the aide said, sidling from the room.

Carla knelt and kissed Janelle's forehead. "Look what we brought you." She held a small bouquet of dyed purple carnations low enough for her daughter to see.

Janelle responded with an appreciative, wavering coo.

In less than a minute, however, Carla was back on her feet. "Come on, Papa, we've got to go," she announced impatiently. Janelle's plaintive eyes bounced from her to Joe and back again. "I'm sorry, baby, but we got a bunch of errands. We got to get to Costco before it closes." She gave Janelle a kiss, scooped up her purse, which she had dropped near the door, and scurried out with an unprotesting Joe lumbering behind her.

The visit was vintage Carla: a cool assessment of how Janelle was doing, a skirmish with the staff, and a quick exit. Fifteen or twenty minutes max. It was not a lack of caring; quite the contrary: it was escape behavior, more avoidance than denial. This was how she handled grief. Around Janelle, Carla was in constant motion, busy fussing with something in the room or getting something from the office or dashing off to talk to a nurse or the Heatherfield administrator. While fiercely protective of her daughter, she kept a safe distance from the intense emotions of dying.

Like her mother, Janelle, too, was unsentimental and shunned displays of emotion. She liked things light and humorous, and turned stoical and snide when strangers expressed sympathy or pity. But temperament aside, she was still a child who craved motherly affection.

Janelle had two best friends: Connie and Davie. Connie was a teacher's aide for Janelle's freshman class when she was still being mainstreamed. They bonded early on, and Connie had continued to tutor Janelle at home when she could no longer attend school because of her deteriorating health.

Janelle's diminished endurance and mild but progressive dementia limited her attention span so that schoolwork was partly ceremonial. Most days Connie spent time reading to Janelle, or playing cards—usually Crazy Eights—or listening to tapes. Officially, however, Janelle remained in school. Connie was a regular visitor at the nursing home, where she acted as her protector and comforter. Davie, who had a serious learning disability, was in Janelle's class at school. They were partners in the special education track in their rural school and became an unlikely but inseparable pair: Janelle, the brains, and Davie, the brawn. He would push her wheelchair about the school, and she happily picked their route and directed their games. Even though distance and his own therapies prevented Davie from visiting Janelle often in the nursing home, their friendship was central to the completing act of her life. Janelle had strong opinions about some things, and her graduation was one of them. She made it clear that she was going to graduate with her class, and that she and her friend Davie were going to be together when they received their diplomas.

Janelle's health rapidly slipped in the nursing home, and a string of harrowing incidents threatened to shorten her time even further. Connie visited one Monday to find Janelle and the nurses in distress. As soon as Connie appeared, Janelle shrieked a grateful greeting. She was on her floor mat, limbs akimbo, her attention roaming between the soap opera on the television and the snowstorm outside.

"Connie! Connie! You're here!" Janelle blurted.

"Hi, Jan, I'm glad to see you, too." Connie knelt on the mat and smoothed Janelle's short, curly hair. Janelle's obvious relief at the sight of her friend made Connie think of puppies in an animal shelter, desperate for attention. "Has your mom been here?" Janelle's forehead felt warm, almost hot.

Connie waited for Janelle's answer, which was a jerky shake of the head, indicating no.

"Oh, Janelle, I'm sorry. Do you want warm fuzzies?"

Janelle's response to the question was a crooked smile. Connie laughed as she grabbed a teddy bear from the bed. "OK, I'll give you one fuzzy, then I want to find a nurse." Connie tenderly rubbed Janelle's face with the bear. She swooned with pleasure.

Connie left the bear in Janelle's arms and marched to the nurses' station at the end of the corridor. A man and a woman in white polyester uniforms were behind the counter talking to each other.

"Excuse me," Connie said, with firm politeness. As neither a family member nor a medical professional, she was on shaky ground to complain or ask for special attention. "I'm visiting Janelle Haldeman, and she feels like she's running a temperature. Could one of you take a look at her?"

The woman, who looked like a seasoned nurse with a hedgerow of instruments sticking out of her breast pocket, looked up.

"Not again," she exclaimed, and headed straight for Janelle's room, talking as she walked. "Janelle had a bad night. The night nurse said her light was on almost constantly, and she was thrashing about a lot. They couldn't keep her covered or figure out what was wrong."

"Did she get her sleeping pill?" Connie asked.

"No, I think she has to ask for it. It doesn't look like she's gotten it for the past few nights."

The nurse pulled a chart from the plexiglass hanger outside the room. Connie dropped onto the mat beside Janelle, who was curled in a ball, totally rigid, with her eyelids fluttering.

"Easy, easy, it'll be over soon," Connie comforted, stroking Janelle's forehead.

"Umm. It says here that Dr. Byock had wanted the sleeping pill given every night and that he ordered an extra evening dose of Tegretol. I wonder why she didn't get it?" The nurse studied the chart.

"Can't you see she's having a seizure?!" Connie interrupted. "Can't you do something?"

Startled, the nurse looked up from her chart. "Oh, Jesus, you're right. Just keep her on her side, I'll run and get some medication," she declared, and hurried from the room.

As she had done countless times before, Connie stayed with Janelle as she endured the electrical tempest swirling through her brain. Her annoyance at the nurse not noticing Janelle's seizure was tempered by the knowledge that, at other times, nurses had thought she was having a seizure when it was just her body jerking as she reached for something or repositioned herself. With Janelle it was sometimes hard to tell. Yet Connie fumed, thinking of how the Tegretol, an anticonvulsant, might have spared Janelle the seizure. She reflected that Janelle must feel this helpless and twice as angry a lot. By the time the nurse returned, the seizure was over. Once Janelle's body relaxed, Connie mopped her brow and stayed with her, saying soothing things and giving her "warm fuzzies" until she fell asleep.

At one point in the afternoon, Connie overheard the nurse talking with a Heatherfield social worker in the hall outside Janelle's room. "We tried to reach her mother last night, but someone said she's away. And we couldn't find the county woman who's Janelle's legal guardian. We didn't know who else to call. And then there's her primary doc and Dr. Byock and the hospice people." She paused. "This stew has too many cooks."

When I finally heard from the nursing home about the delay in Janelle receiving her nighttime medication and the quickening pace of her seizures, I was furious at the nursing home, and I suspected that the staff was avoiding Janelle out of annoyance with the family. I immediately visited her and, after an examination, ordered a blood count and measurements of serum electrolytes and anticonvulsant drug levels. If necessary, I would make daily visits to force the institution to pay attention. I tried to reach Carla, but, without a phone in their trailer, had no success. I contacted Harriet Davis, Janelle's court-appointed guardian, and discussed the situation with her. She agreed with my feeling that this child deserved better care, and I proposed a meeting of the principal players to discuss coordinating that care. The following Tuesday afternoon, seven of us gathered in a conference room off the Heatherfield dining hall.

The atmosphere in the meeting room was tense and frosty, like the harsh early spring outside. I hadn't actually seen Carla in well over a year. She had aged—more salt now than pepper in her hair—and, I thought, looked tired, especially her furrowed eyes. After thanking everyone for being there, I related my simultaneous shock and relief at first learning that Janelle had been referred to hospice. I asked Carla to remind me when I last saw Janelle. She brightened just a bit and recalled a visit to the ER when her daughter had fallen from her wheelchair and needed ten stitches in her scalp. "You complimented Janelle on her pretty purple dress and matching hair ribbon and put her at ease. While you sewed Jan up, I guess the nurses washed the blood out of the ribbon and blow-dried it. After you were done, you tied it back in her hair and gave her a hug. Janelle talked about that for weeks. She always liked you a lot."

"It sounds like the last couple of years have been pretty lousy for Janelle. From reviewing the medical records, I know she's been having more stiffness and jerking, and trouble eating, and now, more seizures and medication side-effects. But all that doesn't tell me what it's been like for you and your family."

Carla had been intently regarding me while I was speaking; now she looked down and paused. "It's been hell." She spoke softly. "Everything I did seemed to make things worse. Janelle is such a trooper; such a fighter. It has killed me to see her lose weight and suffer like this, hurting herself in falls and seizures. I get so impatient and angry with her sometimes." She looked mournfully at Harriet and then fell silent.

"She has been a fighter, and so have you, Carla," I continued. "I think you know that I've always had respect for you as an advocate for your daughter. I can remember times in the ER when you told me that you had brought Janelle in partly to document the need for some protective device or new piece of equipment and to build a case for the state to pay for it. All that she has been able to do in the last five years is a tribute to you and your commitment. Despite whatever happened and the court appointing a legal guardian, I know full well how much you love this little girl." I said these things mainly for Carla's benefit, but I was also deliberately speaking to Harriet and the nursing home staff. They needed to know that Carla could not be dismissed as another dysfunctional or abusive parent.

"From hearing you describe her deterioration in the last year and a half, and from reading her medical records—especially the hospital records from her admissions for aspiration pneumonia—it seems that Janelle may finally be coming to the end of her illness." I waited for a moment. Carla looked up and nodded enough to let me know she wanted me to go on. "I long ago stopped predicting how long people had to live. But as I graph Janelle's decline in my mind, it's hard to imagine her still being with us in the fall." I chose my words carefully, trying to be as gentle as possible while saying the hard things that needed to be said. "Her body seems to be trying to find a way to die." After a moment for all this to settle, I asked, "What do you think?"

Carla was composed but quietly crying. Joe had put his arm around her shoulder and was holding her close. "I think you're right, Dr. Byock. It breaks my heart to say it, but I *know* you're right."

"You know, I think we have some serious decisions to make. Because she is the court-appointed guardian, Harriet now has the final vote on what treatments are given, but I think we have a chance to make decisions we can all agree on."

Harriet quickly chimed in with her support. "I want Carla and Joe and Tommy to all feel we're doing the right thing. That's why I'm here today."

"Carla, I think it's inevitable that some night, perhaps three or four months after Janelle has passed away, you will waken in the early morning dark and remember that she has died. Typically, a person's first reaction to realizing it was not just a dream is a wave of sadness. But at such times people often ask themselves, *Did I do the right thing?* It is my goal that if and when you ask yourself that sort of question you will be able to recall the sequence of events and confidently answer yes. I want to promise you that we will not let your little girl suffer. I simply will not stand for it, and neither will anyone else on our hospice team." Once again, I was speaking to Carla, while putting everyone in the room on notice. "But more than this, I think what we need to do today and in the next few weeks is to create a plan of care that leaves you feeling not only confident that your child is comfortable, but also feeling that she is honored—and even *celebrated*—in her passing. That's *my* goal, and I think we can achieve it. But it will require us to work together—all of us."

I panned the room, making brief eye contact with everyone. For a moment no one spoke, but the mood had notably softened; their faces told me it was safe to continue. "Carla, if we can accept the hard fact that Janelle is dying, what would make the rest of her life the best it could be?"

"Graduation!" The reply was quicker and louder than the conversation had been.

Connie's sigh of relief was audible. "Oh, thank God you said that!" Carla and Connie smiled at each other. "That would make Jan *so happy*! And Davie could wheel her down the aisle."

The tone in the room changed again. A few people had become a bit misty during the last interchange—even, I noted, one of the crusty Heatherfield nurses. Now there was a palpable sense of enthusiasm. Hearing

Carla speak of Janelle and seeing her emotion, every person in the room was moved on a gut level. Despite her faults and demanding behavior, no one there could ever doubt the love this mother had for her child.

Because she was still an aide at the school in Jefferson three mornings a week, Connie knew the when and where of graduation day, and the schedule for the event. We discussed logistics and possible medical obstacles. It was now March; graduation was in late May. It was a long shot at best, and we all knew it. We would need to boost Janelle's nutrition and treat her recurring respiratory infections if she was going to live to see graduation. This would require considerable medical care. Planning for the actual day—from making a special gown with Velcro closures that would fit her contorted body, to transportation, to emergency plans—all would require considerable creativity. A tone of camaraderie now pervaded the multiple conversations that broke out over this or that detail.

We decided a dry run was a good idea, an afternoon trip to Janelle's school to see if she could take the long drive and the excitement of seeing her friends without becoming overly stimulated or utterly exhausted. In addition, a plan was needed for seizures or other medical crises that could arise on the hour's drive between towns. Connie and Carla agreed to be trained in administering medications by injection (through a subcutaneous "button" a nurse would insert) in case Janelle had a seizure. The group was so enthusiastic it reminded me of teenagers planning a prom.

As we talked about Janelle's health and getting up her strength, the previous miscommunication snafus were raised. Susan Brannigan, a Heatherfield social worker, offered a solution.

"I remember when I worked with a patient at St. Pat's and there were lots of people involved, what we did was set up a journal. This was a notebook we kept in the patient's room with absolutely everything written in it. Not only updates of the medical situation, but family notes and communication between the aides, and notes to family and aides from the nurses and doctors, too. That way, everyone knew what was going on."

"Sounds reasonable," opined Lily Day, a staff nurse on Janelle's wing. "We certainly wouldn't have any problem with that. As long as everyone else holds up their end," she added snidely.

The meeting broke with the insistent beeping of my pager. As I stood at the wall phone talking with a hospice nurse about a patient's medication,

I watched Janelle's newly invigorated team gather their papers and purses. Carla no longer looked angry but simply guarded, and the nursing home social worker lingered to assure her she could visit any time, even spend the night.

Connie and I were the last two to leave. "I thought I'd drop in on Janelle," I mentioned.

"Oh, she's not in her room, she's in physical therapy. I'm going there now. I'll show you the way."

Noticing Carla heading down the opposite corridor, I raised my eyebrows to Connie.

"Nope, she's got to get home. Joe's dinner. Between Joe and Janelle, Carla's like a puppet on a string, back and forth. I wish Carla would spend more time with her. Last week, after Carla just flew in, said hi, kiss-kiss, then left because Joe needed cigarettes, Janelle cried herself into a seizure." Connie's voice was sad, not disapproving.

We passed the aviary with its chirping finches and canaries, where many of the home's elderly residents spent hours in wheelchairs, watching the birds. The combined occupational and physical therapy room, tucked into a corner of a wing, was a large open space with crafts benches as well as parallel bars and mats and lots of chrome training apparatus. Janelle, in shorts and a T-shirt, lay on her back on a bright red mat, and a male physical therapist was helping her with stretching exercises. Standing over them and laughing was Janelle's other therapist, a young woman named Diane.

"You're breaking Kevin's heart, Janelle!" Diane exclaimed.

The handsome, muscular Kevin looked crestfallen. "Come on, Janelle," he was saying as he gently manipulated her leg. "My girlfriend doesn't think I look that bad." He implored, "She thinks I'm cute. Why don't you?"

"You're ugly!" Janelle blurted out with a puckish grin, and Diane laughed some more. Teasing the good-looking therapist looked like a favorite pasttime for Janelle and her friend. We did not want to interrupt, so we hung back until a break in Janelle's routine; we said hello, Connie gave her a hug, promising to return, and we left.

Janelle breezed through the pregraduation trial run; she rode up and back to her school and saw her friends, and the excitement and fatigue she felt did not cut the trip short. A week before her real graduation, however, our optimism was dashed when the seizures and another infection hit with a vengeance. Each seizure rendered her more spastic or more rigid, and the infection wracked her with fevers and left her utterly exhausted. As if this were not enough, one night she had a frightening episode of bloody diarrhea. Consistent with the plan to which we had agreed, the hospice team and I jumped in to prolong her life. We ordered tests and gave her antibiotics and ulcer medication to forestall her inevitable demise.

Distraught that Janelle might not live to reach her final achievement, Carla and Connie hastily planned a commencement ceremony at the nursing home. The teacher's aide telephoned Janelle's school, enlisting various administrators and friends, while the mother hurriedly finished sewing her daughter's gown and located a mortarboard.

But Janelle endured, and the mock graduation was canceled. Joe visited that week; lying on the mat beside her, he listened patiently to her halting words. "She never quit," he says in recollection. "I held her and rubbed her and told her it was OK, because she was fighting so hard and she was hurting so bad. I don't think she fought death because of the fear of dying, I think she fought death because she wanted more life." The Monday before graduation, Janelle's temperature completely resolved, the seizures subsided, and her GI upset abated. Connie, following Janelle's direction, decorated her wheelchair with crepe paper in the school colors, purple and gold.

On Saturday the Jefferson High School gymnasium was packed with hundreds of parents and teenagers. Rows of folding chairs covered the shiny wood floor, and a raised platform occupied one end of the gym, right below the basketball net. A sign pasted on the wall behind it read "Home of the Knights" in large block letters, and listed the names of each graduate. Janelle's stood out on the end. The noise of the band, crying babies, and people calling out to one another bounced off the bleachers and almost drowned out the first speaker.

Carla and Joe, along with Connie and Diane, sat in the audience as the school band played a squeaky version of "Pomp and Circumstance" and the twenty-five grads filed in, led by Janelle in her wheelchair, pushed by Davie. Janelle was in deep purple from the top of her head to the spokes of her wheels. Occasionally a spastic leg kicked out, but she did not seem to mind. She beamed and giggled when her mortarboard tumbled from her jerky head. On the way to the stage, each grad carried a single red rose and detoured to present it to his or her parents. Davie steered Janelle to the end of Carla's row, and people scooted back as she rolled up to her mother and presented her with the flower. Carla bawled, and Joe grinned.

The normal order for awarding diplomas was to begin with the eighth-graders and then honor the high-schoolers. This year, consideration for Janelle and the stress of the long ceremony put her at the head of the line. The first speaker was a woman all the kids knew well, a checkout clerk from the local grocery store. In this small mountain town of barely eight thousand inhabitants, Mrs. Macafee had watched each of them grow from toddler to teen. A small, dark-haired woman in a tailored dress, Mrs. Macafee did not have to read her tribute to Janelle. She announced, "Janelle Haldeman: Those of us who know you are better for having known you. We love you, Janelle. God bless you." As Davie and Janelle moved forward to receive her diploma, the entire audience and all the graduates spontaneously rose to their feet and loudly applauded. The ovation lasted for two minutes, but it seemed suspended in time. Another senior girl leaned over to whisper to Janelle as she passed, "That's for you." Davie gave the thumbs-up sign to anyone who caught his eye. Janelle wept with joy.

This recognition was another landmark for Janelle and signaled the completion of her relationship with lifelong school friends and the community. With their standing ovation, these people acknowledged her spirit and specialness, and in receiving it she, in turn, told them how important they were to her determination to be there. There was nothing left unsaid. Love and admiration had been readily given, and received.

Following the ceremony, there was a party for Janelle in the special education room. It was decorated with balloons, streamers, and lilacs from Carla's garden, and Janelle presided over the festivities like a queen. Ensconced in her purple chair, she admired the sheet cake with her name on it and greeted her friends. A classmate brought her a teddy bear, and someone else gave her a new tape player. Connie hovered nearby with a small, battery-operated fan in her hand to cool Janelle. Connie watched for signs of exhaustion or an impending seizure; two syringes filled with exact doses of medication were in a zipped nylon bag close at hand. But Janelle was in a happy, healthy fog, miles from her disease. A couple of times Connie asked her, "Are you tired? Do you want to go, honey?" and each time Janelle shook her head.

Janelle continued to bubble with delight even at the end of the long day on the ride back to the nursing home. She did not want to lie down in the van and nap, but insisted on staying in her chair and continuing her barely intelligible chatter to Carla and Connie about all she had seen and done. In Missoula, the Heatherfield Nursing Home was waiting for her arrival. As Carla pushed her through the front door, they were greeted by a long banners and signs with drawings of her that proclaimed: "Congrats, Janelle!" Purple and gold balloons were everywhere. Janelle roared with pleasure. There were hugs and tears all around. Then, *finally*, Janelle announced, "I'm so tired," and her glorious day ended.

I was afraid of a letdown after graduation, not only for Janelle but for everyone else. Despite the exuberant success of graduation day, Janelle was actively dying, and while we could not alter her fate, we still needed to pull together and attend to her every need. We had to make sure she was comfortable and stay alert for any opportunity to enrich her waning life. I arranged for another meeting at the nursing home; it included the same people as before, plus Janelle's brother, Tommy.

We gathered in the same room, but now, instead of icicles outside, we saw an early spring chartreuse on the mountains. In contrast to the previous meeting, the mood was tinged with sadness and solemn resignation. In the week since graduation, Janelle had been having more frequent episodes of crampy abdominal pain, despite continuing adjustments in her tube feedings and medications; she was losing weight, and anything we gave her to add calories just made things worse. And her seizures had resurfaced, as they did whenever her general condition deteriorated.

Adding emotional insult to physical injury was the news that Janelle's father, long estranged from the family, who had lived for the past three years in another nursing home in town, had just died of complications of Huntington's. We needed to decide whether, and when, to tell Janelle.

Before moving to the more somber decisions that awaited us, I wanted to recapture the spirit of the last few weeks. I suggested that we begin with Carla and Connie describing graduation day for those who were not there. The rapt attention, smiles, and teary eyes of the nursing home staff increased my confidence for the task ahead.

The issues of whether to use antibiotics and whether to diminish and ultimately discontinue tube feedings had been introduced during our earlier meetings but put on hold as we had focused on graduation. Now we had to revisit them in earnest. "Graduation was a wonderful chance for us to honor Janelle," I began. "In the days and weeks ahead, we still have an opportunity to celebrate her in her passing. Right now Janelle is having a harder and harder time. The tube feedings are causing painful intestinal cramps and diarrhea, despite our having tried various different formulas and tricks. And she is still vomiting occasionally. It's only a matter of time before she gets another pneumonia. And her seizures are coming more frequently again. It's as if her body is searching for a way to die. The hard question for us now is: What would be the best way for Janelle to die?"

I turned and spoke to Carla. "The decisions we need to make about her care should be based on Janelle's comfort and pleasure. You have done all you can. Now all any of us can do is love her and maybe even pamper her in her dying."

Carla's flat expression might have been mistaken for a lack of feeling, except for the tear rolling down her cheek. She knew the end was near, and somehow my words gave her permission to grieve for her daughter and, for a moment, loosen her control.

"Carla, now that graduation is over, I want to ask the same question I asked a couple of months ago: If Janelle were to die suddenly, would there be anything left undone?" She dabbed her eyes and sniffled, and Joe held her hand. But she remained composed as she nodded.

"Dr. Byock, the research people have told me about a hospital in Massachusetts where brain tissue can be sent for study. Janelle is only one of seven kids in the world, you know, to get this at such a young age." From her purse she dug out forms from the Brain Tissue Resource Center at McLean Hospital. "I'd like her brain sent here."

Although I suspected that part of Carla's decision was a way to defer her feelings, I applauded the fortitude it took to contemplate Janelle's autopsy and the desire to give further meaning to her tragic life.

And Carla had made another decision. "Janelle needs to be told about her father having died. I'm worried that she'll be confused and frightened if she sees him in heaven after she dies and doesn't know he died. I'd like to tell her with Tommy," she said, casting an inquiring look toward her other child. Her children had never known the reasons behind their parents' breakup, and Carla had been scrupulous in saying only nice things about their dad. Janelle loved her father, though he was almost a fairy-tale figure—almost a fairy godfather—built upon dim memories of early childhood. And she knew he was very sick.

We confronted other tough issues at that meeting. Feeding Janelle via the tube into her stomach was to be gradually decreased, and her morphine would be supplemented by a continuous infusion of a small dose of Versed to keep her muscles relaxed and help control the seizures. I think everyone left the meeting feeling we had done everything humanly possible to make Janelle's passing painless and of value.

Over Janelle's last days, Carla and Connie visited her daily, often more than once a day. Harpists from the Chalice of Repose visited each day. As they played and softly hummed, Connie and Janelle lay on her new thick mattress surrounded by pillows; Connie rubbed Janelle's shoulders and Janelle rested, semiconscious. Carla arrived. As Connie had always done in the past, she indicated she would gladly relinquish her spot beside Janelle. Until now, Carla had always declined. This time, she slid onto the mat beside her daughter and stroked her.

Janelle died two days later, not long after her mom and Tommy told her about their father's passing. "I think it sort of eased it or made it OK with her," Carla says. "I think her dad's dying was like him coming to her and saying, 'Come on, Janelle, it's time for us to run and play. It's OK. It's nothing to be afraid of.' "

The day after Janelle died, Carla, Joe, and Tommy returned to the nursing home for her things. They packed her clothes and teddy bear and music tapes in boxes and carried them out to the car. Tommy asked to keep the purple and silver Mylar balloon that Janelle had got at graduation and that had been floating around her room. He tucked it into the back of the car, but when he opened the door to load more boxes, it almost escaped. He tied the string around his finger. As they were loading the last box, the balloon slipped out the door and floated away.

"Let it go. It's meant to go, Tommy," Carla said. And they sat on the parking lot curb and watched the silver orb climb higher and higher, twinkle in the bright afternoon sun, and disappear. *Everything's OK with Janelle,* they thought.

. . .

The decisions people make to complete their dying days, or to help someone they love complete a life, are rarely easy. They are often gut-wrenching and may challenge basic beliefs about who one is and what is important. Nevertheless, these end-of-life decisions create opportunities for new experiences and discoveries that range from the fairly mundane to the frankly extraordinary. The opportunity for Janelle was to confirm her self-worth and to receive well-earned recognition from her family and community. There were a couple of times in the weeks leading up to her graduation when I doubted whether she would be able to hold out. Some days I was sure her seizures or another pneumonia would consume her.

Like Janelle, Carla found opportunities in ordinary routine and daily struggles. Her emotional calluses prevented her from doting on her daughter, but she showed her love by warring with the bureaucracies that ignored them. And ultimately, when the love was overwhelming, she expressed it with the simple gesture of lying down beside her daughter and soothing her rigid body.

As people struggle to make the right decisions in the midst of the staggering crisis of an imminent, untimely death, startling opportunities may be revealed—opportunities for nurturing, honoring, and celebrating the person departing. Very often I have seen families build living monuments to their dying member by the decisions they make and the care they give. And despite how much these challenges may threaten firmly held beliefs, it is remarkable how often they are made without wavering. To me, this willingness, and even determination, to venture into the unknown is the essence of courage.

Seven

Writing a Personal Script for Dying: Steve Morris

As I learned from Janelle and Carla, heroism comes in many shapes and sizes. They unflinchingly tackled the hardest decisions in life and then pushed on, undeterred by fear or grief. And not only did they embrace their family, but they shared their pain and joy with the entire community. But dying well does not always demand exceptional imagination and tenacity. Occasionally it is a little simpler and a little more private, although no less demanding. For some people, knowing the uncomplicated activities and tasks that can be completed within their individual sphere gives them peace and a final sense of accomplishment.

Such was the case for Steve Morris, a Montana cowboy who typified the western culture of stoicism and deadpan reactions. During the week he punched a time-card as a lineman for the telephone company, and on the weekends he punched cows. What mattered in his life was riding quarter horses in rodeos and into the back country. Skilled with animals and in reading terrain and weather, he was not an introspective person. Showing emotion, much less dwelling on his feelings, was as alien to Steve as an English saddle. Even as he approached the brink of death, he was not one to muse about the meaning of life or to express personal feelings or thoughts, beyond noting concrete facts. However, when I wrote out for him what hospice calls "the five things of relationship completion"—saying "I forgive you"; "Forgive me"; "Thank you"; "I love you"; and "Goodbye"—it gave him a kind of script with which to greet his final days with courage and determination.

Married for twenty-two years, with grown children, Steve was a loyal but unaffectionate husband and a demanding father. When his years of heavy smoking caught up with him and he developed chronic obstructive pulmonary disease (COPD) around age fifty-five and faced the very real prospect of dying, he prepared to die the same way he had lived. Rather than reflecting on what he might have done differently or what he could accomplish in his final days, he stuck to what he knew: maintaining independence and distance from his emotions. But a funny thing happened on the way to the great unknown. Steve did not die as he lived but, instead, changed in remarkable ways. Despite his literal-mindedness, or maybe because of it, Steve gradually came to understand the landmarks and tasks he could accomplish in his last days. He didn't set out thinking of his illness or impending death as an opportunity to grow as a person—indeed, the idea would have seemed ludicrous to him when he was well—but the prospect of dying so scared him that he was willing to try anything that might relieve the terror.

Substantial personal growth often occurs in dying without agonizing soul-searching or questioning of one's fundamental nature. The adage that people die as they have lived is a half-truth. Even as they are dying, most people retain the capacity for change or, more accurately, growth. In Steve's case, this meant acknowledging the emotional impact his impending death was having on both himself and his family. Ultimately Steve courageously tackled the taskwork of completing life as much for their sake as to lessen his own anxieties. Rather than ignoring his sadness and grief and leaving things unresolved, he concentrated on the personal dimension and methodically addressed each significant relationship in his life. Like a roper cutting calves, he learned to identify and isolate from the rumbling herd of his emotions each feeling he needed to convey. In expressing his feelings, Steve found peace.

I first met Steve at the insistence of his wife, Dot. They lived in the hills of North Missoula in a split-level home stuffed with porcelain figurines, plastic flowers, and doily coverlets. While the inside of the house was clearly Dot's creation, the large backyard was Steve's territory. It was large enough for the camper top to his pickup truck, a tall flagpole, and extra horse feed. Although zoning laws forced him to board his horse elsewhere, he kept a couple of dozen bales of hay handy for trips. On the flagpole waved a conspicuous Stars and Stripes.

Taking care of Steve had stressed Dot to the edge of collapse. Ever since his heart attack and angioplasty four years earlier, he had grown increasingly debilitated and dependent. Two medications, in addition to a water pill and a potassium supplement, were required to control persistent hypertension. Much of his lung tissue had been destroyed by emphysema, and a string of infections had put him in the hospital with increasing frequency. Making matters worse, Steve had been a heavy smoker since age fifteen, and he had continued until only recently. As with many people whose habit has progressed to a lung or respiratory disease, his smoking was as much a personality trait as a mindless ritual.

For many lifelong smokers, smoking is self-nurturing behavior. The sucking and immediate oral gratification develop as a way of taking care of themselves; it feels good in the short term, or at least it did when the habit began. Often people who go on to have severe chronic pulmonary disease, those whom doctors and nurses sometimes label "lungers," have a history of being emotionally neglected as young children. Smoking constitutes a calming and reassuring form of self-care. One need not be a Freudian to understand that, for people who fit this profile, smoking is a form of self-mothering. As adults, people like Steve tend to remain emotionally needy, unable to feel affection from others because of a vague sense of unworthiness. As their respiratory disease advances, the very habit that brings brief comfort becomes the cause of their debilitation, and they tend to become frustrated, anxious, and irritable. As people afflicted with emphysema or chronic bronchitis, the two most common versions of COPD, become increasingly dependent on others for routine care, they may become insistent and overly demanding of family and care providers, as if attempting to extract nurturing. Not only does this increase their stress, but for these previously independent, goal-oriented people, dependency brings with it the guilt of being a burden and thus increases their anxiety and frustration. It is a hellish spiral and can lead to a miserable dying. This was certainly the direction in which Steve and Dot were plunging.

Steve's anxiety was intensified by an overpowering fear of suffocation. As his illness had progressed, his inability to catch his breath had provoked anxiety, which left him even more breathless and caused a sensation of air hunger. The situation grew more and more desperate as the weeks and months passed. By the time I saw him, he was so afraid that his blood oxygen level was falling that he was unable to sit still. In the midst of breathlessness, in fact because of it, he couldn't keep from constantly pacing.

Over six feet tall and lanky, with thinning brown hair, amber aviator glasses, and a rosy complexion, Steve Morris looked younger and healthier than he was. Even the clear plastic tubes running into both sides of his nose did not make him look sickly. His voice told the real story. He grunted with each breath, and his words came in short bursts, the speech of someone whose lungs can not sustain sentences.

Steve's growing need for more oxygen and his inability to breathe freely kept him largely housebound. He spent his days in the den, surrounded by rodeo trophies and bronze Remington reproductions, on a La-Z-Boy recliner, watching television. If Dot ventured more than twenty paces away, even into the yard, Steve would yell for her to come to his aid. "Dot, *Dot!*" would come the familiar call. While the tone of his voice never rose above a hoarse C, the panic it conveyed was clearly audible. She would immediately drop whatever she was doing and rush downstairs, to find that he wanted a light across the room turned on or off or a magazine handed to him. What he really needed, of course, but could not say, was reassurance that she was around and would respond. Being naturally laconic only made him seem more gruff. Always the dutiful helpmate, Dot never refused his insistent demands. Her submissive behavior, coupled with a preference for perfect order and cleanliness around the home, had her stretched to exhaustion.

Dot sat on the edge of the couch watching me as I listened to Steve's lungs. With my stethoscope on his chest, my eyes wandered to the tattoo on his arm; I tried to decipher what looked like a barbed-wire design. Very little air was moving through his lungs. The lingering smell of cigarette smoke in the furniture reinforced the suffocating atmosphere.

Steve was never still. He wrung his hands and constantly scratched at his forearms. Clearly, Steve was "hospice appropriate," our euphemism for someone with very advanced, terminal illness. "How are you doing today, Mr. Morris?" Rather than assume what seemed obvious, I waited to hear how he was feeling.

"I'm hurting, Doc."

"Where are you hurting, Mr. Morris?" I asked.

"Don't know, exactly. Don't know. Sort of all over." He spoke in a staccato wheeze. "I'm afraid," he gasped. "Running out of air."

Dot nodded as if she had heard this many times before. He probably had her checking the oxygen tank gauge every hour.

"Is it pain you feel or more of a dull ache?" I asked.

"It's everywhere."

"Are you feeling nervous, too?" I asked, though the answer was evident.

"Oh, God, yes, Doc." He made eye contact with me for the first time. "Nervousness," he said flatly.

I sat next to him and spoke softly, allowing my voice and the relaxed pattern of my own breathing to project a tone of composure and reassurance. "Do you mind if I call you Steve?" I asked.

"Hell, no, Doc. That's my name. Anything but late for dinner." His smile gave me a glimpse of the youthful, vigorous man he had once been.

"Steve, have you talked to your children, told them what's happening?"

"Oh, they know. They know all right."

"What have you told them?"

"That I screwed up. This is all my fault. All that smoking. My kids don't want to talk to me. Who can blame them. The divorce and all." Steve's first marriage had ended twenty-two years ago, but for this lapsed Catholic the guilt would last a lifetime. Dot had disappeared; she reappeared with coffee for Steve and me. She gave me a cup, set one beside her husband, and straightened the stack of *Reader's Digest*s on the television tray beside him.

"It's hard to imagine your kids holding that against you after all these years. You know, Steve, sometimes just bringing things out into the open helps clear the air. You could tell them the way you feel," I suggested.

Steve gave me a blank look and continued to scratch at his elbows. "How are you feeling about yourself, Steve?"

"Lousy, Doc. This is no good. For the birds. I can barely breathe," he declared, not realizing that my question concerned his emotions. He gazed at the bookshelf across the room, which glittered with trophies, plaques, and belt buckles from roping competitions, barrel racing, and rodeo riding. "I'm afraid I'll suffocate. This is no way to live."

After a pensive moment, he continued, "I should blow myself away. Save everybody a lot of trouble. I'm not going to get any better. I've got a revolver in my closet."

While I did not know whether he was testing me with his thoughts on suicide, I knew that his feeling of hopelessness was genuine.

"Do you mean that, Steve?" I asked intently. "Would you really blow yourself away?"

"Nah, I couldn't do that. Wouldn't be right for Dot," he declared.

"Steve, I'm beginning to understand how horrible you feel, and I want to know more. If a time comes when you are thinking seriously about using a gun on yourself, I want you to call me first. Can you do that?"

"Yeah, Doc."

"Promise?"

"Yeah, I promise."

I believed him. As we visited, I also noted that his breathing had become slower, a little deeper, and more relaxed. There was sadness in his eyes and voice, where a few minutes earlier there had been panic.

"I think that I and the other hospice folks can help. But it will take some time. You didn't get into this fix overnight, and it will take some time to find out what works." I paused, letting each point sink in. "I want you to hear, first and foremost, that we won't let you suffocate, Steve. I know that's your worst fear, and over time I hope to prove to you that it's not going to happen. I have helped care for lots of people who are dying of illnesses like yours, and they do not die suffocating or feeling like they are drowning, but peacefully, usually becoming sleepy and slipping away." Steve was looking at me, in a childlike way, as if I were asserting that Santa was real. "It's going to take some time, Steve, but if you're willing to work with us, I think there's a lot we can do."

While Steve's anxiety was as easy to read as a stop sign, I could not decipher what else he might be thinking. His facial expressions ranged from neutral to blank.

"With your permission, I'd like to adjust some of your medications and start you on a very low dose of morphine for your breathing. Also, although I know you've had problems sleeping and becoming even more anxious on prednisone in the past, I think it might actually help you. I'd like to try a tiny dose and sort of sneak up on a dose as your body allows it. What do you think?"

"OK, Doc. I'm willing to try."

"Good. I'm also going to have Vickie, the hospice social worker, come out to meet you, Steve. She is really skilled at teaching people relaxation, and I'd like you to try it."

"I don't need that, Doc. I'd be relaxed if I could just breathe."

"Well, I know that, Steve, and I still think it may help. The more anxious you are, the more short of breath you feel. You know that too, don't you?" He nodded. "Relaxation isn't something that just happens, nor is it something you—or any of us—can force. But it is something that you can learn to do. I think of relaxation as a skill, like riding a bicycle or playing piano. And Vickie is a good teacher. Also, we have some relaxation tapes that are soothing and can be a useful tool when you are alone and anxious and feeling breathless." Knowing that Steve best understood the concrete, I emphasized a factual description of the tapes and accounts of how other people used them.

"What do you think? Are you willing to give it a try? I don't think they have any bad side-effects," I offered, with a teasing smile.

"Yeah, I guess," he replied, smiling in return.

An early therapeutic success, I thought. My goal for this first visit was to establish rapport and lay the basis on which to build trust. Something else happened that day: Looking at Steve, I couldn't help seeing him as he must have looked as a teenager in his first rodeo. Tall and wiry, big ears overshadowed by his wide ceremonial cowboy hat—even then, his bravado hid his tender vulnerability.

I realized how much I liked this guy already.

For the first time Dot sat down, her expression softened, and she seemed tired. Like Steve, she suffered in silence. Dot was a small, bubbly woman with carefully arranged white-blond hair and large gold-rimmed glasses. When stressed, her eyes grew larger and more alert and her brow became knitted. She was fidgety and in constant motion; her busy hands provided a distraction from the painful reality around her. I hoped that any gains Steve made in relaxation would benefit her, too.

Next, Steve and I talked about dying. I asked him how he would like to die, "in the best of all worlds." He said he wanted to simply fall asleep and never wake.

"You have some time until then," I suggested. "Time you can use to do things and be with loved ones. You must carry wonderful stories inside you about your life as horseman and rodeo competitor that your grandchildren would treasure. Perhaps you can record these stories on tape as a legacy for them. Sharing their feelings with their children and other close relatives gives many people who are facing their final days a sense of completion and peace. Some find that saying what we call in hospice 'the five things' to loved ones helps enormously." As I enumerated each one, Steve nodded thoughtfully, but I was not sure whether he had heard them until he asked me to write them down. I wrote them on a blank prescription form.

Before I left I explained to Dot that I was modifying Steve's medications, and I wrote out detailed instructions for giving them to him. According to his chart, his medication regime had been spotty. He had had a bad reaction to corticosteroids three years earlier; he had become bloated, anxious, and sleepless. I suggested that his dose was probably too much and that a lower dose of prednisone would help him considerably. We also talked about morphine, which he did not understand, believing it made him feel anxious. We both agreed that his overuse of the inhaler, rather than the small doses of morphine, might well be fueling his anxious feelings.

I spoke with Dot by phone a few days later. She said that Steve had awakened with an air of grim determination the day after my visit. After breakfast he had disappeared into the den, trailing his long oxygen tubing, and then immediately summoned her. She found him sitting on the couch, close to the oxygen tank, studying his rodeo trophy wall. He did not look well, she thought. Although dressed and combed, he had a pasty cast, accentuated by the yellow tint in his glasses and a moist sheen around his hairline. With Steve, it was hard to distinguish his natural dourness from depression.

"Got to get rid of that stuff," he announced.

"What do you mean? What stuff?" she said.

"Trophies, ribbons, buckles, plaques. All that riding stuff. I'll never see the back of a horse again. Might as well give them away. Maybe the kids would like them."

Dot sat on the couch beside him and gently laid her hand on his forearm. Not normally at a loss for words, she did not know what to say. She held back tears, afraid that they would upset her husband.

"I'm sure they would like them," she said tentatively. "But are you sure? They're no trouble here, and I sort of like dusting them. See that tall trophy on the end, the barrel-racing one? It always reminds me of the time we took the camper over to Billings for that three-day fair and you brought two boots from two different pairs. Remember that? You had one brown crocodile boot and a rough-out boot, and the heels were different? And all weekend you walked around with that funny limp because one heel was higher than the other? That's when you won that barrel race." Dot was struggling to hold in the tears.

"Yeah. Maybe Tom would like that trophy."

"Don't you want to keep any? You must have at least a dozen belt buckles. You know what they say, you can only wear one at a time." Dot wondered if she was babbling. She did not understand exactly why Steve was doing this. Was it a gesture of love toward his children, or was it the act of someone getting ready to die?

As she related this to me, I felt it was Steve's way of communicating his fatalism. Some people use words, and some, like Steve, use gestures to express how they're feeling. Since he could not add to his trophy collection and would never ride again, he was preparing to give up all life as he knew it. As Dot continued to describe the events of that afternoon, this impression was reinforced.

"We have any cardboard boxes around?" he asked.

"There's some in the garage. I'll get them." Dot went to fetch the boxes, as Steve dismantled a lifetime. Unable to move far without gasping for air, he painstakingly took down each item from the shelf and placed it in one of six piles. Dot returned with the boxes.

"Tom, Sara, Cathy, and Jim." She ticked off the recipients. "Who else are you thinking?"

"John at the stables, and Ellen," he added, naming his favorite niece.

"Why don't you just sit down and tell me who gets what? Let me do this. You rest. I'll put them in the boxes," Dot insisted. For the rest of the morning, on and off, they sorted through Steve's mementos. Twice he said he was tired and curled up for a nap. Dot stayed with him, watching talk shows on television, the volume turned low.

That evening Steve telephoned everyone to tell them what he had done and that they could pick up their souvenirs. Over the next week, his children, niece, and friend from Rolling Hills Stables came by in the evenings and weekends. Dot said their visits were unlike any others. Steve not only gave each recipient the mementos but added his memories about when and how he won them. They heard about his favorite quarterhorse, Bar Plank, the countless ribs Steve had broken in competition, and ways to avoid losing fingers while calf roping. I asked her what Steve had set aside for her.

"Oh, I don't need much." She gave an embarrassed laugh. "To tell you the truth, I think he forgot about me. We got to the end of the collection and he says, quick-like, 'What do you want?' The only thing left was this leather belt-buckle with his name carved in it, so that's what I got. It's nice."

Typical Dot, I thought. In her own self-effacing way, she was as emotionally hamstrung as her husband. I took solace in the knowledge that they had been successfully married for many years, and while their relationship might look strained to an outsider, it worked for them. Over the following weeks, I kept track of Steve through reports from my hospice colleagues. Despite our efforts, his anxiety was not abating; if anything, it seemed to be mounting. An obvious problem was that Dot still did not understand his medication doses and schedule, so Steve was not receiving them on time. He had become confused about why he was taking morphine and compazine, an antinausea drug, and had stopped taking both. A hospice nurse made scheduled visits three times a week, but some nights we received three or four calls from Dot, frantic about his breathing. Steve was also having problems sleeping. He was going to bed around eight in the evening, then was up and down most of the night. In the mornings when he woke up—which is to say, when he gave up trying to sleep—he was tired. I made a home visit, examined him, found that his measured oxygen saturation had not changed, and detected no evidence of deterioration. I consulted with his pulmonary physician, and we agreed that anxiety was a major component of his current distress. This was more than merely emotional. Anxiety increases a person's physiological "work of breathing" and, therefore, increases the body's oxygen demands.

About a month after I had first met Steve, at around two on a Saturday morning, I was in the ER working a night shift. It had been quiet, and the nurses and I were chatting and eating reheated pizza when an ambulance crew radioed that it was en route with a man who had fallen in his home and was complaining of chest pain and severe dyspnea. From the vital signs and description of distress given over the radio, I knew the person was in extremis, on the verge of death. When the emergency medical technician radioed their arrival—"We're at your door"—I went out to meet them, pulled open the ambulance doors, and had grasped the end of the gurney before realizing who was under the oxygen mask.

"Steve! What are you doing here?!" Mercifully, the absurdity of this question was lost on Steve. He was drenched in sweat and semiconscious. It took only seconds to confirm that in his fall Steve had fractured a rib and "dropped a lung," an expression for a pneumothorax, that is, air trapped between the outermost lining of the lung and the chest wall. When the lung is punctured, as it was by Steve's broken rib, the wound acts as a temporary flap valve, and each breath forces more air between the lung and thoracic cage, gradually compressing the lung.

Rarely have my hospice practice and my emergency medical practice intersected so directly. During the next few minutes, the ER staff and I performed a well-rehearsed role. An IV line was in and an X-ray taken before Steve was even undressed. He was given IV morphine as I quickly prepped his chest with Betadine, numbed his skin, and surgically inserted a sterile plastic chest tube that decompressed the space between the chest and squashed lung. An audible *whoosh* was followed by an instantaneous improvement in Steve's condition. A few minutes later, as I was sewing the tube in place, he looked up and weakly exclaimed, "Jesus Christ, Doc, you didn't have to knife me. I thought we were friends!" His breathing and sense of humor were back.

"Oh, Steve, we are. But you sure know how to scare the hell out of your friends!" The multiple ironies of this situation were not subtle, even at two A.M. Here was a guy I had promised would not die suffocating, and he damn near did. When I asked Steve what had happened, he told me he had awakened anxious and unable to sleep, had started down the stairs for the den, relaxation tape in hand, and had tripped on his oxygen tubing. The relaxation tape I had stressed had almost caused his demise. And then there was the notion of "intensive palliative care." I frequently use the phrase in my lectures when I discuss the importance of planning for the occasional situation that requires intensive medical intervention to control pain or breathlessness among the dying. But I rarely include chest tube insertion in my discussion. Were his injury and near death necessary for the universe to teach me another lesson in humility? Steve's case would continue to defy many of my assumptions about not only medical care but also palliative care.

Being admitted to the hospital turned out to be a good thing for Steve, and for Dot. It forced him to stay still for a time, allowed us to readjust his medications, and gave Dot a much-needed rest from his constant demands. While visiting him, however, I saw no indication that he had yet confronted any of the sticky emotions that were making him so anxious and physically uncomfortable. During his stay in the hospital the Chalice of Repose harpists visited him daily, and the music relaxed him dramatically. When they entered the room Steve was usually hyperalert, his nervous system vibrating with anxious energy, but reliably, within minutes of their beginning to play and softly hum their "prescriptive music," he'd be soundly snoring. He frequently mentioned how wonderful it was "when the angels came to play," and I detected more than a hint of optimism in his voice.

Steve was in a double room on the third floor of Community Hospital; fortunately, the other bed was empty. I wanted to have a heart-to-heart with him and felt he would be even more inhibited if a stranger were six feet away behind a curtain. It was late afternoon when we talked, and the sinking September sun flooded the room with warm yellow light. What relaxed Steve the most was company, especially people who appeared calm and in control. I wanted to let him know that time was wasting—the initial hospice report had given him less than six months—without my voice or body language revealing apprehension.

I studied his chart for a moment. "How do you feel?"

"So-so," he said.

"How about the anxiety, the nervousness you mentioned before? That still bothering you?"

He shrugged.

"You know, if it was me lying in that bed, I'd probably be scared. You're still very sick. Even surrounded by all this medical care and help at a second's notice, I might well be afraid. It's only natural." I chose my words carefully and left lots of pauses for him to fill. "I know you're worried about suffocating," I continued. "But, honestly, most people with this type of illness do not die in a sudden crisis. Usually they go peacefully, getting sleepier each day, then slipping away quietly without too much discomfort."

I shifted gears. "Have you given any thought to what we last talked about? Taping your recollections for your family? Saying the five things?"

"No," he said sheepishly. Then he added perfunctorily, "I'm not afraid of dying. We all got to go sometime."

"You're not?" I gently challenged.

"I *have* been thinking about those five things, Doc. They make a lot of sense. Maybe I should do them more often." He reached into the drawer of the nightstand, retrieved his wallet, and pulled out the prescription slip I had written them on. Although he was dodging the amorphous emotions swirling around thoughts of dying, he liked having what amounted to a written script.

Steve had recited the five things to his wife, and he had ticked off the items as he spoke with his children, nieces, and friends. His style was awkward and mechanical, but his intentions were deeply felt. On one level the process seemed to get the job done. From what he said, it seemed that his affairs were in order. Yet, clearly, something continued to gnaw at him. He was frequently agitated and at times sullen. When I asked him at various times how he felt, he often replied, "Pretty shitty, Doc, pretty shitty," without being specific. Asked if he felt anything would be left undone if he died tomorrow, his automatic response was no.

One nurse on the hospice team who had known the Morris family for years made us aware that Steve had had a son, Andrew, by his first marriage, who had died of AIDS almost ten years earlier. We wondered about the specter of that fractured relationship, but whenever Andi, Vickie, Tom, or I gently inquired about Andrew's death and his feelings, Steve would deflect the conversation, saying, "Some things just can't be made right."

Steve's agitation spread, sometimes making him confused and even disoriented. The only things that calmed him were someone's soothing presence or the music of the Chalice harpists. From a physical perspective, Steve's injury shouldn't have kept him in the hospital for more than a day or two. But his anxiety was a more difficult matter. As it was, several more days of care and the addition of new medications, such as Haldol, were needed before I considered discharge.

With a great deal of attention and reassurance, Steve gradually became more calm and actually quite cheerful during the week he was in the hospital. He ate well and slept through the night; a nurse noted in his chart that he slept with a smile on his face. While it was premature for him to return home, he agreed as an intermediate step to be transferred to Sky View Nursing Home, a twenty-bed institution resembling the vintage 1955 elementary school it had once been, just three blocks from his home.

He was initially happy with the move to Sky View, and medically he was improved compared with when I had met him. Yet the faint whisper of panic grew progressively louder, and within days his nervous tension covered him like a nasty rash. He continually asked about going home, and it gradually became a fixation, the focus of nearly all his energy. Between his lung condition and, even more, his anxiety, he could not even walk to the bathroom without wheezing, labored breathing, and a couple of puffs on his inhaler. Nor could he function at rest. He paced his room and the corridors, usually with an oxygen tank in tow. He had sores on his arms from compulsively scratching at his elbows. At night he complained of not being able to sleep, despite extra doses of Ativan, an antianxiety medication. At four A.M. he would be wide awake and dressed and repeatedly asking when he could go home. Complaining of "nerves" and breathlessness, he ate little. He was almost literally bouncing off the walls. Anxiety tends to be infectious, and he was agitating other patients and driving the nursing staff nuts.

One evening around seven o'clock Steve exploded. Dot had left about half an hour earlier; while she was there, his fears had been contained, but only superficially. As soon as he was alone, the anxiety and fear rose in him like a dangerous high tide. It crept upward, each wave threatening to drown him. He felt claustrophobic and couldn't breathe;

he was sure that any moment he would gulp for air and feel drowned. Terrified of suffocating, feeling the need for fresh air on his face, panicked and confused, he lifted his oxygen tank with both arms above his head and heaved it through the window. The shattering glass summoned an alarmed nurse and an orderly. They found him leaning against the window frame, gasping and wheezing, and hugging a pillow to ease the pain of his labored breathing. The frigid December air had quickly knocked ten degrees off the room's temperature, but the thin, pale man in a pale blue bathrobe did not seem to notice. His exhaustion and the cold had brought a measure of composure. While the orderly went for another oxygen setup and a wheelchair to move him to another room, the nurse sat with Steve, trying to soothe him further. She had never seen a patient so afraid.

The nursing home notified Andi, and she arrived shortly thereafter. Her presence and reassurance calmed both Steve and the Sky View staff. By the time she left, Steve, who was physically drained, had fallen into a deep sleep. Andi paged me and relayed the details of the panic attack by phone. The crisis had passed, for the moment. Together, we sketched a two-pronged approach for Steve: boosting his Haldol, and bringing back Vickie, who had introduced him to the relaxation tapes.

Steve liked Vickie, who mixed her warm encouragement with strict practicality. She alternately mothered him and scolded him. A middle-aged woman with long, straight brown hair lightened by many fine strands of gray, Vickie is both savvy clinical counselor and nurturing earth mother; she always lets patients know where they stand with her. She visited the next morning, and in her presence, Steve's emotions loosened up. He warmed to her demonstrative nature and would acquiesce when she insisted on a big hug every time she saw him. With Vickie this weather-beaten cowboy was more a frightened adolescent boy than the Marlboro Man he resembled. Her complete acceptance of who he was, without judgment, allowed Steve to admit having feelings, even if he could not easily give voice to them. To her, he tenderly acknowledged feeling helpless and afraid. While Vickie didn't push Steve to talk about Andrew or his feelings, she let him know that it was OK to have feelings he couldn't reconcile or even talk about. If and when he could and wanted to, she would be there to listen.

The hospice team and I decided to try channeling Steve's determination in a concrete, constructive manner. After extensive discussions with Steve, Dot, their children, and Dr. Levering, his pulmonologist, we developed a plan of care that detailed what he had to master in terms of his own care in order to go home. Before Steve could leave the nursing home, he had to be independent enough to get by without yelling for Dot every time he wanted to scratch.

Like a teacher laying out lessons for a homebound pupil, Vickie presented Steve with a description of the skills he had to learn. He had to be able to dress and undress, shave and bathe without help, walk up a flight of stairs without gasping, know how to use and refill his inhaler, be comfortably alone for two hours, and sleep through the night. These criteria for discharge were written out.

Now Steve knew what he had to do. With a list of tasks to master in order to leave the nursing home, he got to work. One afternoon, just a few days after his night terror, Steve called Dot and implored her to allow him to come home for a day. When Dot asked Andi what she should do, Andi, Vickie, and I had an impromptu meeting and agreed it was worth a try. He spent the day at home; that evening, Dot called the nursing home to report that things had gone pretty well but that Steve refused to return. I heard about his refusal the following day and immediately made a visit to their home. After a look from Dot confirmed she was not ready to have him at home, I was able to convince Steve that he was making real progress, but for the moment it was best for him to return to Sky View.

The trial day at home did have a positive effect on Steve. He was calmer, more focused, and more resolute about learning to live within his physical capabilities. Within ten days we were able to assure Dot that he had achieved a measure of personal independence and could be alone when she was off doing errands or visiting family. Steve went home.

Bad news was waiting for him. His brother, Harry, in Kentucky—the older sibling who had protected him and taught him how to ride—was dying of cancer. I gathered that Harry was as impassive as his brother and, despite their affinity and warm memories, they had not been in close touch. Steve telephoned him as soon as he got word. They talked for nearly an hour, longer than they had collectively in the last twenty years. In an ironic reversal, Steve effectively calmed Harry's fears of dying, telling him they would soon be together. He also confided that he had put his life in order: sold the camper and pickup truck, paid off the mortgage, and made sure he was up-to-date on his life insurance. The dying brothers dispassionately discussed suicide, and Steve offered his practical rationale for rejecting the idea: "If I blow myself away, Dot won't get any insurance." Midway through the call, Steve brought out his worn slip of prescription paper and methodically explained to Harry about saying the five things.

"That made me feel good," Steve said. "Harry's my big brother. He was always taking care of me. That was something I could give him. We never talked that way before." Harry died six weeks later. Although Steve remained stoical and concealed his grief, he seized chances to talk about how close he and his brother had been as children. In his Montana cowboy way, Steve confronted the loss he was feeling over his brother, and his own dwindling life.

On my next visit, I first heard about what would become the next astonishing turn of events in Steve's saga. On a morning television talk show, Dot had seen a report about an experimental surgery for people with advanced emphysema. Called "lung reduction," this procedure removes the overinflated, severely damaged portions of a person's emphysematous lungs, which rob space from the remaining functioning, gas-exchanging lung tissue. While it makes eminent practical sense, any procedure that removes part of a vital organ is highly risky. Dr. Levering got a call from Dot, and within a day he had tracked down one of the two lung reduction programs in the country, which was fortuitously located within driving distance of Missoula, at the University of Washington Medical Center in Seattle. At a hastily arranged office visit, Dr. Levering informed the Morrises that Steve might qualify, but a number of tests would be needed to make sure his heart hadn't been badly damaged by longstanding lung disease and hypertension. Other tests would require preliminary trips to Seattle, and the entire process would take time and careful planning.

Within three weeks, the surgeon directing the program had reviewed Steve's medical records and the requisite tests, and Steve had been accepted and scheduled for surgery. Lung reduction surgery lasts six hours, and patients are warned that they could die during the procedure. If the operation is successful, however, a patient may leave the hospital free of twenty-four-hour oxygen and with years of life left. To say that the prospect of this operation gave Steve newfound optimism is an understatement. Once again he had a concrete goal, and he had hope for years of life. He was calmer, more collected, and more upbeat than I had ever seen him. He was still often sleeping in the den and dependent on oxygen, but happily counting the days. Every morning before the trip he announced to Dot, "One more day less." One less day of difficult, painful, frightening breathing.

I visited Steve a few days before the trip to Seattle and did a routine examination, listening to his lungs and asking about his medications. Centered on the wall over the couch, where before had been photographs of Steve and horses, was a fine ink drawing of two hunting dogs. I remarked on its craft and artistry, and Steve told me proudly that his son was the artist.

In a look, I realized, indeed, that this was the missing piece! Now he admitted to me that he had never made peace with his "queer" son who had died years earlier from AIDS.

He added, "Andrew was such a good boy." I never again heard him mention this son. I can only speculate on how he came to it—Steve was not one to engage in introspection or psychological discussion—but the ease with which he referred to his son told me that he had finally arrived at a degree of resolution in that central relationship.

Before I left, Steve made a heartfelt confession. "Doc, I'm kind of embarrassed, but I got to apologize. I've been telling you for months that I'm not afraid of dying. Well, I was lying. I was."

I laughed easily and responded with a confession of my own. "Oh, Steve, that's OK. I never believed you anyway."

"Oh, you didn't! That's good!" he said with real relief. I'll never forget the way he looked at me, his sad eyes smiling in appreciation, like a little boy who had confessed to doing something naughty and had just been forgiven.

Steve not only survived the surgery but arrived home two months after it with new color in his cheeks. His prognosis had improved so markedly that he was being discharged from hospice care, so I stopped by for a last official visit. Dot showed me into the den, where Steve was still camped out in the hospital bed with his oxygen nearby. I examined him, checking for signs of infection from the long scar down his chest and listening to his lungs, which were moving more air than I had ever heard.

"You look great, Steve," I declared. "Your scar's healing very well. How do you feel?"

Perhaps it was the yellow tint in his glasses, but his eyes looked flat and watery. He shook his head in resignation. "Not good. Still hurts to breathe."

I sat on the side of the bed and Dot hovered on the other side, helping him button his pajama top. She smoothed his hair and straightened his collar.

"I'm hearing parts of your lung that I've never heard before, Steve," I said. "The operation worked well. It's just going to take time for you to adjust. Your fear of suffocating is rooted pretty deep. Please be easy on yourself. You've just come back from the brink and accomplished some extraordinary things. And you've earned my lasting respect—you've wrestled with demons and come out on top. Not many people could have done what you have accomplished. I'm not blowing smoke, Steve. You've done something truly remarkable here. And I hope you know that."

"Yeah, well," he tentatively agreed. He added, with a hint of enthusiasm, "The biggest thing in the world is saying those five things. If I hadn't been dying I never would have cleaned up all the crap in my life. I think of my kids and Harry." His voice trailed off, and I noticed again that in giving voice to his sadness he was calm. It had taken the specter of dying, and the loss of his brother, to tear away the retaining wall around his own emotions. He grinned sheepishly, and I squeezed his shoulder affectionately, wishing I could will him to feel better. But tincture of time is often the best medicine for what ails. Steve's depression would lift eventually as he learned to live again. I said goodbye to the Morrises and promised to stay in touch.

Although he probably could not articulate exactly what had changed, Steve's encounter with dying altered his life forever. The balance of emotions within himself and his family will never be the same; they will be more stable and more satisfying. Much of the terrible anxiety that plagued his days and nights evaporated, and he became able to welcome each day with a new sense of peace. While Steve hardly mastered all the possible developmental landmarks of life, he unmistakably grew as he lived toward his expected death. He faced his fears, confronted the emotional rattlesnakes that lay hidden in the brush of his past, expressed his love, and said the five things to the most important people in his life.

Relationships that are reconciled and brought to completion need not cease; rather, this sense of resolution can form the basis for a new beginning. The next time the Morrises sit down at the family dinner table, the ties will surely be stronger. No one needs to wait until the end of life to resolve the emotional business of relationships. One key to living well lies in expressing the essence of the five things in our daily interactions with those we love. Now this is true for Steve, too.

Eight

Accepting the Gift of Dependence and the Burden of Care: Jake Edwards

Often when I ask patients to tell me about their suffering, they talk about being afraid of becoming a burden to their loved ones. Sometimes, more than dying, people dread becoming dependent on caregivers and making them feel responsible for both financial and physical needs as well as the inevitable emotional demands. Of course, caring for someone who is dying requires fortitude. Family members may have to provide constant attention to physical comfort, such as easing dry lips and fever. They may sit for hours and days with someone, offering love and reassurance with their presence. The dying person may moan incomprehensibly or breathe noisily, adding to the caregivers' ordeal. This is all made even more poignant and intense by the nearly universal sleep deprivation that caregivers endure.

However, to speak of this time solely as a "burden" misrepresents the nature of the experience. Although a patient may feel that this care and attention is unduly taxing or unpleasant, caregivers frequently tell me that they regard this time as precious. The burden is rarely too heavy. Far more often, they say it feels like a sacred responsibility that they want to shoulder—that they *need* to shoulder. I frequently ask patients to imagine how they would feel if they were well and another family member were dying. "Oh, I would be sad, but I would want to care for them," they often reply.

Caring for a dying loved one is a powerful way to express love, devotion, and reverence. Allowing a spouse or grown child to care for one becomes a final gift from the person dying. The physical acts of caring can help family members in their own grief. This was certainly true for Jake Edwards and his family. Jake had always felt like an outcast, and he had left Missoula as soon as he was old enough. So when he contracted AIDS, he came home reluctantly. He loved his mother and sisters, but he abhorred the idea of them having to care for him. His feelings of unworthiness reinforced the feeling that his care was a burden, and for a time he adamantly refused to let them tend to his physical needs. But at some point, Jake realized the nature of the burden he presented and allowed his mother and sisters to nurse his deteriorating body. Jake's act of self-sacrifice—giving up his desire for independence and allowing himself to become defenseless and vulnerable to his family—might, at first, appear passive. In fact, it was a difficult, active decision and a conscious gift he gave to his family. By accepting their care and their love, he helped ease the pain of their grief in a way only he could. The healing and growth that Jake and his family experienced in his dying can only be adequately conveyed by telling the story.

Jake lived in the old part of Missoula, which was carved into the edge of the winding Clark Fork River and built around the flour mill and sawmill that served homesteaders coming west. The people of Missoula have always been a collection of unconventional characters. In its frontier days, it lured railroad tycoons and wranglers, Indians and artists. Its immigrants today are writers, film stars, medical professionals, fly fishermen, and students. Nevertheless, Missoula's old section, fenced in by highways, seems immutable. It is easy to get lost in this part of town, with its assortment of one-way streets chopped up by railroad tracks and overpasses. The dwellings here are an incongruous mixture of Victorian houses and pastel-colored mobile homes on bare lots. Landmarks tend to be things like a large vegetable garden or a new motorcycle in a front yard.

After numerous wrong turns, I found Jake's house in the shadow of an interstate overpass. The air was heavy with the smell of sawdust from the pulp mill on the other side of the highway. He lived in the first-floor apartment of a two-story house with a barbecue grill on the front porch and a laundry line around the side.

I had first learned about Jake, who was forty-three at the time, from Charlotte, a home health nurse, who had cornered me in a parking lot outside the hospital. "I've got this AIDS patient," she said. "I'm going to talk to his doctor about referring him to hospice. I think it's time for you to see him."

"What can you tell me about him?" I asked.

"Well, he's having lots of problems." She paused as if she had thought of something more important to say. "He's a problem patient, giving everyone fits, but I just love him." I raised my eyebrows in surprise. Charlotte was a veteran of the oncology units, had cared for countless dying patients, and had the gruff exterior of a traffic cop. In the coming weeks I would come to understand. Jake Edwards was ill-tempered and irascible, but he grew on people and melted even the coolest professional.

As the hospice's medical director, one of my jobs is to review each patient's regimen of pain and other medications and make sure patients are as comfortable as possible, while coordinating with a hospice nurse and a hospice social worker. We function as a team; each of us plays a different position, but we all work toward the goal of comprehensive care. At times I feel like the conductor of a small, talented orchestra, keeping everyone in tune and in tempo. I have a strong sense of what the finished piece should sound like. I want patient and family to feel emotionally safe enough to regard the final weeks or days as an opportunity for meaningful interaction. In Jake's case, my job became especially satisfying, because ultimately the music sounded far better than we could have imagined.

Jake lived alone with a rambunctious mixed Labrador retriever named Kate, although by this point in his illness, his mother Pauline was at his home constantly. This was a sore spot between them. Jake hated losing his independence, and Pauline refused to back off, even for a day. A small woman with white hair and tender eyes greeted me. She was agitated and distressed, and glad to see me. Jake had had an awful weekend, with recurring nausea, vomiting, and an unremitting headache, and he had been blaming her, his only target, for his discomfort.

His bedroom at the back of the house was tiny, with a mattress on the floor and bookshelves on both sides within easy reach. On this cold January afternoon Jake lay in bed smoking cigarettes and, occasionally, pot, a heaping ashtray on his chest, the room hazy with smoke. A country-western song wailed from the radio. He looked like he had led a hard life, and he reminded me of the frayed people I see going into Narcotics Anonymous meetings. His hair was sandy, long, and stringy, and his light blue eyes were deep-set. It was his face that spoke volumes: a fierce visage with pale, sunken cheeks and a pitted and pocked complexion.

I introduced myself and asked how he was feeling, expecting to hear about his pain and weakness, and braced for his wrath. I have grown used to angry patients, especially patients with end-stage emphysema, AIDS, or cancer. Sometimes they lash out at me just because I am there, or because I represent a medical system that cannot save them. They may be irate over a string of bad experiences with doctors and hospitals, feeling they have been deceived and ignored, and suspicious of any new medical person. But anger is often more than a reaction to a cruel fate. It is a mask emotion, and behind it lies sadness. People can become angry when they are losing something or someone precious and when the fundamental emotion within them is sadness, an ache they can do nothing about. Anger is a way of directing this pain outward.

Jake gave me the details of the rough weekend, but said he was feeling better. He could take fluids, and a small appetite had returned. Nevertheless, he was bedbound and extremely weak, and lancing pains down his legs, plus nightmares about tubes being inserted into his head, made sleeping fitful.

"That gancyclovir really kicked my ass, it really messed me up," he declared angrily. He complained about his various drug therapies, an intestinal tract infection, and the gradual loss of sight in his left eye. A few days earlier he had blasted his primary doctor about the "stupid medication" and had demanded an herbal treatment. He spoke in a hoarse, bitter tone, and occasionally paused for sips of water and long silences. Pauline stood near the doorway, offering to help each time he moved. "Stop hovering!" he snapped, as he struggled to reach for a glass of water. She disappeared into the kitchen.

I asked what I could do for him, and we talked about his headache. Jake was dehydrated, which was probably adding to his headache, and had enough medical savvy to ask for a liter of IV saline.

With many terminally ill patients, I find that my responsibility for helping manage their symptoms is my ticket in. It allows me to talk about what's happening to them without getting touchy-feely—it gives us both a safe, somewhat impersonal way to broach the subject of dying.

I wondered if he had any questions about the course of his illness. He stated brusquely that he knew AIDS was fatal, he had seen others die from it, but he was going to beat it, at least in the short run. I hoped he was right and that his optimism was not complete denial but more the suppression of painful possibilities. Jake's path to the end was unclear, and I was going to try to make it safe for him to look beyond denial, when and if he chose to.

We talked about ways to help him feel a little stronger. "I think it's likely we can get you feeling better," I began. "But what if something unexpectedly happened today or tomorrow? What if you suddenly became more ill or if there was a hurricane and the roof caved in and you were trapped, knowing you had only fifteen minutes to live? What would be going through your mind as you lay dying? What would be left undone? Is there anything you haven't done or said to someone important?"

"Yeah . . ." he began slowly. "There are some things I'd like my kids to have." I explained that we could help him with the formalities of a property will and a power-of-attorney form. He kept coming back to his daughters. "There's so much I want to tell them," he said, barely able to lift his head, his urgency muted only by weakness. With the mention of his daughters he seemed to relax; the anger faded like a receding wave, and he talked of his life.

Jake had grown up in Missoula, the only son in a family of six children. Number two in the string, he had been fiercely attached to his older sister, Gerri, serving as her confidant and protector throughout their childhood. The bonds with his younger sister, Arlene, were more tenuous, strained by the wounds of previous years of impulsive behavior and sibling strife. She had not visited him since the AIDS diagnosis. Jake was a born musician. His mother remembers him as a toddler banging on pots and pans. Unlike most kids, he did not grow out of it. The family was poor, living in the country, getting by on little. There were no tears when Jake's father, an alcoholic who had regularly beaten his only son, died of a heart attack when Jake was seventeen. As soon as Jake was old enough he had left Montana for California and the life of a drummer in a rock band. Living in the world of late-night clubs and with the stress of uncertain employment, Jake fell prey to the family predisposition for alcoholism. Nevertheless, he struggled and survived years of heavy drinking and IV drug abuse.

Jake was complex, more than just a burned-out musician, and his California years had been an emotional roller coaster. He had married Jeannie, a small, dark-haired woman, who, like his music, would be a passion for life. They had two daughters, Cecilia and Shawnee, two years apart, whom Jake had alternately spoiled and disciplined harshly. The marriage had been stormy and rancorous. He fought constantly with Jeannie and was mercurial around the girls. At Jeannie's insistence, he gave up his music and the late nights. The pain of sacrificing one love for another ultimately proved too much for the marriage to bear. Even before the divorce, Jake resumed his drums—and drugs—with enthusiasm. It was during this time, he figured, that a dirty needle had sealed his fate.

Jake returned from California after twelve years. Though he told his mother he had come back to play in a band with childhood friends, I have always suspected that somehow, even then, he knew he was coming home to die. Finally, when he had a sore throat for five weeks straight, his mother's nagging forced him to see a doctor, and he was tested for HIV. At first he did not tell his mother that he tested positive; he claimed that he had emphysema, and, before he was old, was going to be "one of those people dragging a tank around." I think he feared she would smother him if she knew the truth. He kept the news to himself for three days. When he finally told her, after she finally stopped crying, he extracted from her promises that she would not move into his house and that she would never hospitalize him.

Part of Jake believed he could beat the disease, repeatedly reassuring his mother, "Don't worry, something is going to happen." Maybe it was just a front to give her hope. Occasionally the tough exterior slipped, and he would castigate himself for being "such a fool," the doctors for their useless medications, and even his mother for her constant crying.

Jake and I talked for over an hour that first visit. I sat on a kitchen chair at the foot of his bed. He insisted that all he wanted from me were IV fluids to stem the headache, and a drug for his infected mouth sores. While we talked I wondered whether he had stashed away a supply of painkillers, just in case he wanted another option, another possible ending. It is a common reflex with AIDS patients, given their indefinite, though unequivocally finite, prognosis. And Jake's life certainly reflected a man independent perhaps to a fault, who made his own decisions. A note in his medical records written two weeks earlier by a hospice nurse revealed some of his thoughts. He had said to her, "I want to be in control of the situation, then find the correct drugs to make me die."

Ironically, I believe his drug history pushed him away from attempting suicide, however. In California he had been through detox at least three times, and the excruciating withdrawals had left him with a strong distaste for drugs, except pot. This aversion explained his rejection of anything his primary doctor prescribed, and his seeking out a naturopath for herbal remedies.

As I left Jake and his mom, I felt both hopeful and overwhelmed. My hope arose from the aching familiarity of Jake's case. There was so much to do, so much ground for Jake to cover, and I feared we only had a few weeks. I could ensure that he would not die in pain, and, along with the hospice staff, help him finish his will and maybe write a final letter to his daughters. But Jake's life had been tumultuous and troubled, an endless string of shattered dreams and fractured relationships, and there was much unfinished business. Yet his humanity shone through. As I had been warned by coworkers, I found I liked Jake. I could see in this hardened young man the boy his mother still saw. Behind the mask of fury, I could see his innocence and I could see his love. I did not want him to die alone, save with his mother, and I did not want him to die feeling unworthy. Without denying the seriousness of his mistakes, I perceived a fundamental beauty in him, and I hoped he could experience unconditional love before he died.

Jake's ordeal was on my mind the following day at the regular hospice team meeting. Every week about a dozen hospice workers gather around a large conference table in a windowless conference room at the hospice offices. It is a sterile, stuffy room, but we have humanized it by hanging framed photos of patients and their families on the walls. Tom King, the chaplain, usually starts the meeting with a brief description of the patients who have died, followed by a few words of memory and moments of silence; then we launch into discussion of the current cases.

I clipped through Jake's medical condition—his diagnosis, symptoms, treatment and medications—because I wanted to press the team to think about his personal situation. They did not need a lecture from me on tending the dying. They are pros in gently steering patients and families toward achieving the landmarks that underlie dying well—saying "I'm sorry," asking forgiveness, accepting forgiveness, saying "I love you," acknowledging self-worth, and saying goodbye. Inching toward these achievements is as fundamental to our daily visits as taking vital signs. But I was worried about Jake, so I slipped into the role of the stern maestro.

"Let's not lose sight of how much opportunity we have here," I urged, anxious for everyone to understand Jake's plight. I wanted to make sure they were all listening. Throughout the meeting we circulate sympathy cards for families, and each of us writes a note; it's easy to become distracted.

"Look, this guy has been the family outcast, the black sheep. He left Missoula years ago, propelled by his own surging impulses and the stormy family dynamics. But now he's come back to die. He could have stayed in California and shot himself, or OD'd on something, or died in a hospice in L.A. or San Francisco. Why didn't he? Why did he come home to die? Because on some level, this family means a lot to him. We've *got* to help him reconnect. And we'd better hurry; I don't know how much time there is." I don't harangue often, so they were duly attentive; even writing in the sympathy cards ceased. Jake's case was one of eight we covered that day—at any one time we care for fifty families—but it made an impression.

Over the next two weeks I followed Jake's progress through the hospice team. Andi Dreiling had been assigned the primary nursing responsibilities, Vickie Kammerer covered the social-work tasks, and Tom was doing his chaplain thing. After Jake took a bad fall, his mother moved in, sleeping on the living-room couch. Her closeness only heightened his feeling of embarrassing dependence. He could not accept her help or tolerate her unrestrained emotions. "Don't be wimping out on me," he cautioned, whenever she started weeping.

One afternoon he flew into a rage when he realized that she was scrubbing the bathroom floor; he had given her permission only to clean the floor in his kitchen. Pauline was as persistent in her care as her cleaning. "He knew I wasn't leaving," she told me during a later home visit, when

Jake was sleeping. "Knew it didn't matter what he said, what he did. Wet his bed, whatever. I would always be there."

She never backed off. As the days passed, his outbursts were followed sooner and sooner by tender apologies. Ultimately, I think Jake taught himself the real value of being cared for—that it was not so much for him as for her, and accepting care was the most important thing he could do *for her.* His mom needed to clean and dote on him as a way of caring for herself; it was her way of dealing with the inner turmoil and grief she felt. During the last few weeks, Pauline was never far from his room—"floating," as she called it. When she sat by his bed, stroking his head, he complained one minute about her messing up his hair, and the next minute would gently squeeze her hand. "This anger comes on me and I've got to get it out, then I feel so bad," he explained to Andi.

Self-loathing sometimes consumed him. He berated himself for being stupid and foolish about drugs and AIDS, and for overdisciplining his precious daughters. Nothing had gone right in his life, and his weaknesses and failings had just made it worse. Vickie visited regularly, and they seemed to be kindred spirits. A gentle earth mother who lived on a farm outside of town, Vickie also eschewed conventional living and prodded him into reminiscing about his days as a musician. With his OK, she took notes as a keepsake for his daughters. She sat on the only "chair" in the room, a portable bedside commode, and they frequently joked about his thrift-store furniture, sharing tips about the best alleys in which to find castoffs. They talked about what possessions he wanted to leave to his daughters, and together they began to compile a list. This led to making out a written will. Each of these tasks inched toward completion as the days drifted by and he lay in bed, semiconscious much of the time, his eyesight failing and his memory dimming. Aside from the hospice team, his only visitors were two friends from his band-playing days, Heather and Starlight. Although he was usually too weak to converse, they would sit on either side of his bed, one massaging his feet, the other stroking his head, and talk quietly to him or with each other.

As Jake's body deteriorated, Pauline grew exhausted from the round-the-clock changing of bed linens, doing wash, cooking, and cleaning. Vickie arranged for a hospital bed to be delivered to the home. She also persuaded Pauline to allow a hospice volunteer to stay with Jake for a few hours during the day while she got some rest. And Vickie proved her mettle in managing the practical matters of dying when she helped Pauline contact the International Red Cross, enabling Jake's beloved older sister, Gerri, an army nurse stationed in Italy, to come home.

The household changed with the arrival of Gerri, who took over the daily caregiving duties from their drained mother. She remarked that Jake had "mellowed out like an old man." His cantankerousness now flared only sporadically. Gradually, he had stopped resisting and, instead, began letting his family express their love by caring for him. At times their attentiveness reached comic proportions. One night when Gerri had been dozing beside Jake's bed, she woke up, touched his arm, and asked if he was cold. Although he said no, he felt cool to her, so she tucked his blanket over his shoulders and asked if that was all right. He nodded slightly. A few minutes later Pauline came into the room; noticing that his arms and shoulders were uncovered, she asked if he were cold. "No," he said, but he lifted his arms, knowing she would cover him up. After she left the room, Gerri glanced at her sleeping brother and saw that his arms and shoulders were once again lying exposed across his chest.

His younger sister, Arlene, arrived, and they had the makings of a family reunion. The three women fussed over him like a new baby, and Jake, still crusty, tolerated their nurturing. The care and tending of Jake was more like a blessing than a burden. Even his bedwetting gave Pauline a chance to freshen his sheets and fuss over him. He and Gerri frequently watched their mother putter about his room, folding and arranging everything. "Yup, Mom's *sure* tidy," Jake wryly joked.

Andi was also a regular visitor, and Jake won her over immediately with a mixture of charm and honesty. When they met he was smoking pot; instead of hiding it or apologizing, he teasingly quizzed her on where to find more. Andi always had a soft spot for people like herself who used charm deftly to get their way. They developed a routine. As Andi took vital signs, emptied his urine drainage bag, applied ointments, and swabbed sores, Jake recounted the previous night's dizziness or nausea or leg pain. After attending to medical matters, she would draw him out, and he would eagerly offer his views on a variety of subjects, from the topical to the philosophical.

Andi was a good listener. Jake's divorce had soured him on religion, and he insisted that he would allow no "Bible-thumpers" in the house. But he agreed to meet our chaplain, an ordained minister and gifted counselor. She astutely described Tom as someone "who used to be a hippie and doesn't have a church." Tom visited Jake a couple of times, slowly learning about the family and Jake's history. While Jake expressed strong opinions about everything and was not reticent about religion, he surprised us by accepting Tom's offer to celebrate communion.

The afternoon Tom brought communion for Jake and his mother marked a dramatic turn. Jake acted indifferent to the service and seemed unmoved as he sipped the wine and ate the wafer, his mother kneeling beside the bed. He looked steeled against any spiritual experience. Yet at the end, he let out a long sigh, gratefully thanked Tom, and muttered to no one in particular, "I've made my peace with the church."

Tom sat with Jake after the service; they had previously spent many hours sitting in peaceful silence. As Tom was about to leave, Jake told him that he felt the end was near and that he was ready to die. Tom's response took Jake aback: "You can't die without saying goodbye to your daughters. I think you need to call them or ask them to come."

Later Tom told me, "You know, I'm almost never that forceful, I don't know where that came from. It was intuitive, I guess, but it was clear to me that it was something Jake *had* to do."

It was as if our chaplain had looked into Jake's soul and knew his dearest wish. Jake had long been estranged from his family. The divorce had been messy, with many recriminations, and he had hardly spoken to Jeannie or his younger daughter in years. Nevertheless, Tom's emphatic encouragement moved him to take the first step toward reconciliation. He asked his mother to call California. The family's meager resources posed a challenge, but the hospice team devised an affordable plan.

In the meantime Jake grew sicker, unable to leave his bed, drifting in and out of consciousness. At times he stared into space, as if watching an invisible tableau of people. On the wall over his bed, his mother taped pictures of his daughters. Everyone knew he was holding on, waiting for his "girlies," as he called them, to arrive.

Jeannie and the girls traveled by bus from Long Beach, arriving in the early evening. Stepping into Jake's bedroom, they hung back, shocked by and unprepared for the sight of his emaciated, diseased body. Jake opened his eyes and slowly focused on his ex-wife. As she came closer, he held out his arms to embrace her, and he whispered, "You have always been . . ." Jeannie bent into his arms and then lay down beside him.

I saw Jake again two days before he died. The outside of the house had not changed; it was still wrapped in the pungent smell of freshly cut lumber and surrounded by a blanket of dirty snow. Against the gray winter sky, however, the inside of the house was aglow. This family had not always been close or warm, but the atmosphere in the home that day would have thawed the coldest cynic. Jake's illness had refocused the Edwards family. Now that the children were grown, it was their turn to take the full share of responsibility for making this family what it could be. The knowledge that Jake was dying caused grief, but it also provided a critical opportunity. They reminded me of something psychologist and theologian Gerald May said: "Grief is neither a disorder nor a healing process; it is a sign of health itself, a whole and natural gesture of love. Nor must we see grief as a step towards something better. No matter how much it hurts—and it may be the greatest pain in life—grief can be an end in itself, a pure expression of love."

Pauline and Gerri greeted me at the door, eager to talk about Jake and introduce the latest family arrivals. Over the past few days he had been semiconscious, but at times clear and alert. When I arrived he was sleeping, so I sat with the family for a little while before going into his room.

"He hasn't lost his orneriness," his mother noted, almost with pride. "He's just putting up with us better." She and Gerri recounted the latest incident, each adding a piece in an affectionate duet. The night before, Gerri had crawled into bed with her brother and tucked her arm around his frail shoulders. As she snuggled her head next to his, he remarked in a hoarse voice, "I crapped on that pillowcase, you know. Crapped on the sheets, too." She chuckled. "I don't mind, I'm sure Mom cleaned them," she said.

Each daughter spent hours with him, sometimes lying down beside him. "Cecilia told him how she loved him," Pauline recounted, "and he told them about his AIDS and drugs, and how sorry he was and how much he loved them." Her eyes teared up, but she smiled with the knowledge that Jake had finally forgiven himself for the pain he had caused his daughters.

Andi described Jake's growing peacefulness: "One afternoon, out of the blue, he turned to me and said, 'You're beautiful.' But he wasn't really talking about me. He had that dreamy, faraway look. I know he was talking about himself." At last, Jake was at peace with his imperfections; he could accept and love himself.

Jake had withered since I last saw him. His skin was gray, and his hands and feet felt cold. He was alert only a fraction of the time and swallowed only small sips of water and tiny bites of food. He shook his head when I asked if he was in pain or uncomfortable; earlier he had accepted Andi's suggestion of a simple pain medication and could swallow Dilaudid, a morphine-type drug.

Over the next two days, his sisters, mother, ex-wife, and daughters stayed close, taking turns sitting beside him, mopping his brow, wetting his lips, holding his hand. In hushed tones they giggled about the time he cut Arlene's finger with an axe, and both of them worried more about their mother's wrath than the sister's injury. Each time someone entered or left the room, they hugged, but their eyes were dry. They were letting him go. Jake died on a Friday afternoon around four o'clock, surrounded by his family.

I spoke with Pauline a number of times in the months following Jake's death. She missed him terribly, and it would take her more than a year to relinquish his ashes and scatter them over Blue Mountain, as she had promised him. Nevertheless, she was grateful for those final days with her son. If I was the conductor for this concerto, then surely Pauline was its first violin, its virtuoso. Despite Jake being unconscious most of the time, alert for only moments and unable to see, Pauline described it as a "special, special time. We all shared with him what was happening. We have never before been that close, that intimate, as a family. If there is such a thing as a wonderful death, Jake was blessed with it."

Nine

Growing Within Tragedy: Michael Merseal

One of my heroes in medical school was a professor named Mary Anne Guggenheim, who was world-renowned in her field of pediatric neurology. Dr. Guggenheim had a mesmerizing way of teaching the medical facts of a case, then stepping back and adding a human dimension. After explaining a condition or neurological function, she offered a patient's perspective of what this might mean in terms of behavior, personality, or emotions. She continued to climb in my estimation during my residency, and later when I began my practice. In the course of researching patients' problems in the medical library, I was led to salient chapters and articles she had authored. Over the years she came to represent for me the importance of humility and keeping an open mind when faced with a difficult case. Though I had not spoken with her since medical school, her teaching and practice never let me forget that there are more unknowns than knowns about the human body and spirit.

A few years after I settled in Missoula, I heard that Dr. Guggenheim had retired from the University of Colorado Medical School teaching faculty and moved to Helena, Montana, just two hours east of Missoula, to establish a regional center for childhood neurology and to pursue her love of fly fishing. When hospice received a patient, an eight-year-old with a brain disease, who was being seen in consultation by Dr. Guggenheim, I felt a bittersweet excitement. Sadly, my patient was a little boy with a fatal illness, but I looked forward to working with my mentor again. She did not disappoint.

Dr. Guggenheim had first examined Michael Merseal at the request of his Missoula pediatrician, Bruce Hardy, when Michael was three, and she saw him regularly after that. Michael's brain disease was so rare that even she could not assign a name to it and had to settle for the label "degenerative polio dystrophy." Nevertheless, she knew more than anyone else about his illness, and I telephoned her with questions about what to expect from his decline. I vividly remember an early conversation about Michael's vague diagnosis. She explained that while he showed symptoms of what is called Fragile X syndrome, such as mild retardation and seizures, it was not an exact fit, and she was still mystified and would continue to hunt for a more specific diagnosis. She said, "This little boy is trying to teach us something." The refrain stuck in my mind and echoed louder and louder as Michael's illness progressed.

Michael Merseal did, indeed, teach me and everyone around him many things. As a child robbed of intellect and language by his disease, Michael was an innocent, seemingly incapable of intention or design. Nevertheless, in his dependence and dying, he became a fountain of lessons.

Michael's appearance was deceiving. A cheerful, apparently happy child throughout his young life, he was enormously engaging. He captivated people with his big smile and two flashing front teeth, and when they looked into his large, brown eyes, they were moved. For some, he revealed the power of human connection. For others, he was a mirror, reflecting their own soul.

At Michael's funeral, Andi Dreiling described this special quality: "He opened people's minds to possibilities. Those who came to him, supposedly a damaged child with no capacity for consciousness, found themselves first asking 'Who am I?' and shortly wondering 'Who should I be?' He brought together people who were far apart. People around him changed their attitudes, their philosophies, and even their lives. Caring for this totally dependent child became first satisfaction and then joy, a privilege, and finally, a sacred honor."

Michael's dying formed a crucible in which people were purified and forever altered. As he lay dying, his family was transformed from a collection of related people to a process. Family became a verb, an action or a quality coming into sharper focus. And those of us on the periphery of the family circle contributed to transforming "community" into a coordinated process of committed caring.

One of the early lessons of Michael's dying had to do with the nature of tragedy. At first glance, his dying appeared to be a horrible tragedy: A little boy with no childhood or future was suffering and dying from something totally beyond anyone's control. But his own and his family's suffering and devastation shrank compared with the joy and growth he engendered. While Michael's illness and dying were tragic, they were not *only* tragic. What we experienced was far greater and far richer than sorrow alone.

Michael began showing the first signs of misfortune at age three. His head was abnormally small, he was having seizures, and he was not developing normal toddler skills. His CT brain scan, which was not quite normal, pointed to a degenerative and potentially progressive central nervous system disease. Suspecting a congenital, genetic condition, Dr. Hardy sent Michael to see Mary Anne Guggenheim. Her initial diagnosis was the poignantly named Fragile X syndrome, and she detailed for Mike, the boy's father, what he could expect to see in his son. Yet from the beginning, Michael did not follow any predictable patterns. Despite the forecast, he slowly learned to walk, speak a few words, and use the toilet. But at around age five he stopped growing, and within two years had regressed into infancy, unable to feed himself or move around without help. For the rest of his life he would be a cheerful, babbling, bedridden baby with the mental age of a ten-month-old.

A single parent, Mike Merseal was raising Michael and his older sister, Krystle, by himself. Their mother had led a troubled life, and she and Mike had separated when the kids were four and five years old, so Mike provided both the mothering and the fathering. Parenting came naturally to him. He instinctively knew when to discipline and when to listen, when to expect childishness and when to demand maturity. Michael and Krystle looked like siblings. Both had dark red hair, freckles across their noses, and fair, pink complexions. Michael's frequent smile radiated from two large buck teeth. Krystle's face usually bore the expression of a sunny nine-year-old, but at other times she exhibited the solemnity and wisdom of a grandmother.

The Merseals lived in a yellow frame house on the north side of Missoula with a dog named Ginger and a large black-and-white cat named Pooh that Krystle adored. Her attic bedroom was plastered with posters of cats and kittens. Before little Michael had become bedridden, Mike and the kids loved to pile into his pickup and drive to Seeley Lake for picnics and fishing. When Michael's seizures, which often involved incontinence followed by long "post-ictal" periods of being dazed and confused, with episodes of gagging, kept them close to home, the family still enjoyed times together. Mike taught Krystle how to cook their favorite desert, Buffalo Chip cookies, made with chocolate chips, marshmallows, and oatmeal. Together Mike and Krystle liked to read Dr. Seuss to Michael and sing to him. Michael loved music, and the household was never quiet. From rock-and-roll oldies to contemporary country tunes, the radio or record player was always going. During the day, a nurse paid for through a state fund cared for Michael while Mike worked as a custodian at the University of Montana. When Mike and Krystle got home in the late afternoon, she helped her dad prepare the liquid supplement for Michael's tube feedings and played with her brother. She rattled his toys, and he gurgled and reflexively grinned, giggled, and chewed on anything within reach.

I met the Merseals when Michael was eight and his health was rapidly deteriorating. He had just been hospitalized because of persistent vomiting, and the doctors at St. Patrick's had recommended surgically inserting a tracheostomy tube into his neck to prevent choking. When Mike refused to approve the surgery, declaring that his son had already been through too many procedures, the family was referred to hospice. Mike had long known that his son's illness was terminal, and possessed equal measures of fatalism and practicality. When he heard from Dr. Guggenheim that Michael had only months to live, he grimly accepted this turn of fate and concentrated on ensuring his son's comfort and contentment, no matter how short-lived they might be.

When hospice became involved, Michael's seizures were occurring back to back, and his vomiting and choking were becoming almost hourly events. His son's suffering tormented Mike. Even moistening Michael's lips and mouth provoked a reflexive gag, and tears welled up in his eyes before he stiffened dramatically and finally went limp. Although little Michael could not speak to express his pain, Mike read the signs in his son's frantic eyes during his seizures and choking and in his listless body afterward. After he was discharged from the hospital, Michael was put on a number of medications to control his seizures, and his father cut back on his tube feedings and fluids in order to diminish the horrible gagging. But neither measure worked. Dr. Hardy had kept in touch with Dr. Guggenheim by phone, and now, in the final phase of his patient's illness, he asked me to help.

When I called to set up an appointment, Mike said that he had been expecting my call and asked me to the house to talk about further reducing or stopping tube feedings and fluids. It was early afternoon; I sat with the family—Mike, his sister, Kathy, and their father, Ted—around the kitchen table. Krystle was in school. James Taylor was singing on the radio. The kitchen was tucked into an alcove off the living room, where Michael slept on the couch. As we talked, we could hear his rattling breaths. At one point, we had to interrupt our discussion to suction phlegm from Michael's windpipe. I noticed that Mike performed the task adeptly.

Ted Merseal apparently was a recent addition to the household. Before Michael's hospitalization, Mike and his father had not spoken for ten years. When Michael was hospitalized, Kathy had telephoned their father and told him what was happening to his grandson. He had come to the hospital within an hour. Since Michael had been discharged, Ted had shown up at the house daily. Although he looked like a working farmer, always dressed in denim overalls, flannel shirt, and a cap with a feed company logo, he was mostly retired, and he readily volunteered to run errands or sit with Michael. He usually stayed in the kitchen and made sure there was always hot, fresh coffee. Ted and Mike mostly spoke to each other in clipped though not unfriendly tones. They exchanged practical words about things like meals, the day's shopping list, or a new problem with one of the cars. Whatever had caused their estrangement had been buried and replaced by Ted's support of the hard decisions Mike was having to make, and Mike's appreciation of that support and his father's presence.

Mike and Kathy bore little resemblance to one another. Mike was short and stocky, with straight blond hair long enough for a ponytail, and although Kathy was also broad in the shoulders, she was taller, with short, coffee-brown hair. Nevertheless, they interacted like twins, sharing unspoken thoughts and emotions. They often mirrored each other in their reactions to situations or people. Michael's illness had brought them even closer, if that was possible. Kathy had moved in after Michael's first hospitalization, and she and Mike juggled their jobs and caring for Michael in a carefully choreographed duet.

As our visit began, we chatted about who had visited Michael, breaking the ice by gossiping about a new pizza place in town before the conversation shifted to Michael's condition. As we got down to business, the mood was glum. Michael's seizures were not abating despite a barrage of anticonvulsant medications, and his choking was worse despite the reduction of tube feedings. Mike was sleeping only a few hours each night, often getting up to check on Michael's breathing. The worst time was the early morning when he came into the living room. If Michael was feeling well, he was awake and chirpy, but in the past few weeks, Mike had always found him silent and listless.

In the middle of the table, Mike had assembled all of his son's medications. He ticked off the names without mispronouncing a syllable: Reglan, Tegretol, Felbamate, Depakote, plus a multivitamin. "It seems to me that the medications are making him throw up, not the other way around," Mike said. "He had twelve seizures yesterday, and they're getting worse, putting him out longer and longer."

"How much Jevity are you giving him?" I asked about the liquid nutrient he was getting through his tube.

"Only a can a day, and about four hundred cc's of electrolyte solution," Mike responded. As he mashed one cigarette he lit another, and cradled his coffee cup.

"Does propping him up help at all?"

"Not really," he answered, and waited.

"It is hard to say what Michael is able to sense or experience," I began. "Certainly, his seizures trigger a physiological response. His body stiffens, and there are tears in his eyes. But beyond that . . ." My voice trailed off. Everyone was gazing into a coffee mug, heads bowed. "As you know, cutting back further, or stopping his tube feedings and fluids, is an option. I want you to know what all the possibilities are, Mike, and I will tell you everything I know. The decision will remain yours. You're driving the bus here." We had a lot to discuss, but I paused before continuing.

"Clearly, Michael will die of some complication from his neurological deterioration. It may be an infection or the result of a prolonged seizure that causes hypoxia, that is, robs the oxygen from his brain. Cutting back on calories and fluid may be an option worth considering."

"You mean starve him to death?" Kathy whispered, her eyes wide.

I explained that the reality did not match the gruesome image the word *starvation* brings to mind. Kathy, like most people, harbored understandable misconceptions about this way of dying. People imagine that malnutrition and dehydration are painful, horrible ways of dying. But with an advanced illness like cancer, heart, or lung disease, kidney failure, or AIDS, the reality does not match the awful image. Over the years I have seen that malnourishment and dehydration do not increase a terminally ill person's suffering, and can actually contribute to a comfortable passage from life.

"Kathy, I would never suggest that we refuse Michael his baby bottle or food if he could take it, but now even his bottle causes him to gag uncontrollably. The tube feedings are also causing him to choke, and we've tried all the things that should be making it better. It's unlikely that Michael will feel much discomfort or suffer if you decide to cut back on his feedings further. Hunger disappears after a day or two of withholding calories, and dehydration in someone terminally ill is usually experienced as a dry mouth and throat, which we can easily relieve with tiny sips or a spray of fluid. Although there's no way of knowing exactly what Michael is feeling, my experience with other patients has been that this is a comfortable way to die. Often people even experience mild euphoria, probably because of the change in their chemistry from not taking in calories."

For years hospice people have avoided this subject, fearing that it might be misinterpreted as encouraging suicide. But it is not suicide to refuse an operation when one can no longer swallow, nor is it suicide to decline food when hunger is a distant memory and death is one's immediate future. The social climate is rapidly changing, and one good effect of the assisted suicide movement has been to make discussion of suicidal feelings and not eating more common. The family of a person who can no longer eat normally or communicate his desires often struggles with decisions about life-prolonging procedures such as surgery to place a tube for formula feeding. In deciding that a loved one will not be allowed to die of malnourishment, a family is making a tacit decision to let the person die of something else. Thus, the declaration by the daughter of an eighty-seven-year-old comatose patient, "I would never let Mom die of starvation," is a decision that Mom must, therefore, succumb to infection or stroke or seizure or blood clot or gastrointestinal hemorrhage. Each complication that is treated merely shifts the physiology of the person's dying, it does not halt it. A patient who is artificially fed and hydrated may live longer but is more likely to die with episodes of acute pain or breathlessness or, as in Michael's case, from a seizure. For Mike, the issue was not about how, precisely, his son would die but the quality of his life in the final days—that is, how much physical distress he would feel.

"You have done a magnificent job taking care of Michael," I told Mike. "You've given him more love and attention in his few years than most people get in their whole life. And I recognize how tough it must be, trying to take care of him and at the same time making sure Krystle does not feel neglected. But somehow, you've managed. I know of no institution or medical people who could have done it as well as you have. You have earned my lasting respect. Whatever you decide, you should feel confident that you have done everything for this little guy. I don't think there are any wrong decisions to be made here."

Mike's eyes watered. "He's not holding down any of his food. I can tell it's really hurting him when he throws up," he said. As if on cue, Ted rose from the table to check on Michael's breathing while Mike briefly diverted himself by pulling a Mountain Dew from the refrigerator.

"You don't have to decide anything this moment," I said. "This is wrenching stuff, so take as much time as you need. None of us, in the months to come, and especially after Michael has died, wants to look back and wonder whether we did the right thing. Think about it. We don't need to make any changes today. One thing I would like to do right away, Mike, is to begin to back off on his usual seizure medications and start him on a low dose of Versed around the clock."

I explained that Versed was a fast-acting, powerful medication like Valium that would have to be given by subcutaneous or intravenous infusion but would very likely control Michael's seizures. This was another big topic we needed to talk about today, and I was glad that Andi had discussed it with him when they were preparing for Michael's discharge from the hospital. She had introduced Mike to Versed and the other drugs included in the hospice "crisis pack." The medications and syringes, and the idea that he would eventually learn to use them, had intimidated him. "Am I supposed to use these needles?" he had asked her, his mouth open and brow arched. The person she had described then was different from the resolute man sitting across from me now.

"The Versed will give him relief from the seizures. But he'll probably be pretty sedated. We'll start at a fairly low dose and adjust it to keep him from convulsing. You need to know, however, that if a large dose is required, there's always a chance that it could suppress his breathing and he will die. It's not likely, but there's a chance," I said.

"I understand. Andi and I talked about this for a long time. Whatever it takes, we've got to stop his seizures. I'd like a day or two to think about the tube feedings and fluids. Maybe tonight we can put him on Gatorade and water. You know, gradually cut back to see how he does," Mike said. "I've just got a feeling that he might snap out of this. I don't know why, just a feeling."

Mike would not be human or a father if he did not hold a kernel of hope. I knew he was looking for middle ground between this sliver of wishful thinking and the desire to end his son's suffering. And, as happened time and again with this family, little Michael showed the way.

Before I left the Merseals that first day, I told Mike that I would talk with Dr. Hardy and get in touch with Dr. Guggenheim as well for any new thoughts she might have on controlling the seizures, and any other suggestions. In truth, I did not expect to hear anything new, but I wanted to give Mike as much time as he needed to decide which way to go next. As important as Michael's medical care was, my treatments as a doctor—and those of the other hospice people—had become secondary to the family's emotional needs. In this respect, hospice care differs noticeably from the modern medical approach to dying. Typically, as a hospice patient nears death, the medical details become almost automatic and attention focuses on the personal nature of this final transition, what the patient and family are going through emotionally and spiritually. In the more established system, even as people die, medical procedures remain the first priority.

With hospice they move to the background as the personal comes to the fore.

Andi gave me daily reports about the effects of the Versed; it was slowing the tempo of the seizures. Michael slept most of the time but occasionally shifted to groggy wakefulness. Finally, the gagging stopped. Mike spoke about the various treatment issues with Kathy and Ted, and debated the pros and cons aloud with himself and with the hospice chaplain, Tom King, who had become a trusted friend. A couple of days after our talk, he asked Andi to lower Michael's fluid intake to three cans of Jevity and five ounces of water a day. Three days later, they cut it to one-and-a-half cans, and after another three days Mike decided to stop the nutritional supplement completely.

Less than a week after the decision was made, I was finishing dinner at the Hob Nob Cafe in the old Union Hall downtown when I received a page from the Merseal home. Joy, the hospice nurse on call, needed to speak with me. "Michael's making these strange noises," she reported. "I don't know what I'm listening to. I think you should come over."

"Is he in distress?"

"I don't think so," Joy said.

"Has he been seizing?"

"Mike says Michael hasn't had a seizure in three days."

"I'll be over in a few minutes."

Every light in the Merseal home was on. The family, along with Joy, a friend of Kathy's, were clustered around Michael's couch. He slept here for two reasons, one practical and one symbolic. The couch offered more space for the stuffed animals, pillows, and dog that crowded it, and the living room gave everybody easy access to the medical tubes and machines Michael needed. Symbolically, this was the center of the home and the family, and it had become Michael's place. Installed in the living room, beneath a blue quilt on the wall pinned with pictures of Barney and a rocking horse, he was the first thing people saw when they visited. Here, everyone who entered was reminded that this boy was the polestar of the family.

Mike greeted me at the door; for a few moments I stood there, watching Michael and his sister. Krystle, pigtailed and in her pajamas, was snuggling beside her little brother and making silly noises, mimicking his own. She whistled and popped and screeched to him, and Michael watched, his eyes wide open. I was stunned; he was *watching* her.

Mike gave me a quizzical look, and Joy shook her head in mystification. I knelt beside Michael and tested his eyes. Sure enough, they were tracking, something he hadn't done in months. My mind raced as I listened to his chest and heart. Finally, it struck me; I stood up and declared, "I think he's cooing!"

Krystle was shaking a rattle for Michael; his eyes got wider, and he kept reaching out to grab it. "He wants to chew!" she said excitedly.

I had never seen anything like this before. This little boy was supposed to be in a coma and dying. He had not had any nourishment to speak of for days, only a few ounces of water a day, and was now on no antiseizure medications other than the Versed, which was supposed to sedate him. But "supposed to's" aside, here he was, awake and ready to play.

"He hasn't had a seizure since the day before yesterday," Mike volunteered.

"My best guess is that until we started the Versed the seizures had been coming so frequently that he's been in that post-ictal, sort-of-irritable, 'gorked' state almost continuously for weeks. It was like a hibernation. And now that he seems to have stopped seizing, he's woken up." I shook my head with amazement and grinned at Mike. "The good news is that I think, for the moment at least, your son's doing great! The bad news is, I also think he's rested, and you're going to be up for awhile!" Mike gave me a lopsided smile.

The improvement was dramatic. With Michael temporarily resurrected, we all changed gears. He was offered his baby bottle and drank without any choking or gagging. We steadily increased his fluids and formula. Mike now discovered that his son, like a growing infant who has outgrown the bottle, was hungry for solid food. The family resumed its picnics, now in the backyard, with Michael wearing a brightly colored baseball cap in his wheelchair and Krystle climbing a tree or chasing Pooh. Michael was very thin and his father was anxious for him to regain his strength. He spoon-fed him macaroni salad, ham, cereal, marshmallows—virtually anything in the pantry. The day his son punched him, he was delighted. "He had finished eating, and I asked him how he was doing, and he doubled up his fist and hit me in the mouth! He didn't mean it, but I'd never seen him do that before. I grabbed some toilet paper for my bloody mouth, and started laughing, because he was getting his strength back," Mike recalls.

The Merseal household came alive with visitors, people who were eager to see Michael when they heard about his astonishing comeback. Mike was having to juggle all the people who wanted to sit with and care for his son. A nurses' aide who had been assigned to another patient asked if she could come by on weekends. Michael's teenage cousin brought tapes of his favorite music. Preschool teachers from years past visited with coloring books and toys. Even Krystle's friends hung around after school just for the chance to giggle and play with her brother. Soon after Mike rose every morning, someone would appear at the door to see Michael, and the traffic continued through the day and into the evening. Michael's night-owl hours kept the lights on, coffee brewing, and company coming until well after midnight.

Mike felt more than one reason to welcome all the visitors. Michael loved the company—the noise, the voices, the activity—and frequently squealed with delight. A lively house also enabled Mike to avoid stewing about his son. "If there wasn't anybody in the house, I would sit there and think about Michael and what was going to happen. Anybody could walk through my door and I'd be happy to see them. Anybody except Michael and Krystle's mother," he said.

Through July, August, and into September, Michael flourished. He was doing so well that Mike resumed working at the university, from which he had taken unpaid leave months before. I marveled at Michael every time I visited. Except for his size, he was like a happy six-month-old child. He defied medical axioms. Although an MRI showed deterioration of cerebral tissue, with the current dose of Versed, his brain looked relatively calm on an EEG. I told Mike that his son might be on a long-term plateau.

As we both knew, this was not entirely good news. The uncertainty of Michael's present condition and the certainty of his demise in the uncharted future pushed Mike and Krystle into an emotional roller coaster. Mike had no illusions about his son's prognosis. He read a copy of a letter Dr. Guggenheim had written about Michael to his pediatrician and myself so many times that he memorized phrases, especially the last paragraph: "I am sure that we all appreciate how complex this is for Michael's father and other family members when we had anticipated that Michael was in the last few weeks of life. Now, we have to reassess and recognize that part of his terminal state was apparently caused by the anti-epileptic medications and at this point, I cannot accurately judge his actual life expectancy."

Mike reiterated his plan not to do anything dramatic if Michael suddenly became ill again, relinquishing any wistful ideas of a complete reversal and lasting good health. Nevertheless, every time he saw Michael laugh or grab a toy, he hoped it was forever.

Krystle's roller coaster traveled higher peaks and deeper lows. Some days she was inseparable from her little brother. She would curl up beside him on the couch and whisper into his ear or prop him up, and with her arm guiding his, fill in a coloring book, repeatedly removing the crayon from his mouth and chattering sweetly to him. Occasionally he drooled on her, and she nonchalantly wiped it off. Yet on other days she declared that she did not want to play with him or she ignored him. Out of self-protection, part of Krystle was withdrawing from her dying brother.

For me, Michael's fluctuations in health were a repeated lesson in humility and the potential arrogance of supposed knowledge. I could not make any assumptions about how this little boy would fare from day to day, or even week to week. Instead of imposing on the situation what I already knew about his medical condition and prognosis, I had to admit to the myriad unknowns and stay open to the next lesson. I felt like a surfer catching huge waves and trying to stay upright in a rolling sea. With each successive wave, I wondered what Michael would teach me next.

Michael remained stable through the fall, and we began to wonder if we should transfer his care from hospice to the less intensive services of home health. All of us on Michael's hospice team agonized over the thought of withdrawing from this family we had grown to love. But the plateau did not last beyond Thanksgiving. Michael's seizures gradually returned, stealing a couple days of sentient life each time. After the initial shock of a seizure, he became irritable and lethargic and vomited frequently. His fluttering eyelids would signal a coming seizure, and his father would hold his son and rub his head as his body stiffened and shook like a marionette with a cruel master. "Hang in there, Tiger," he soothed. "We'll get through this one, we've been through worse. Hang in there."

While the electrical storms in Michael's brain grew worse, the love around him grew stronger. People who had known him through the Medicaid office or his preschool formed a constant stream of visitors. Virtual strangers to Mike would drop by the house, introduce themselves and their connection to Michael, and ask if they could sit with him for a few hours. As I witnessed this parade of pilgrims, I marveled at how Michael's dying belied medical wisdom. His chart and medical history—the description of a boy with a hopeless illness whose life was a litany of misery and debilitation—looked like only tragedy. Yet when I removed the medical filters from my eyes, I was struck by how powerfully his life was affecting his family and friends and by the loving relationships he inspired.

Around the middle of December, Mike realized that his son was slipping away for the last time. The light in his eyes dulled. Mike told his son to hang on and make it through Christmas for his sister's sake. Mike took Krystle out of school a week early and they decorated the house with colored lights, red ribbons, and pine boughs.

I stopped by the house to check Michael and take his vital signs. Mike paced and chain-smoked as I sat on the edge of the couch.

"Are you getting out at all?" I asked.

"Not much. It makes me nervous to go anywhere." He lit another Newport and looked straight at me. "In the last twenty-four hours, he's had three of the hard seizures and at least twenty of the fluttering ones, Ira. They *have* to stop, he can't take it anymore. I can't watch it anymore. They're getting worse and longer."

Krystle was puttering around the kitchen as we spoke, and I watched her scoop out a mound of chocolate ice cream for lunch. She fiddled with the radio and found a station playing Christmas carols.

"I understand, Mike. We can increase the Versed infusion further and give a bolus injection each time you see a sequence of the milder seizures that tell us he is beginning to kindle. That way, maybe we can stop the grand mal seizures from happening." I smoothed Michael's brow and saw that someone had pinned a sticker that read "Don't Ever Give Up" on the quilt over the couch.

"You understand that full sedation may be necessary to control the seizures." This step meant crossing another major threshold and giving him intravenous barbiturates, something we have very rarely had to do. But I did not have to tell Mike this. By now, he was achingly familiar with the signs of suffering and the potential consequences of treatment.

"Yup, I know. But they have to stop, even if he's in a coma," he insisted. "The look in his eyes last night, the pain and stuff. He can't take it anymore, even if it again means stopping the feedings and fluid. They're not making him feel any better, and they're just prolonging the agony." I nodded as he traversed this sad, familiar ground. I said that for the moment we would adjust the Versed dose and start liquid phenobarbital through his peg tube. The front door opened and Ted and Andi came in, having driven up simultaneously. Andi was starting her shift, and Ted carried a bag of groceries. Ted gave a soft hello; Andi sat down beside me. She took Michael's hand, noting his pulse and skin tone.

"You saw we're up to two milligrams an hour?" she asked me, referring to the Versed.

"Yeah. Mike and I are talking about holding off on the tube feedings and cutting back on the fluid."

No one said anything for a few minutes. Krystle came over to the couch and sat on the end. Ginger hopped up beside her. She held a music box that played "When You Wish upon a Star."

Ted was in the kitchen, and I smelled coffee. The house seemed enveloped in a blanket of calm. I packed my medical bag and prepared to leave. I reassured Mike that we were doing everything humanly possible to make his son comfortable. Once again, I said I thought he was acting carefully and out of love in reducing Michael's tube feedings. But I had a further concern.

"Mike, even though I feel you are doing the right thing, and I think I would make the same choices if Michael were my son, I want to present this case to the ethics committee at St. Pat's. Because Michael is a child, and because his treatment plan goes beyond ordinary measures, I want to make absolutely certain we leave no stone unturned. I want to do this in the light of day, so to speak. If someone criticizes your decision, or our care, after Michael passes away, it will be important to all of us to be able to say we asked everyone we could think of for help and made these decisions in the open. OK with you?"

Mike's response was immediate and unequivocal. "Sure, I've got nothing to hide."

As a doctor treating a terminally ill child, I felt it was important that our actions be known and understood within the medical community. Michael's story was receiving some public attention. The *Missoulian* was planning to run a front-page account about him, and a film crew from Maysles Films, a production company for Home Box Office, was capturing his story for a documentary about hospice. The spotlight on a child who was dying and whose family and doctor have decided to cut back on nutrition made all of us sensitive to appearances.

I had already discussed my decision to solicit input from the ethics committee with the hospice team. No one had any doubts about the rightness of Mike's decision, and I took some heat for my insistence that the ethics committee discuss the case. A few members of the team feared that the committee's questions would intrude on this family and might result in a second-guessing of their decision. I held firm. Three or six months after Michael died, I did not want anyone, his family or us, accused of killing him. Any inconvenience or intrusion on the Merseals now would pale in comparison to the sort of inquiry and fuss they might be vulnerable to later. I felt it was imperative to anticipate, prepare for, and prevent such a possibility. Without violating the bounds of medical confidentiality, we had to make people understand the situation. It was paramount that, if anyone in the medical community—or the community at large—investigated, they understand that we were not euthanizing this little boy but remaining focused on his comfort and the support of his family. At times in hospice care the line between ensuring comfort and hastening death becomes fine; in Michael's case, I felt it was best to walk that line in bright light.

In my letter to the chairman of the ethics committee, I explained: "This case is not controversial in the usual sense. There is no conflict with the family. Indeed, relationships with the family are warm and supportive. However, all involved realize the poignancy of the situation. While this decision seems within the ethical and legal authority of this patient's father to refuse unwanted medical intervention, we are aware that the situation might appear to an outside observer as constituting euthanasia."

I was braced for a lengthy and arduous session with the committee. Instead the meeting lasted just over an hour. The two doctors, the nurse, the social worker, the nonmedical businessperson, the hospital administrator, and the community pastor who comprise the committee had all read my letter and a summary of the medical aspects of the case. They asked pertinent questions and probed to find out whether all available options had been explored. They did not question the family's motive or decision but marveled over the exceptional care of Michael. At the conclusion of the meeting, the committee asked me to communicate to Michael's family and the hospice team its understanding, continued interest, and support.

Less than a week later, the *Missoulian*'s front-page story, "Michael's Gift: Dying Child Leaves Family Stronger Still," described what was happening in the Merseal household. It quoted Andi: "Michael has taught a lot of people, hospice workers included, not what dying is but what living means. This is not a sad house. This is a remarkable place." The story had unexpected consequences. Michael's mother, Leslie, read it, called Mike, and asked to see her son.

Four years earlier, Leslie had left behind an angry husband, a frightened daughter, and an uncomprehending son. Even after years of peace without her, Mike's anger still burned, and Krystle was still terrified that she might be forced to live with her mother. Krystle happened to answer the phone when Leslie called, and in a few short minutes, Krystle was terribly upset. Mike refused to let Leslie come to the house.

Michael lived through Christmas, still very much a part of the family, though he was sedated most of the time. Santa Claus gave him a big brown stuffed bear and a Lion King T-shirt, and gave Krystle a new pair of skates, a cookbook for kids, and a stuffed kitten. On Christmas afternoon, a day gray and drizzling outside but lit inside with candles and colored lights, Michael opened his eyes for the last time. Mike was immediately by his side with a cool washcloth for his sweaty brow. His eyes briefly tracked, picking up a Snoopy doll Mike wagged for him.

When Andi and Tom King came by later that afternoon, Mike and Krystle were baking Christmas cookies. But Mike was clearly on edge.

"This is scaring me real bad," he said, after describing Michael's condition. "I don't think he'll last another week. I can't let him go on anymore, he's gone through too much. I've got to let him go. I've been thinking about it for days. This is making me nervous, it's got my whole body shaking. I can't sleep."

Two days later Mike left a note on Leslie's windshield saying that she could visit her son the following evening. When he told Krystle that her mother was coming over, the little girl insisted on going to her grandfather's house. Leslie appeared around eight o'clock—petite, with long brown hair, delicate, fine features, and a doll-like beauty. Mike let her in with a cold hello and retreated into the kitchen area. He had asked Andi, Tom, and Kathy to be there. Mike and his sister stood in the kitchen, leaning against the sink, and mostly avoided looking at Leslie as she sat beside her sedated son and rubbed his back.

"Michael's in a sleep-like state," Andi explained. "He was having terrible seizures, and this was the only way to make him comfortable. But I always act as if it's possible he knows I'm here and can hear me," she suggested. "We keep his mouth moist, so he won't be thirsty." She showed Leslie a sponge swab. "He's also getting a little fluid through the tube."

Crying as she spoke, Leslie remarked on how much Michael had grown and pulled back the blanket to caress his legs and feet. Although Michael had been bedridden for months, his many caregivers had made sure that he had no sores or raw spots. The only physical sign of his failing health was a bluish tinge at the ends of his limbs and other extremities. Leslie noticed that the tips of his ears looked blue, and Andi explained that it was due to lack of oxygen. With tears silently running down her cheeks, Leslie studied Michael's hand, which looked waxy, kissed it, and began to wail.

"I wanted to read him a story," she said helplessly.

Tom King knelt beside the couch and wordlessly held Leslie's hand.

"It'll be OK, I believe that with all my heart," Andi said, and left to get fresh syringes from her car. The house was crammed with people, but the loudest sound was the gurgling of Michael's breathing. When Andi returned, Mike stepped forward to help her. Adept with tubes and needles, he helped her give Michael his nine-o'clock dose of liquid phenobarbital through the tube. Leslie watched as Mike then gently slipped a soft plastic suction tube into Michael's mouth and throat to clear the collected saliva. As Mike suctioned him, he intoned, "It's OK, Tiger. You'll be OK, Tiger."

When Mike finished, Leslie marveled, as if she had not known what her ex-husband was capable of.

Over the next two hours Mike, Andi, Leslie, and Tom hovered over

Michael, tending to his every twitch, his every irregular breath. Concerned about a seizure breaking through the sedation, Andi checked and rechecked the subcutaneous Versed infusion line. Mike changed the Foley catheter bag, even though it contained barely a cup of urine. Together, they cleared his mouth and throat. Throughout it all, Michael's mother grew visibly hollow-eyed and pale.

When they could do no more, Andi said to Mike, "He's not suffering. He's in a different place."

"Do you think he's going?" Mike asked.

"Yes," Andi replied softly. "I'm not sure tonight, but it feels like it."

The need for suctioning became more frequent, and Mike worked the tube while Andi held Michael's head from behind at a slight tilt. Frightened by the long plastic tube that disappeared into her son's nose, Leslie stood back and watched. But as time went on, she edged closer and closer.

Mike, Andi, and Leslie hovered over the comatose boy. His hands and face were turning grayish blue. Andi softly murmured, "It's all right, sweet boy." Mike sat on the edge of the couch close to his son's head and held his hand. On the other side, Leslie leaned close to her son's face, almost lying down beside him. The room jangled with discordant sounds: light rock on the radio, Michael's talking bear reciting a story, and the slurping and rattling of the suctioning tube.

Through his tears, Mike urged, "Let go, Michael. You're beautiful." Leslie was beyond words; she wrapped her arm around Michael and wailed. The two hospice workers moved closer and enveloped the grieving parents in their arms.

Sensing that Michael's heart had finally stopped, Andi consoled them. "He did more than fight the good fight," she said.

Bereft, yet composed, Mike agreed. "Yeah, he needed to rest."

I was not there when Michael died, but I had been visiting almost daily. As Michael was dying, the Merseal household felt like a sacred place, almost a temple, where people selflessly poured their love into a little boy. The family dynamics—Mike's enormous growth as a father, Krystle's uncanny ability to be both child and mature sibling, Ted's and Kathy's coalescing into a tight unit—evolved by the day and changed what some might have considered a dysfunctional, disparate family into a committed whole. This family grew immensely in the face of this seemingly senseless tragedy. Even as a vital part of it was being amputated, long-festering wounds and previously severed relationships were healed, and the family assumed a new and stronger identity. Clearly, this was neither a painless nor perfect process. People and families all have their flaws; certainly the Merseals were no exception. Mike never reconciled with or forgave his ex-wife for leaving. Nevertheless, for the sake of his son, he put aside his burning resentment of her. When Krystle returned home after Michael had died and Leslie had gone, her first thought was that her mother had taken her brother. She was relieved to learn that he had peacefully died. Although Krystle could not forgive or forget that her mother had left them, she recognized this special time in her family's life and suppressed her nine-year-old emotions. Leslie, too, transcended ancient emotions, at least for a few hours. Despite being surrounded by rejection, she did not flee or back away. It was too important to stay with her son.

Many people believe that the dying of someone who is unconscious has little value and that it stresses family members and caregivers far beyond the usual sadness it brings. What is the point, they wonder, of allowing an unconscious, terminally ill patient to linger? The patient is mentally gone, and the family is suffering from emotional and financial demands. Isn't this the kind of situation that cries out for euthanasia? Michael's story certainly attests to the value such a dying can hold for a family. As Mike cared for his comatose son on Christmas Eve, I remember someone saying to him, "You must wish it was over." He replied, "Oh, no, I still have hope, I still have my family." Mike would not have wanted Michael's death to have come any sooner than it was destined to. Up until his final breath, Michael united and fortified the family.

Ten

Facing Unbearable Pain, Unspeakable Losses: Terry Matthews

The following story, which tells of the dying of a thirty-one-year-old mother with advanced kidney cancer, may be difficult for some people to read. While the details of anyone's demise can be hard to digest, this story is about someone wrestling with the outer limits of human endurance. Everything about Terry Matthews's dying was larger than life; nothing was small, neither her disease (renal cell carcinoma that had metastasized to her pelvis, lungs, bones, and brain), nor her pain, nor her emotions. Life, in Terry's final days, became a crescendo of agony that reverberated through her family and the community. Terry Matthews never found a transcendent peace in this life; she never "let go." Ultimately, life was forcibly taken from her. As if following Dylan Thomas's exhortation, she "did not go gently into that good night," but raged "against the dying of the light."

Terry's was not the way I would choose for a relative or loved one to die. By my personal values, Terry did not die a "good death." Yet how Terry and her family felt, not my values, is what ultimately matters. In this respect, she died well, because she died her way—fighting for life and time with her family. In her dying, she remained true to her spirit and true to her values. It was her way, thus the only way.

. . .

Terry was twenty-four years old and the mother of a toddler when she learned she had a fatal illness. She had been admitted to the hospital to have a growth on her right kidney removed, a growth her doctor had earlier assured her was benign. After the surgery, he crisply told her that kidney cancer in someone her age is very rare, adding, "It's also very difficult to cure." An oncologist subsequently told her that, even though the surgeon had removed all of the visible tumor, this type of cancer often reappears within a year. Terry and her husband, Paul, rejected his gloomy prognosis and found a more optimistic oncologist, who talked about occasional complete remissions and recommended a course of chemotherapy. When this was completed, he told the young couple they could get on with raising their family. And they did.

For a time it seemed like a miracle had occurred. After the birth of Scotty and Jenny, who was conceived shortly after Terry finished chemotherapy, they adopted a baby girl they named Sally; along with two dogs, the family was complete. They moved to Missoula to be close to Paul's family and rented a ranch-style tract house in a development that had overtaken a cornfield on the western outskirts of Missoula. Paul, a well-muscled man with a ruddy complexion and deep brown eyes, worked as an assistant operations manager for UPS, which meant he worked from late evening until mid-morning. On weekends during warmer months, the family went on picnics and outings to a cabin on Trout Lake. All year round, Terry devoted her days to her children, baking cookies, crocheting dolls, and sewing clothes and party costumes. She and, whenever possible, Paul attended every school and sporting event and volunteered to help with field trips and holiday shows. At home she organized arts and crafts projects and created toys and a steady stream of birthday and holiday gifts for grandparents, cousins, aunts, and uncles. She also made sure the children did their household chores, helped one another, and said their prayers before bed every night.

Terry often declared Friday night was "kids' night," rented their favorite video, made popcorn, and let them stay up late and sleep together on the couch. She would be there in the middle of it all, laughing and munching, giggling at the funny parts and snuggling at the end of the night. A sweet, affectionate person, Terry also had a devilish side. She could imitate Beavis and Butt-head and delighted in wisecracks and teasing with her children. She intentionally set high standards for the children, but she could also make fun of herself, slaying her family, for example, with an exaggerated impression of her own compulsive organizing.

For six years Terry was healthy and nurtured her family as lovingly as she did her bright flower garden. It was just before Thanksgiving when she developed a persistent, raspy cough and occasionally spit up streaks of blood in her phlegm. The doctor in the mall thought she had a bad chest infection and gave her an antibiotic. Christmas was now approaching, and gifts and holiday activities occupied her mind, but the hacking continued. Try as she might, she couldn't ignore it. Reluctantly, she saw Dr. Stevens, an oncologist in Missoula, and a chest X-ray was done in his office. Even though he was accustomed to giving bad news, Terry's youth and the images on the X-ray viewbox left him shaken. Terry noticed that he appeared upset when he was telling her what he saw. Multiple shadows in her lungs confirmed their darkest fears. After years of lying dormant, the kidney cancer had returned with a vengeance.

This time, Terry could not avoid the ominous forecast by finding another doctor. A lymph node biopsy removed any shadow of diagnostic doubt, and a three-week course of radiation therapy to her chest did not halt the progression of the disease. The cancer was moving quickly. By the middle of January it had spread to her face and sinuses, and by Presidents' Day painful spots had appeared in her shoulder and hip.

The family reacted to the reappearance of Terry's disease with anger. A casual churchgoer but deeply spiritual, Terry railed against God or blamed herself. "Why did God let us adopt Sally if he knew this was going to happen? She's going to lose two mothers! Why does God want this to happen to me?" she lamented to Jane Taylor, a hospice volunteer who had become close with her while driving her to and from additional radiation therapy. At other times, Terry felt that she herself had brought the recurrence on: maybe she should have eaten differently, or not yelled at the kids, or kept up with the naturopath's shark cartilage treatment. As the weeks and months passed, she began all sorts of remedies, including coffee enemas, seaweed potions, and herbal tonics.

Paul turned his frustration on everyone, including his wife. Some days the mood in the house was as cold and gray as the late winter sky; they barely spoke, and when they did, they argued. The family bill-payer, Terry struggled to keep their accounts up-to-date. One evening, as she sat on the living-room floor surrounded by piles of paper and two cardboard boxes, she begged Paul to pay attention and be more responsible about money and paying bills. He slammed a soda can on the kitchen table and declared, "I'll just burn them until a new batch comes in. You don't have to worry!" He stomped from the house and tore off in his van. Whenever she talked about death or what would happen "after she was gone," he accused her of giving up. At work, he itched to pick a fight with anyone who looked at him crosswise.

The children—Scotty, who was now nine, Jenny, seven, and Sally, four, reacted with ire, too. Scotty became argumentative and defiant; he hit his sisters, talked back to his parents, and even struck out at walls and furniture. He also sneered at doctors and medical people because they had not cured his mother. Jenny buried her pain and grew sullen, often avoiding Terry. Her voice, frequently a whisper, revealed her sadness and depression. Even the baby, Sally, lost her sunny cheerfulness and clung to her mom, becoming tearful if Terry was out of sight.

As Terry grew sicker, the couple's extended family rallied around. Terry's parents, Arthur and Diane, still lived in Butte, where Terry had grown up. Arthur moved into the basement and helped with chores, including cleaning and laundry. Although quiet and often at a loss as to how to help his daughter, Arthur doted on her. He spent much of the day at the kitchen table, waiting for her to call out. More than once, late at night, Terry could hear him crying himself to sleep. Her mother, who managed a beauty parlor in Butte, was less eager to come to Missoula, even on weekends. Time was not her only impediment to visiting. She had already lost one child, Cal, who had died at age six of a cerebral aneurysm, and she could not bear to watch her bubbly, energetic second child succumb to cancer. Some weekends she did not make the two-hour drive, begging off for work reasons. When Diane was at the house, she dwelled on the beauty parlor, rambling on with stories about customers and tips. She was outwardly oblivious to Terry's declining health. Terry's sister, Rebecca, who lived in Anaconda, floated in and out when her job and responsibilities in her own home allowed.

Within this large family, it was Paul's sister, Candy, who was most attuned to Terry's growing pain. As Terry became more incapacitated, relying increasingly on a cane, then a walker, Candy was there to run errands, help bathe her, and, later, help her to the bathroom. Other relatives gathered at the periphery. On the weekends the Matthews home became a hangout for aunts, cousins, and in-laws. The men gravitated to the carport or basement, where they talked in low voices or watched television. The women clustered around the kitchen and the adjoining dining room while they kept the coffee fresh, cooked, folded laundry, mended the children's clothes, or engaged in other minor household chores. It was not unusual for fifteen or more relatives and friends to be milling about the house on any given weekend evening.

Despite the obvious reason for all the company and activity, few of Terry's relatives treated her as if she were an invalid. During the winter and for most of the spring, she did not look sickly; she was youthful, still able to get around, and, most of the time, able to hide her pain from everyone except her father, Candy, and Paul. This false picture of health encouraged the atmosphere of denial that pervaded the house. While people might talk about an upcoming trip to the doctor, her medications, or some other aspect of treatment, the terminal nature of Terry's illness—the fact that she was dying—became an elephant in the living room that no one admitted seeing and no one spoke about. In avoiding what was obviously most real and mattered, Terry and her family also avoided what needed to be said and done before she passed away.

Terry fought the disease every step of the way. Since the chemotherapy had apparently contributed to her remarkable remission years before, it seemed reasonable to try again. She immediately agreed. This time, however, all it seemed to do was make her lovely thick brown hair fall out in clumps and contribute to her disgust and frustration. One morning in April, Paul arrived home after a night at work with his head completely shaved in sympathy. Terry did not laugh, as she would have in better times, or thank him for this act of solidarity. Instead she upbraided him for acting foolishly. She would not admit that her disease was getting worse. By this time, her pain was such that she could not tolerate sharing the waterbed with Paul, so she moved into Scotty's room and he shifted to the basement with his grandfather.

One morning a month later, Terry awoke determined to finish sewing the girls' Easter dresses. On attempting to get out of bed, she felt something give way on the right side of her pelvis; she collapsed in excruciating pain. Strapped to a spinal immobilization board by the ambulance crew, Terry cried out as much in distress at failing her family—yet again—as in physical pain. At the emergency room at St. Patrick's Hospital, the admitting doctor wrote in her chart: "No fractures are evident today; however, this patient obviously has very rapidly progressive renal cell carcinoma with several known foci of metastatic involvement to skeletal areas . . . and attendant secondary problems with extreme pain, malnutrition, weakness, fatigue, and severe depression. Unfortunately, her prognosis with all of this is quite horrible, and therapy is only palliative." A surgeon inserted a Portacath, an intravenous line to deliver medication directly into Terry's bloodstream, and Dr. Stevens ordered high doses of Decadron, an anti-inflammatory medication, and a constant infusion of narcotic. Radiation therapy to her pelvic bone and hip was begun. Terry rapidly improved, and within three days she was discharged to continue daily radiation as an outpatient. Two weeks later, Dr. Stevens started her on interferon, a chemical therapy to shrink the tumors and slow their growth.

As the disease and the drugs undermined her once-balanced moods and flawless memory, Terry battled back. She started keeping three journals, one to organize her day, one for her medical care, and another for her thoughts. She made a daily entry in each, noting things like who was coming to visit, the times and doses of medications, and how she felt. When she began forgetting people's phone numbers, she bought a machine with memory buttons. Her children remained the focus of her life, her lifeline in the maelstrom of illness. Although I heard Terry's attitude referred to as denial, it was far more complex than that. For instance, she undertook to create a treasured final gift for each of the children. She was crocheting a big bed doll for Sally, and she was knitting afghans for Jenny and Scotty in their favorite colors. Jane Taylor helped by transcribing letters for her children to read years hence. They included memories of each of them when they were little, motherly discourses about personal values and family traditions, and touching imaginings of how she would have wanted to celebrate their graduations or weddings. Fueled by a superstitious hope that God would not let her die until she finished her children's last gifts, she never came close to completing the afghans or Sally's doll. The children gave her gifts, too. Jenny, the quiet, introspective child, wrote and gave her a story called "Feelings." Sally gave her a cuddly teddy bear she had been given at the cancer center. Scotty gave her a tiny, gift-wrapped box that contained "his love" with a note that said "If you're feeling bad, just hold this and think of me and know that I'm in your heart."

Terry was referred to hospice in late spring, when the family was going through more bad than good days. By June, she often felt too sick to leave the house and missed most of her appointments. However, she undertook another round of radiation therapy for yet another crop of painful bone metastases. On the occasional day when Terry had enough energy, she worked in the garden, bending, kneeling, and turning small spadefuls of soil despite fierce discomfort.

Even as her pain mounted, Linda Simon, her primary hospice nurse, had to negotiate with her for days before being allowed to increase her medication by the smallest possible increment. They would talk about how the new doses would make Terry feel—she hated anything that made her fuzzy or sleepy. Together they weighed the pros and cons of using frequent boluses of pain medication (a bolus is a large, single dose given when needed) versus increasing the steady drip of her analgesia. The infusion rate of her Dilaudid was set at two milligrams per hour, nearly half what it had been in the hospital, and her boluses were set at .8 milligrams up to four times per hour. Linda promised Terry, "We can go up, and if tomorrow you're not using very many boluses and you're too sleepy, we'll take it back down." Terry hated increasing the pain medication, because it meant she was getting worse, and she delighted in the few times the doses were reduced. A triumph for Terry was the time they were briefly able to drop the Dilaudid drip from 2.6 to 2.3 milligrams per hour.

Vickie Kammerer was the hospice social worker assigned to help the family. In addition to her role as a counselor, one of Vickie's main functions is that of administrative go-between for patients. She knows bureaucracies, and she helps people navigate through institutions, agencies, and the maze of private insurance and government payment systems. In an early visit with Terry, Vickie told her about the Montana health directive called Comfort One. By law, this program allows someone with a terminal illness to carry a legal release or to wear a bracelet declaring that she does not want

CPR in the event of an impending or full-blown cardiac or respiratory arrest. Though Vickie knew of Terry's fierce drive to stay alive, the topic required discussion. As she had with hundreds of patients with advanced cancer, Vickie gently explained to Terry, "If you had a massive heart attack in your current condition, it might be somewhat futile even if you could be briefly revived." Terry's reaction said it all: "If they could bring me back to life and I could have one or two more days, that is what I would want."

Terry refused to be bedbound; she even hated to be alone or to sleep. Sleep was too close to death for her; the magical-thinking side of her psyche feared that if she came too close to death, it might somehow take her away. Furthermore, being in bed was a waste of time, and she had lots to do. When alone, she felt cut off from friends, family, and life, so she virtually lived in a blue crushed-velvet recliner in the corner of the living room. From here, she greeted visitors, wrote thank-you notes to people who had sent flowers or food, and supervised the children's games and chores. She and Paul still regularly skirmished over trivial issues: bills, tax forms, school clothes for the kids next fall, even whether the television should be on or off.

Through the early summer, Terry and Paul continued to live in a state of emotional defiance of what was happening to her. While they did not deny that she was dying, they felt that giving in to her symptoms and letting the illness rule them would be an acquiescence that would only hasten her demise. During a doctor's visit at which Paul was present, Dr. Stevens jolted the couple out of their superstitious suppression of the truth. Terry's Dilaudid dose had gradually inched up to four milligrams per hour—roughly the equivalent of twenty milligrams per hour of injectable morphine—yet she admitted to him that she still had substantial pain in her shoulder and back, had a nearly constant headache, and felt nauseated much of the time. He was disturbed that the couple did not seem to be facing the reality in front of them. He drew Terry and Trevor a diagram, a chart with a straight line across the bottom representing the weeks ahead and a vertical line along the left edge representing her life.

Starting with an X at the middle of the left axis, he drew a diagonal line across the page toward the bottom axis, and told her, "Terry, this is your life, this is the down slope of time left. You're right here, and"—he pointed to the bottom right corner—"this is death. I don't think you have too long to live at all. Maybe two or three weeks." Three weeks took her to July 14, Paul's birthday.

Doctors usually refrain from making exact predictions about the course of an illness. For one thing, accuracy is almost impossible. Diseases and people have a way of defying odds and belying even the most knowledgeable opinion. Yet there was nothing equivocal about Dr. Stevens's drawing, and this was deliberate. He wanted to shake them up. At the very least, he wanted Terry to become more accepting of the pain medication she needed if she were to have a semblance of comfort and be able to function. His note on this meeting stated that he felt that no one in the family was sufficiently focused to give Terry the emotional and physical support she needed.

Although he called the family "dysfunctional," they were, more accurately, suffering from the turmoil of grief. From an outsider's perspective, the family appeared to be overwhelmed by the chaos of their emotions. Yet Terry, Paul, and their children were handling their tragedy the only way they knew how, with great energy and emotion—namely anger, sadness, and love.

Dr. Stevens's blunt illustration shocked the family into openly accepting that Terry would soon no longer be with them. Paul took off time from work and, for the first time, took on household duties such as learning to run the washer and dryer and paying bills. He coddled the children more, and he became more assertive in supervising and disciplining them. One morning he watched Scotty sass his mother when she asked him to get dressed and pick up his clothes, and he saw himself. It was a sobering moment, he recalled later. "I was very angry in the last few months. There were plenty of days I wanted to hurt something or someone. It was the same with him." He took Scotty out to the carport, a good place for a private conversation, and told him, "I'm angry, too. But instead of yelling at Mom or being mad at the world, we've got to find a better way of dealing with it. Let's do this together."

The couple decided to tell the children about Terry's condition, and the short time remaining to her, on a Sunday when both her parents were there. While Arthur and Diane played downstairs with the two younger children, Scotty was asked to come upstairs alone for the solemn talk. The fact that their mother still did not look very sick made the task even more difficult.

Petite, with an olive complexion and huge brown eyes, Terry always prided herself on her well-kept, attractive appearance. Her curly brown hair had begun to grow back after chemotherapy, though straighter than before, and the Decadron had plumped her up. Most days her strikingly dark features were enhanced by skillful makeup. Scotty sat on the edge of the recliner footrest, and Paul sat in a chair beside Terry, holding her hand.

"You remember last winter when we told you that your mother has cancer?" Paul began, in a storylike fashion. "And that she was very sick and might not get well?" The little boy nodded gravely, and Terry picked up the narrative.

"That's why I've been going to St. Pat's every day. The doctors have been trying to make me better. But, Scotty, it hasn't been working, honey. It's getting worse, not better." She leaned hard against the door of her closeted emotions.

"Mom is probably going to die," Paul continued, while Terry collected herself.

"Positively, for sure?" their son asked.

"Yeah. Unless there's a miracle, which is probably not going to happen. Most likely, Mom is going to die," Paul answered, without faltering.

"When?" Scotty wailed.

"No one knows for sure, but it could be soon," Terry answered. For a moment, her son was incredulous, his expression disbelieving. Then it slowly melted into tears and sobs. Paul squeezed Terry's hand, and they wrapped their arms around Scotty and wondered if they had the strength to go through this with the girls.

They spoke with Jenny and Sally together. The four-year-old sat on Paul's lap and played with her dolls, outwardly oblivious to what was being said, though she was quietly listening. While Jenny was attentive when they reviewed her mom's illness and the treatments she had been getting, she interrupted them when they said that Terry was probably going to die, soon. "Don't die, Mommy," she implored. "Don't go. I need you, you're my Mommy. I don't want you to go away."

Terry cried, and held her, saying, "I don't want to, Jenny."

Other family members in the home absorbed and adjusted to the announcement of Terry's impending demise. Arthur had been devastated, but also had been a helpless spectator to her deterioration and blind to her needs. When Linda Simon had arrived one morning, Arthur, sitting at the kitchen table, had said that Terry was resting comfortably in bed. He hurt too deeply to sit with her for too long, so he was popping in and out of her bedroom. Linda found Terry in extreme discomfort because she could not get to the bathroom on her own, and her father had not heard her calls for help. "Art doesn't have a clue that Terry can't get out of bed," Linda thought. She pointedly asked him to lend a hand a couple of times, and he began to stay longer in Terry's room and to offer help.

As July 14 neared, Terry grew moodier. More than once she yelled at Paul when he was busy doing the laundry or defrosting the freezer, "You're going to regret this. After I'm gone, you're going to wish we spent more time together." Paul understood what she was going through: "She didn't want to die. She didn't want to leave me and the kids. She didn't want to leave the family. And she was unsure whether I could handle things."

In her typically organized way, Terry made funeral plans, deciding what she would wear, what the kids would wear, whether to be buried rather than cremated (she chose burial), what music was to be played, and what scriptures read. She wondered whether the funeral home would let Paul pay in monthly installments.

Terry's favorite aunt, Clarice, arrived from Alaska for a long visit. Cheerful, energetic, and loving, Clarice swept into the Matthews household like a fairy godmother. She made sure that the kids behaved and were clean, the meals were more than pizza and Coke, the house was tidy, and Terry was treated like a cherished infant. Throughout the day she checked on Terry and blanketed her with kisses and hugs. Every time Terry left for her radiation treatment, Clarice walked her to the car, perched in the window as if she could not bear to lose sight of her, and declared, "I do love you!"

Terry did not die in July, although she came close. Late in the month, her pain intensified almost to the point of total paralysis. It had crippled her right arm and shoulder and forced her into a wheelchair. Late one Friday night Linda made an evening visit to the house, and wanted to increase her medication. Once again Terry resisted, but by early Saturday morning she was in a pain crisis. Mary McCall, the nurse on call for hospice, tried to administer an extra dose of medication and became concerned when she was unable to establish flow through the Portacath, the intravenous line delivering medication directly to the superior vena cava, the largest vein in the body. The Dilaudid was switched to a subcutaneous infusion setup, and Terry quickly became more comfortable. Mary, however, asked Paul and Clarice to take her to St. Pat's emergency room for an X-ray and to see if the catheter could be unclogged. Although the ER doctor attributed Terry's increasing right shoulder pain to local invasion by a tumor, Clarice asserted herself and conveyed Mary's request. The picture showed that a five-inch section of the Portacath wire had broken off and migrated to the right atrium of the heart. As soon as the doctor saw it, he paged the cardiologist on call. Within the hour Terry was in the "cath lab," and, in a procedure similar to the angiograms and angioplasties performed many times a day at St. Pat's, the fractured segment of the catheter was extracted.

Dr. Stevens and everyone at hospice were dismayed at the event. Most of us had never heard of central venous lines breaking. It seemed that of all the families we were caring for, the Matthews did not need any iatrogenic—that is, medically caused—disasters. Surprisingly, Terry and her family took the episode in stride. She stayed overnight in the hospital and the next morning drove home with Paul.

A full house of relatives and friends awaited her. Diane and Arthur, Paul's mother, Bea, Clarice, and two cousins crowded around Terry's bed and remarked on the pretty flowers sent by Paul's boss, then fell awkwardly silent. Before anyone else could fill the gap, Diane told a complicated story about a customer who had mistakenly or deliberately (she did not know which) left a $20 tip after a $20 haircut. Clarice listened incredulously. Before Diane segued into her familiar worst-kind-of-customers anecdotes, she wedged herself in beside Terry and asked, "How are you doing, dear? Are you feeling better? Do you need anything? Are you comfortable?"

Terry looked at Clarice and smiled. "Thank God, I'm home!"

Terry was comfortable for the moment, but over the next few days, relief became an elusive goal. She was still trapped by her pain, now mostly concentrated in her left shoulder, as if she had been cornered by a wildfire. From the deepest sleep she would awake in spasms, screaming "I'm burning up, I'm on fire!" Each time this happened, she or whoever was with her would touch the bolus button on her infusion pump, administering a rescue dose of medication. Although she preferred to be in the recliner in the living room, looking out over the cornfield, she now slept in the hospital bed in Scotty's room. Some nights Paul dozed alongside her so that when her arm began to twitch and seize, he could hold it down and help contain her pain.

The house was now constantly buzzing with visitors, the men gathered around the carport and the women around the kitchen table. When Terry was awake, if she heard the kids elsewhere in the house, she would call out, "What are you kids doing? What's that noise? Are you dressed? Let's see you get dressed!" in a voice that recalled the cheerful mothering of days long since passed. She arranged with Diane, Clarice, and Bea to buy birthday and holiday gifts for times far beyond her expected survival.

By the third week in August Terry was clearly slipping, but she steadfastly refused to let go of her family life. At the end of life, most people turn away from the world toward whatever lies beyond and find a peace with that new vision. They acknowledge to themselves, "I've done my best, but I'm clearly being drawn elsewhere." With Terry, I kept wondering and waiting to see if and when that would happen. It never did. She stayed focused on living as long as possible, clinging to life. She knew the score, she knew that she was dying. But she consciously chose to live every moment until her life was ripped from her.

Terry's pain again reached crisis proportions on a Friday night. Kenneth Groth, the nurse on hospice call, paged me to report that, while Terry had been accepting increases in her Dilaudid infusion, she was approaching the limit of what was currently ordered: fifty milligrams per hour. Dr. Stevens had also ordered doses of IV Valium to calm Terry's nerves. Despite all this, Kenneth said that Terry was comfortable only for ten or fifteen minutes at a time, and at least twice an hour she would suddenly call out and grab her left shoulder. Kenneth needed new orders from Dr. Stevens, and he asked me for suggestions.

I called Jack Stevens directly. We had worked together on difficult cases over the years, and it was obvious that this one was extraordinary. We both had questions, such as what exactly was causing the extreme pain in her left shoulder. Curiously, her right shoulder had been the problem earlier. Was the new pain caused by a tumor growing into the nerves below the clavicle, a seizure due to a brain metastasis, or something else? We knew that we would never know. Clearly, Terry was going to die within a few days, and we would avoid putting her through further tests and procedures that required transporting her to and from the hospital. "Unless she wants to go, let's try to keep her in her own home. There's nothing that can be done in the hospital that isn't being done at home," her doctor asserted, and I agreed.

Jack Stevens and I also agreed on a basic principle of palliative medicine. With severe pain, there is no maximum dose of pain medication; the right dose is the one that works. While the current regimen of drugs was obviously insufficient, medication still seemed the best route to pursue. We formulated a set of parameters for the nurses to follow during the night, enabling them to rapidly increase the infusion rate based on the number and size of bolus doses required to keep her truly comfortable.

From this point on, Terry's condition would require twenty-four-hour hospice nursing care as we struggled to stay on top of her searing pain. At ten P.M. Dr. Stevens made a home visit. With key family members gathered around her bed, he asked Terry, ever so gently, whether she wanted to stay at home or go to the hospital. He left no doubt that he was asking her where she preferred to die. Paul asked Dr. Stevens again if there was anything the doctors and nurses would do in the hospital that wasn't being done in the home. "I don't think so. We have, or can get, anything we need right here." Terry looked to Paul, who thought his wife looked exhausted. The T-shirt she had slept in was dark with sweat; her dark eyes were sunken into her skull. The fan on the dresser barely stirred the dead summer heat. The curtains hung limp. "It's up to you, babe. Whatever you want. I'd like you to stay here, but I'll do whatever you want." Terry closed her eyes, as if to relax, and slowly nodded her consent.

During that long night, the family suffered as much as Terry. Her intermittent shrieks—"I'm on fire! It's burning me up!"—could be heard on the street. Paul had already sent the kids across town to stay with Grandma Bea. Every time Terry yelled in pain, he thought of prisoners being tortured in foreign jails. His sister and parents, as well as Terry's sister and aunts, plus assorted cousins and hospice volunteers, were all at the house taking turns being with Terry as she squeezed their hands and grappled with the fire inside her. In her other hand she clutched the tiny, gift-wrapped box Scotty had given her.

Arthur could not stand to watch; he stood by the bedroom door and sometimes briefly caressed her foot, then left. Clarice hardly budged from the room; she crooned repeatedly, "It's going to be better soon, honey." At times, Terry cried out, "Where is my mother? I want my mother!" Arthur telephoned Diane, and she left Butte just after midnight, arriving in record time.

Hour after hour the fire raged inside Terry's ravaged body. The hospice shift changed and the new nurse, Andi Dreiling, took over. The interval between Dilaudid boluses had dropped to five or ten minutes and the doses of Valium increased to ten and then fifteen milligrams as needed every fifteen minutes. As the night dragged on, punctuated by Terry's screams and brief periods of eerie quiet, Andi and Paul continued to pump Dilaudid into her. Paul had been warned that she might overdose and, at first, he worried. But when nothing quieted her screams and moans, he found himself wishing he could put her out of her misery with a massive final injection.

By three A.M. we had depleted the supply of injectable Dilaudid from all the private pharmacies, as well as the two hospital pharmacies, in town. After a telephone call to Dr. Stevens, the Dilaudid dose was converted to an equivalent dose of morphine. The fluid volume of medication would be larger using morphine sulphate, but we could still deliver whatever dose was required. At the time of the change, this thirty-one-year-old mother was absorbing—and her pain all but ignoring—more than nine hundred milligrams of morphine per hour.

For brief moments, Terry awakened and smiled weakly. She would doze comfortably but awaken with a start every five to twelve minutes. "I'm on fire!" she would yell. Then, as the next bolus of medication was taking effect, she would whisper to Paul or Candy, "I thought I didn't have to hurt." In the moments she was awake and not in pain, she would gaze around the room and seem interested in taking part. "What's going on? Where is everybody? How are the kids?" Paul was at her side, trying to reassure her. Only when she was asleep did he rest his head on the bedrails and sob, in his own agony.

Just after daylight Saturday morning, Jack Stevens telephoned me to review the Matthews family's horrific night. "Don't you folks have a protocol for a barbiturate drip?" he asked. I responded readily. "We certainly do, and for situations just like this." I was grateful, but not surprised, that he had made the suggestion. I had begun thinking along the same lines, and his instincts confirmed mine. Push had come to shove.

The idea of sedation is controversial when caring for the dying, because some people believe that it is tantamount to euthanasia. When our hospice developed this protocol, with the help of pharmacists, nurses, and other doctors, I insisted that it be formally reviewed by the pharmacy and therapeutics committees of the medical staffs at both of Missoula's hospitals. I felt it was important that the community understand that we were committed to caring for people and would act decisively to quell the most extreme and explosive pain. Ironically, it is the very availability of such extraordinary measures that allows us to ensure that euthanasia is not required to end a person's misery. As stated earlier, I frequently promise patients, especially those with potentially excruciating illnesses, that they will not die in pain. Fast-acting sedatives, particularly barbiturates, are, literally, the bottom line of a safe, effective protocol for going beyond the normal pain relief of opioids and other analgesics, and they let me and others in hospice care fulfill that promise.

I headed for the Matthews's to explain to Paul and the family the procedure for giving Terry an intravenous barbiturate drip, an infusion of the drug thiopental, which would put her into a deep, painless sleep. As I approached the house, I could hear Terry screaming. A couple of men I recognized as cousins were standing in the carport, nervously smoking. Paul and Arthur greeted me at the door, and we huddled on the couch as I described the thiopental infusion. Clarice, Diane, and a cousin huddled in the kitchen. The family's Lutheran pastor, Bob Brownlee, hovered at the periphery, prayer book in hand. The house felt stuffy and smelled of burnt toast. The windows were closed, probably because it was a cool morning for August, or maybe to muffle noises drifting out. Neither of the men had shaved. They looked haggard, and they winced every time a noise came from Terry's room. Paul muttered something about being grateful that he had had the foresight to take the children to his mother's house.

I studied Terry's chart and the medication she had gone through. "This is a very late-game strategy, after we've tried everything else," I said. "She will go into a deep sleep and probably will not be aware of us. And, you should know, it's likely that she will not wake up from it. Unless you tell me otherwise or we decide for some reason to lighten the sedation, it is the usual course in these situations to allow people to peacefully sleep away." I paused to invite their questions.

"Will she be out of pain and comfortable?" Paul skipped to his bottom line.

"I promise you that. I'm not going to leave until I know that she is no longer in pain."

"That's what I want," Paul declared.

"I know this is a hard decision," I cautioned. "And if you want to think about it, please take as long as you need. What you have done for Terry has been incredible. I have enormous respect for the love and care you have been giving her. I think you did the right thing, taking care of her here instead of in the hospital. Too often, in hospitals, the medical aspects of things get all the attention and the personal stuff gets shoved aside. The thiopental infusion will eliminate Terry's pain and give everyone some peace. Do you want to talk to her about it?"

"Yeah. Would you come with me?"

Terry's bedroom was a shambles, with dirty dishes on the dresser and nightstand and clothes scattered across the furniture and floors. She was dozing, lying on her back with a sheet covering her. Paul lightly touched her hand, and her eyes popped open.

"Honey, Dr. Byock's here. He's going to help you."

I pulled a chair close. "Hi, Terry," I said softly. "I'm sorry you're in such misery. I think I can make it better. I can give you a sedative, a steady drip of thiopental, that will make you drowsy and then put you into what we call a 'twilight sleep.' It may feel like that floating time just before you drop into a deep sleep. You may be able to hear or be partially aware of people around you, but probably you'll just be sleeping."

"But will I still wake up sometimes and be in pain?" she asked.

"No, Terry, not if you don't want to," I said.

"I just want to go to heaven," she said, with weary resignation.

As we talked, her left shoulder began to tremble and, like a ripple moving across a lake, the spasm inched down her arm and produced a strong twitch. Terry grimaced and let out a long noise—"Ooh, whee"—as if marveling at the intensity of what was coursing through her. Whenever there was a pause in her pain, Pastor Brownlee opened his prayer book and began to read; he then stopped abruptly, often in midsentence, when Terry cried out.

"Please make it stop," she begged. She squeezed Paul's hand, almost folding it in half.

"I promise," I said. I left the room to call in the medication order. The seventy minutes it took for the medicine to arrive and be set up felt like seven years. I sat with various family members by her bed and waited for the pharmacy to prepare and deliver the thiopental. While we waited, I heard people arriving and greeting each other. Family and friends were coming to say goodbye. Many could not bear to stay with her for long, even Paul. At times he broke into heaving sobs and raged against God.

"Honey, please don't be angry at God. God did not do this to me," Terry pleaded.

As we awaited the delivery of the medication, Terry was determined to use even these last few minutes of time. Clarice sat for long stretches with a note pad and pencil, jotting down Terry's last wishes, which she dictated in lucid intervals between the pain: "The stuff for Sally's doll is in the closet. You'll see how far I've gotten on the afghans; Scotty's is going to be a little bigger than Jenny's."

Terry would drop off for a few minutes, then wake up and continue. "Be sure the kids have nice clothes for the funeral. I want Sally to wear her baptism dress. And, don't forget, I want piano music, no organs."

Each time someone new came into the room, Terry whispered, "I love you so much. I don't want to leave you."

At around nine-thirty A.M. the medication arrived. I enlisted Ellen, the hospice nurse now present, and Jane Taylor to help reassure Terry and keep her arm still while I found a vein. Paul hunched over her in a hug as we worked on the other side of the bed, and they gazed into each other's eyes. Terry repeated over and over, "I'm so sorry, honey, I'm so sorry." Paul convulsed in sobs and left the room.

The sedative took just minutes to work; it visibly relaxed her. Her eyes were closed and her breathing steady and quiet. When her left arm twitched briefly, she moaned and tightened her brow. I carefully adjusted the medication upward to make sure there would be no more twitches, no more spasms of pain to jolt her awake. Her good right hand gently held the little box containing her son's love. Her breathing settled and her pulse steadied to 110 beats per minute. I stayed by her side for about half an hour, making sure no pain broke through, and I discussed further changes in the thiopental infusion rate with Ellen, instructing her to regulate the rate to prevent the visible twitching of the left shoulder that had heralded each explosion of pain.

Diane, who had been so frightened by Terry's screams, came in the room, stood beside her daughter, then sat on the side of the bed.

"Is she asleep? Is she OK?"

I nodded, and Terry's mother began to cry. As I held my open hand against her back, I realized that her sobs were not of pleading or pain, but of relief. Her daughter was finally at peace. When I was certain that we had full control of Terry's distress, I joined the family in the living room.

Like the warm Chinook winds that blow through Montana in the dead of winter, a peaceful quiet settled on the Matthews home. For the first time in days, people were talking quietly among themselves and looking relaxed. No pained glances toward the bedroom, no stricken faces, no tense bodies braced for another cry.

I touched Paul's shoulder to acknowledge his ordeal, and I hugged Clarice. "She's much better now," I reassured them. "She's sleeping. She's not in pain. I promise you, her pain is finally over."

A little later one of Paul's brothers asked, "Do people often suffer this much?"

"No. This is as hard as it gets. I don't think I have ever seen anyone endure so much pain. For what it's worth, I want you to know how much respect I have for all you have done. Families sometimes buy large headstones as monuments to their loved ones after they die. This family has built a monument to Terry in the commitment you have all shown and in the incredible care you have given, and are giving. It is truly privilege to be part of it and to know you all."

I accepted a cup of coffee and spent another half-hour or so visiting with other members of the family and satisfying myself that everything was in place. Before leaving I conferred again with Ellen and poked my head into Terry's room to watch her for a few moments to again make sure the pain was truly gone. Paul was beside her, curled up around her, and he had dropped off to sleep, probably the first sleep he had had in days.

When Paul awoke, confident now that Terry was comfortable, Clarice and Candy tidied her room and bathed and shampooed her. Diane gave her a pedicure and painted her toenails. They debated what she would want to sleep in and be seen in and opted for a fresh oversized T-shirt. Later in the day the children came home, and they said goodbye to their mother. Vickie arrived; she helped Paul, Candy, and Clarice explain things to the kids, and she stood with them as they went into their mother's room one by one. When Sally's turn came, she was not around. Vickie found her rummaging through her bedroom closet.

"Can I help you, Sally? What are you looking for, sweetie?" she asked.

Sally was busy making a pile of goodies, including a doll and a stuffed puppy. "I need these for my Mommy. This is for my Mommy," the four-year-old said plaintively.

"You know, Sally, your mom is sleeping very deeply. And she may not wake up again. She may go to heaven very soon," Vickie explained, as she had already a half-hour earlier.

"I know that," Sally affirmed matter-of-factly. "But she might need these in heaven."

Terry Matthews slept for thirty hours, while aunts, uncles, cousins, and friends spoke softly to her, caressed her, and, each in his or her own way, said goodbye. The children finally saw their mom at peace and told her that they loved her.

Paul simply sat and watched her, content that his dear wife was beyond pain. "I feel like this place was a war zone and now the all-clear has been blown," he told Vickie. Terry never regained consciousness. She died peacefully on Monday morning; her breathing became ever more faint, and finally ceased.

Terry's defiance of death defined her exit from this world. She did not "die well" in the usual sense of the term. Instead of reaching the landmarks that I would have wished for her, she chiseled out different ones for herself. Instead of experiencing a deeper love of self, she manifested a deeper love for her family. She never went through the ritual of completing her relationships with her husband and children, yet she allowed them to feel a sense of finality and resolution by allowing herself to be sedated and cared for—and enabling her family to say goodbye. Terry's personhood, her sense of herself, never wavered; she never outgrew her identity as a mother of young children. Toward the end, she realized that after she was gone, other women would mother her children and, for their sake, she accepted this. Life had to be plucked from Terry; she never did let go or turn inwardly to leave the way most dying people do. This was the crux of her life: she died with arms open and outstretched toward her family. Her reluctance to leave will always be part of her legacy to them.

. . .

As helpful as the model of landmarks and taskwork is, it is just that, a helpful guide. Terry's dying demonstrates that dying well is fundamentally about people experiencing something that has meaning and value for them. Her story also reveals how intricately entwined dying can be with a person's family attachments. In her dying, Terry served her family.

At the funeral Clarice said tearfully, "We all grew so much in this. I feel like Terry brought us all together. We're gonna take care of those children, don't you worry. And I love that boy," nodding toward Paul, "more than I have words for." She gave me a big hug and added, "Thank you so much. I don't know how you can do what you do." It is a statement I hear often. I hugged her back and wondered, with tears in my eyes, how I could do anything else.

Months after Terry died I asked Paul to think back on the choices they had made, particularly in the last few days. "Everything just seemed natural, caring for her ourselves. My love for her—I mean, I would have done anything for her, you know?"

"Has it made it hard for you to be in the home, knowing she died there?" I inquired.

"No, I'm sure glad we didn't go to the hospital that day. You know, even though we went through that horrible night, I'm sure it would've been the same thing in the hospital. We did everything they could have done—it just would have been an uncomfortable place to be for us all," he said.

"It has been strange a time or two, though," he said. "I may be crazy, but I've heard her there. The first night the kids were out of the house—I had them stay at my mom's, because I had to work Friday until midnight—I'm lying in bed, and I'm hearing all this slamming going on in the kitchen, like doors opening and closing. And I look out, and the dogs are lying there next to me, there's no one else around. And the dogs usually bark at noises. And it didn't disturb them at all. My mother stayed with us quite a bit in the month after Terry died, and the last night she stayed with us she heard stuff moving around and got spooked. But, you know, I like it. At first it startled me; now it really relaxes me to think that she was there.

"It's as if she's still trying to help me. One week I had to find the kids' birth certificates and I'd put it off to the last day, and I didn't know where those were in a million years. Then everything came to me. I opened the dresser drawer and they were sitting right there. And the social security cards, in a completely different place—again, I had no idea."

"How are the kids doing, Paul?" I asked.

"They're doing OK. They've been part of the kids' group at hospice with Vickie and Monica, and I think that's helped a lot. They have hard times, of course. When Sally is tired and frustrated, she says she hates us all and wants to go live with Mommy. But I hold her, and we take each day at a time, and together we get through it."

"How are the rest of your and Terry's family? Do you see them much these days?" I continued.

"You know, I'm really closer with the family now, even my family, including my brothers. We've always been fairly close, but it seems like we're closer now. We do things together more often, I think. And everyone's always checking up on me, making sure I'm OK. The kids are getting lots of love; so am I."

When a person is dying, pain is never purely physical. Pain that goes on day after day without relief understandably generates fear, anxiety, sleeplessness, and irritability. Also understandably, this emotional distress feeds back on the pain and heightens one's misery. It is a tenet of palliative care and hospice that the nature of pain is subjective; pain is what the patient says it is. While accepting that anyone's distress will always have physical and emotional components—and often social and spiritual elements—I believe that a patient's pain is not better until she says it is.

The cancer that invaded Terry's body caused physical agony that became impervious to the usual pain medications, even megadoses of morphine. Yet, while the physical aspects of her distress were enormous, I have no doubt that Terry's blinding grief at the thought of losing her husband and three young children contributed to her pain. She refused to adjust to her illness. Instead, she chose to claw at every possible route to survival, to defy death by seeking every life-prolonging option, and for this she paid the price of extreme physical distress. She clung to life far beyond the point at which most people surrender to the inevitable. Her connection to her family, being with them, was more important than the pain—and her resistance to letting go gave the disease more time to inflict its cruel torment. By the end of her life, Terry's pain was as bad as it gets, as severe as I have ever witnessed.

Medicine, especially the emerging discipline of palliative care, has devised a wide array of medications and techniques to alleviate even the most profound and persistent pain. Mercifully, situations of such extreme physical misery are rare. The constellation of factors that conspire to cause pain as severe as Terry's is highly unusual. Think of it as winning the lottery from hell. For instance, had the site of Terry's pain merely been in the lower part of her body, rather than at the base of her neck and shoulder, spinal nerve blocks could have been used to provide relief with relative ease.

For the person who is suffering, of course, it doesn't matter at all that the severity of their pain is unusual. The existence of physical agony becomes the overwhelming truth. At this extreme of physical suffering, pain seems uncontrollable.

Eighteen years of clinical hospice experience has taught me, however, that physical distress among the dying can *always* be alleviated. The word "always" in this context may sound facile, but I use it deliberately. Medical care for the dying stops working only when we give up. Pain is only "uncontrollable" until it is controlled. Pain and other physical symptoms caused by advanced disease usually yield to relatively simple treatment. This is not to say that symptom management is routinely easy. Effective therapy may require the efforts of a physician skilled in palliative medicine and a team of hospice-trained nurses, consultant pharmacists, and others. As Terry's story shows, sometimes pain is so severe and so resistant to customary medicines and therapies that a patient is forced to accept sedation as the cost of comfort.

However, as Terry's story also shows, comfort is *always* possible. Although—as in the case of Michael Merseal—it is considered from time to time, over the past ten years, as I have helped care for hundreds of hospice patients in Missoula, I have needed to resort to full sedation utilizing an infusion of barbiturate only once. Terry's pain typifies the sort of nightmare that motivated our program years ago to develop a clinical protocol for barbiturate use.

The story of Terry and her family explores the fine line between sedation for the treatment of extreme terminal pain and euthanasia. Life beyond the ability to respond in a meaningful way, and the care it demands, can both be burdensome. People unfamiliar with the purposes of palliative care may see little difference between sedation to control persistent physical distress and euthanasia. What may appear philosophically to be a fine line is, in practice, a chasm.

Eleven

Letting Go, Growing On: Maureen Riley

I first met Mo Riley at her insistent request, which is unusual. Only occasionally do terminally ill patients ask to meet me. I suspect that some people regard "the hospice doctor" as a harbinger of death who appears on their doorsteps after modern medicine has exhausted its arsenal of possible cures and treatments. My presence may confirm their darkest fears. But not Mo. She had heard about me from friends whose families we had served in town, and she fearlessly asked me to visit; she was full of questions about me and hospice care.

Everything this woman did in her dying days reflected not just acceptance of her impending demise, but curiosity, anticipation, and even pleasure. She typified full, rich living through her very last breath. Mo also showed me how someone who is dying can transform herself from a vibrant, loving mother and person living in the world into an almost lofty being of beauty and spirit. The butterfly metaphor that is overused in hospice logos and sentimental pamphlets surely has its origin in passings of this type. In her dying, Mo epitomized a blessedness that comes with letting go of both the burdens and the delights of daily life—ultimately letting go of life itself and willingly slipping into another realm.

Yet for all its beauty, in fact *because* of its beauty, I hesitate to tell the story of Mo's dying. My hesitation relates to feeding critics who say that in focusing on dying well I am sugarcoating the dying experience. Skeptics of the idea of dying well like to remind me that death is hardly beautiful and is often messy and unpleasant. And I readily agree. Even for people who do die well, the process of dying is rarely enjoyable; indeed, it is commonly a wrenching time in one's life. Many people do struggle for a period of time in their dying. Every now and then, however, I meet a person who while dying seems to flow smoothly out of worldly concerns and relationships and toward an ethereal, spiritual state. Such people may have worked hard earlier in their lives on relationships and on aspects of themselves, acquiring in this way the skills to accomplish the taskwork of dying. Their lives were, thus, fairly well in order before the time of dying, freeing them to focus on growth within the realms of spirit and soul. Growing up, growing old, growing on—this was Mo Riley. Her confidence in who she was and what she had accomplished, and her faith, enabled her to let go of her worldly self and move into another sphere of existence. This experience for her, I believe, was marked by a joy and exhilaration that deeply touched all who knew her.

Yet even Mo's dying was not a fairy tale. Relinquishing her life and letting go of her sense of self were not effortless. An elegant and outgoing, yet private, woman, she suffered assaults on her sense of dignity during her physical decline and dependence. Before letting go, she had to say goodbye to six grown children and grandchildren. But she approached these tasks unflinchingly, with love and acceptance. Having created a life that brimmed with family and community responsibilities, she adjusted not willingly, but gracefully, to her infirm condition. She consciously shed anger and personal resentment, including any bitterness toward those who had failed her. Throughout her life and relationships, Mo did not lug around a lot of emotional baggage. She tended to express her feelings early and often, rather than allowing them to fester. And she took care of herself, cultivating a healthy, independent, and satisfying life apart from her grown-up children. Not surprisingly, the same values predominated as she was dying. Rather than struggle against the waning of her strength and her life, Mo transformed the experience into an adventure full of wonder.

Months before we met, Maureen Catharine Riley had begun her journey, when she noticed a seemingly innocuous tingling pain in her wrist. After three weeks of trying to ignore the sensation, she saw her doctor, who diagnosed the problem as carpal tunnel syndrome and fit her with a brace. Yet neither this nor subsequent visits to a chiropractor, acupuncturist, and naturopath helped. Instead the discomfort moved up her arm into her shoulder and neck. Mo (as she insisted on being called) suspected something was wrong, but she hesitated to trouble her doctor again. She did not like to complain. But she began having difficulty with daily activities. Her fingers felt like hot dogs, she could barely work a zipper, and she had to stop wearing earrings because her left hand felt so clumsy. It was a great nuisance, interfering with her stretching class, her volunteer job at the jewelry counter of the Bargain Corner shop, and helping out at Loyola Sacred Heart High School.

When the numbness spread and became a throbbing pain in her shoulder and neck in early June, two months after her first visit to Dr. Campo, she returned to him. He was concerned that her symptoms had not improved. He seemed irritated when he told her, "I wish you had come back sooner." Mystified by what ailed Mo, he referred her to a neurologist, who took an even more extensive history and examined her thoroughly. When he had finished, he did not tell her what he thought was wrong, but instead said simply that he strongly recommended an immediate MRI.

Until now the only notable entry on the list of problems in Mo's medical chart had been hypertension. She did not smoke, she barely drank, and her only habit was a great fondness for chewing gum, which she was never without. Sixty-five years old and retired, she had raised six children on her own, and she thoroughly enjoyed a healthy independence.

One of her favorite lifelong pastimes was collecting sayings, epigrams that she clipped from magazines and newspapers. With construction paper and paste she arranged them and inserted them into a premade wooden frame. Although gathered from a variety of sources, many of these sayings expressed a similar theme: "Do not dwell on the past but forge ahead." I wonder if she had these words in mind in the days following the MRI scan of her brain.

The scan showed a large intramedullary lesion, that is, some kind of mass or tumor at the base of her brain. The medical team at St. Patrick's Hospital moved quickly; within a day Mo underwent an angiogram to map the blood supply to this mass. Three days later she was taken to the operating room for an open surgical biopsy of it.

Mo's children had already mobilized, making sure she was not alone when she heard the pathology report. She had called her oldest son, Bill, who also lived in Missoula, before going into surgery, and he had alerted his siblings. Twenty-six-year-old Emily, seven months pregnant with her first child, immediately drove down from her home in Glacier National Park.

The biopsy revealed a grade four glioblastoma, a very fast-growing cancer lodged at the top of her spine and entwining the base of her brain. Dr. Campo told her that she probably had only a handful of weeks to live.

Being naturally reserved, Mo quietly absorbed the news and mulled over the implications. Over the years, the one saying that had become her mantra was: "Don't worry about the mule going blind, just load the wagon." True to her temperament and lifelong style of not fretting over what she could not change, she was pleased by the diagnosis in a perverse way. After hearing it she told the doctor, "This is great. I thought I would go quickly in the middle of the night, and never wake up. But actually, with a few weeks, I can say goodbye to everybody. This is better."

Remarkably, Mo never expressed any regret or irritation over the delay in diagnosis; anger was simply not a color on her emotional palette. Now that she knew what she had, it seemed to her that a month or two would not have made that much difference. Furthermore, women of Mo's generation were raised to believe that it was disrespectful to second-guess a doctor or question a doctor's advice. As far as she was concerned, her physician still knew best. After the surgery and biopsy, Mo stayed at St. Pat's to begin radiation therapy. The treatment was not going to eradicate the cancer, only temporarily shrink the tumor and ease her pain.

Mo's room at St. Patrick's resembled a florist's shop, with huge bouquets and vases of cut flowers lined up along the window sill and on her bedside table and dresser and spilling into the corners. Every day, she asked her children to take the flowers to other patients' rooms, and every morning, more were delivered. She had legions of visitors: women who knew her from the Bargain Corner, fellow volunteers and other parishioners, and her sizable family, which extended beyond her six children, with assorted spouses, to five siblings, assorted aunts, uncles, nieces, and nephews, and a handful of grandchildren. Mary McCall, a hospice nurse who was a friend and regular customer at Mo's Bargain Corner jewelry counter, stopped by to see her pal almost daily. On her first visit, she brought flowers, and a card on which she had written "If you're going to die, you can't do it without tattoos!" enclosing a washable "tattoo" of Betty Boop. The two women howled with glee as they debated where Mo should put it; long ago they had promised each other that someday they would decorate themselves with something permanent. Upbeat yet honest, with a quick wit and an easy laugh, Mo had many fans.

The day before she was to be discharged, a meeting was held in Mo's hospital room. The two sons who lived in Missoula, Bill and Bud, crowded around her bed, while daughter Emily occupied the sole chair, and Dr. Karen Stegner, the radiation oncologist, stood at the end of the bed. Blond and tanned, Emily looked remarkably trim for a woman in the third trimester of pregnancy. The men fussed with Mo's pillow, checked her water pitcher for fresh ice, and straightened the arrangement of greeting cards propped up on the dresser.

With Mo's chart in hand, Dr. Stegner spoke in a dispassionate but respectful tone as she described the cancer in medical detail: its exact location, size, and shape, and its effect on nearby tissue and the spinal cord. She reviewed the potential benefits and possible risks of radiation and chemotherapy. It was evident that this doctor had had these sorts of discussions many times. She avoided outlining Mo's prognosis in terms of cold statistics, as is so often done. Although she presented the relevant numbers, Dr. Stegner intentionally painted what lay ahead as an impressionist might—in broad strokes, shaped by expectations of disease progression and colored by likely symptoms and diminished functions.

"This is a high-grade astrocytoma. It is likely that very soon it will begin to affect your gross neurologic functions: balance, coordination, movement, sensory loss. You may experience headaches or more of the electrical sensations you had initially. We'll be asking about these things frequently, and you should be sure to let us know whatever you're feeling. We can adjust your medicines or do whatever is necessary to make sure you're not hurting too much." She paused and softened her voice. "You probably know the outlook is not good. We can possibly buy you a little more time, but there's no guarantee."

Mo listened with a slight smile. She had prepared her children for this day years ago. As a single mother, she had always been concerned about what would happen if she died. She had made plans and told the kids about her will, funeral preferences, and organ donor wishes. She had clipped and given to everyone an article from the *Missoulian* about grown children caring for terminally ill parents, writing marginal notes like "Yes! Let's talk" alongside an explanation of Comfort One, Montana's "do not resuscitate" directive.

"Is it all right for Mom to be at home?" Bill asked anxiously.

"No problem at all. We'll get the hospice folks involved." The doctor looked at Mo, acknowledging a previous conversation they had had about hospice. Mo had brought the subject up, having heard about our hospice through Mary McCall. Dr. Stegner also knew that this would be the first time the family would be hearing hospice mentioned with regard to their mother's care.

"And we'll discharge her with a small moving van of stuff. Hospital bed, commode, quad cane, wheelchair, walker," she continued.

"I don't like a lot of mess and fuss," Mo said, with good-natured sternness. "I don't think we have enough room for all that stuff! Sounds like you're outfitting me for a garage sale!"

"Don't you worry, Mom," Emily interjected. "We'll find a place for it."

"If I know you," Mo teased, "you'll just shove it anywhere, and the place will look like a junkyard." Emily chuckled and rolled her eyes; when she had lived at home, this had been a constant arm-wrestling match between them. The daughter was a casual housekeeper with a healthy tolerance for chaos and clutter, and the mother loved order and clean surfaces. Now Emily had decided to move to Missoula to live with and care for her mother, while her husband stayed in Glacier Park. Their two temperaments would initially clash again. But this time the conflict would be a source of amusement more than acrimony. Emily's brothers in Missoula had offered their homes, but their complicated family lives made her move the best arrangement for everybody.

The group would have continued to banter and tease each other if Dr. Stegner had not sobered them up with her next remark.

"Your mother tells me she has decided not to pursue any further treatment. No more radiation therapy, no chemotherapy. She will accept medication for pain and other symptoms, but that is all." She waited a moment before continuing.

"Of course, the decision is hers, and I have no doubt that it is an informed and considered decision. I and the rest of the doctors will certainly respect it. But oftentimes family members have lingering doubts, and I wanted to meet with you all so that I might answer any questions."

She flipped through Mo's chart as she spoke and made no eye contact, but waited.

The three children looked at their mother. Mo waved her right hand in dismissal, breaking a bubble of tension.

"They know everything I know. I'm dying, and nothing's going to change that, so let's get the show on the road. I'm tired and I want to go home." Mo was not glossing over this momentous decision but summarizing hours of earlier conversations with her children over the last four days. While she had made up her mind that she did not want more treatment, until now she had hesitated to say so, because Dr. Campo was pressuring her to continue radiation therapy. Emily, irritated by her mom's reluctance to assert herself, had been urging her to do what *she* wanted to do. They had argued about what Mo should say to Dr. Campo.

At one point, while defending her acquiescence to beginning the radiation treatments, Mo had exclaimed, "But it seems so important to him, Emily!" Hearing her own words, she had looked sheepishly at her daughter, shook her head, and smiled slightly. Her expression admitted she would ultimately have to do what *she* thought was right. "I'm the one who's dying, after all," she softly chuckled.

In preparing to meet Mo and reviewing her chart, I was struck by two notes written just before she was discharged. The consulting neurologist summarized her condition and concluded: "Prognosis is abysmal." But his last progress note included the entry: "Patient cheerful. Has decided against further treatment."

My visit with Mo was at the house that she, and now Emily, occupied in a neighborhood of duplexes with carports, small lawns, and broad-limbed maple trees. Her home was sparsely furnished, with area rugs over hardwood floors and a few simple pieces of Scandinavian-style furniture. Mo's penchant for order and simplicity was apparent. Most of the walls were bare; centered on one wall was a colorful God's eye, a remnant of Emily's counterculture days, I suspected. A chair in the corner of the living room, however, was selected for comfort as well as function. Large, upholstered, and pink, it reclined or contracted to help the occupant lie down or stand up. This was Mo's throne. On both sides of it were tables stacked with note cards and stationery, and behind it, underneath the window, was a full bookshelf. She spent most of her waking hours here, writing thank-you notes or watching the hang gliders who soared in the summer skies over Mount Sentinel. At her side was a schedule book to manage the daily flow of visiting friends.

Petite, white-haired, and perky, Mo presented her medical history succinctly, in a businesslike manner, the way an intern might present a case to an attending physician. "The pain began as a tingling sensation—at times it burned—in the thumb and index finger; that's the C7 and C8 nerves," she explained. We reviewed the various medications she was taking: Tegretol to prevent seizures, Decadron to reduce swelling around the tumor, Lortab to treat her pain. She reported little current discomfort, except for a stiff neck and feeling like "a board is pressing on my shoulder." Not only was her appetite healthy, but she was enjoying regular splurges; probably a side-effect of the Decadron, I thought. At one point during our conversation she said, "When you visit again I'd be most grateful if you would stop by the Dairy Queen up the street and pick me up a Nut Whip. Of course, I'll reimburse you. They're awfully good—my days just aren't complete without a Nut Whip!" Mo had let me know that I was OK, one of the people she would like to have come around. I felt honored.

When I broached the subject of the limited time left to her, she expressed a unique sadness.

"I'm a bit disappointed that I'm still alive or not sicker," she declared. "When I found out about this astrocytoma, I was glad it was this great big tumor rather than some dinky little polyp that was going to get me. I've said my goodbyes, my life is in order, the kids are taken care of. Actually," she reflected, "I've been ready for a while."

Her high-spirited conviction took me aback, and I wondered whether the Decadron was also causing a touch of mania. I asked Emily, who was pregnantly propped on the edge of the couch, "Does your mother's attitude shock you?"

"Oh, no," she laughed. "That's normal for Mom! Nothing by half-measures and no regrets."

Still, I wondered whether it was totally true. "I gather that you're due soon," I commented.

She beamed. "Yup, at the end of August. We're going to have a little girl."

"Perhaps you would like to record or write down some of the stories from your youth," I suggested to Mo, "for your new granddaughter and other grandchildren. You might enjoy telling the stories, and I am sure your family would love to have them."

Mo frowned. "I don't think so. It would be nice if I'm still here when the baby is born, but if not, so be it. I don't think a tedious account of 'the old days' would be of much interest to her or anyone else. As I said earlier, Dr. Byock, I've had a wonderful, full life, and if I died right now, there'd be no regrets or loose ends."

We talked about the timing of her passing. I explained that if her symptoms ever reached the point where the quality of her life was untenable, she could selectively choose to stop taking her Decadron medication, and probably hasten her demise. By reducing the tumor swelling, the Decadron was providing Mo with a relative plateau of function and comfort; its withdrawal would result in a steeper angle of decline. I emphasized again, for them both to hear, that under no circumstances would I or the hospice team allow her to suffer physically.

Patients often exhibit an uncanny control over the timing of their death. The basic time frame seems to be fixed by the primary diagnosis and the patient's general constitution, but a person may consciously or unconsciously decide to stay alive for an anniversary, Christmas, or another special holiday, or to complete an important relationship. In my experience, one person may live weeks or months beyond initial expectations in order to accomplish such a goal, while another with a similar condition may die suddenly during a period of apparent medical stability after an important occasion has passed. If anyone could exert this kind of control, it would be Mo. Yet she denied any such motivation. I probed a bit, wondering about the upcoming birth of her new granddaughter, and hoping her conviction to die quickly was not a facade that obscured deeper reservations.

After talking for at least an hour, Mo said she was tired and wanted to take a nap. I rose to leave; Emily helped her mother from her chair and readied the walker. We said goodbye, I gave her arm a gentle squeeze, and then I stood aside.

As they shuffled toward the bedroom, Mo told her daughter, "Now, I just want to make one stop. I need to fold that towel and put it in the linen closet."

"All right, Mom, but just one," Emily replied. They paused at the hall closet, and Emily casually stuffed the towel into the cupboard.

"Dear, not that way! *Folded*." Mo affectionately swatted her daughter. "Now, one second. I need to move that vase—it doesn't belong there."

Emily snorted in amusement. "OK, just one more detour, then you're really taking a nap!" I quietly slipped out the kitchen door.

Despite the doctor's prediction and Mo's desire to "go out like gangbusters," she lived through June and July and well into August. I visited twice a month, mostly to check on how she was doing, adjust medications, and continue our ongoing discussion of her preferences regarding one detail or another of the treatment plan. On a visit in late July, I met Mo's newly arrived granddaughter, Lindsey. Emily took me into the baby's room; Lindsey cooed and gurgled as I stroked her downy newborn hair. It was an usually hot August; a small fan whirred over the crib and swung the mobile suspended above it, mesmerizing the baby.

"How's your mom doing? She must be very happy to meet her new granddaughter," I ventured.

"Oh, definitely. She can't do much, but she loves just holding her, and rocking her with her cane." Emily replied. She looked tired. Given the dual responsibilities of caring for a newborn and an ailing mother, she was no doubt running on adrenaline. The brothers who lived locally, Bill and Bud, came over in the evenings to relieve her, and the Seattle siblings, Jason and Greg, drove over to visit and help out on the weekends, but the bulk of the care still fell to this exceptional young mother.

"I'm surprised she's done as well as she has for as long as she has," I said. "Do you think the thought of Lindsey was keeping her going?"

"You know, we never really talked about it after that first discussion with you. She's been very accepting of whatever's going on, living one day at a time. If Lindsey's birth was a motivation, it wasn't a big one. She isn't the type of person to set herself up for disappointment. It wouldn't be in Mom's nature to say, 'I want to live until the baby comes.' " Emily spoke without sentiment, but I could not help wondering whether little Lindsey would add a new note of sadness in Mo's dying.

Emily picked up her cherubic daughter and joined Mo in the living room. The curtains were drawn to keep the room cool, and the air was still, with a faint smell of talcum. Gail Kerscher, the hospice nurse, had just finished changing Mo's urinary catheter and was tidying. Physically, Mo's appearance had changed since I had seen her just two weeks earlier; her face was more edematous, having puffed up from the medications. Her clothes, once neat and tucked in, now tended toward oversize smocks and casual shirts. But she was still ensconced in her pink throne, looking cheerful and comfortable, if slightly sweaty. Wisps of white hair were matted against her temples. I gave her a small hug and sat down beside her. Emily put Lindsey in a rocking crib on the other side of Mo, then disappeared into the kitchen. Mo gave her granddaughter a brief, tender glance, then smiled at me.

"Gorgeous, isn't she," she declared.

"Yup, sure is. A little doll." I paused. "How are you doing?"

"Oh, not bad. Better now that Gail's changed that confounded catheter," she said.

Mo had lost control of her bladder and required a catheter to stay dry, but she had enough residual sensation in the area to be bothered by annoying catheter irritation. While these plumbing problems had begun before her first hospitalization, they had been aggravated in the hospital when an X-ray technician had inadvertently pulled on the tubing of her urine bag in transferring her from her wheelchair to the radiology table and nearly yanked the catheter out. For days afterward her urine had been tinged orange, and she had intermittent discomfort from bladder spasms. The nurses changed her catheter several times in an attempt to quell the symptoms—procedures that, for someone as modest and particular about her appearance as Mo, were surely upsetting, I thought.

"I'm sorry you're still having so much trouble with all this. Do you need any more supplies, like the soothing gel, or those B&O suppositories?" I asked, referring to some of the things that had recently been helping.

"You'll have to ask Emily. She's in charge of that kind of thing." She chuckled to herself. "Whenever she changes Lindsey, I'm next, no matter who's around. I might as well be walking around the house with no clothes on!"

I shook my head in amazement. Out of necessity, Mo had shed her modesty as one might set aside a favorite wool coat for the spring. Emily served us a cup of herbal tea, and we talked about the new baby. After a time, Mo asked me to look out the window; she pointed to a hang glider high above Mt. Sentinel and told me she had read about one who had sailed all the way to Bozeman. As I prepared to leave, Mo's sister, Ruth, arrived. An older, sterner version of Mo, wearing a long, shapeless skirt, starched blouse, and a small cross pendant, Ruth was a nun. She visited Mo every day. A weekly churchgoer and active parishioner, Mo nevertheless was quiet about her religious beliefs. She never spoke of spiritual matters, and I never saw any of the usual signs of Catholicism—crosses, rosaries, prayer books—around the house. We exchanged greetings, and Emily showed me out as Ruth sat down and, while speaking to Mo, deftly extracted a rosary from her bag.

Emily and I stood next to my car for a few moments in the hot, dry sun.

"I usually slip out when Ruth shows up," Emily said.

"Oh?" I said neutrally.

"Yeah, I'm not much for church things. My brothers and I did the whole bit growing up—Catholic schools, catechism, Sunday school—but none of us stayed in the church. I guess I'm an agnostic now." She pushed her blond hair off her forehead and squinted into the sun.

"How does your mom take that? Do you think it bothers her that you and your brothers are not more Catholic?" I asked.

"Nah. Mom's amazing. She never said a thing when I stopped going to church. I've got my own ideas of faith and spiritual matters, which have a lot to do with nature and the land, and Mom knows this and it's fine with her. She really respects that I have my own beliefs. Mom's own spirituality is strong. She's not threatened by my brothers and me making our own choices—she doesn't need our agreement to boost her own faith," Emily softly boasted. I got into the car and she waved goodbye.

Two weeks later Emily telephoned me, sounding worried. Reflecting on her confidence and competence, I knew that something serious must have happened. She explained that for days Mo had been sleeping a lot more and feeling lousy. She was bothered by headaches, which were not severe but were interfering with her ability to sit up and enjoy visiting. At times they lasted for hours, despite the current pain medicine, and they made her so dizzy that she could not stand up. Her vision was so blurry that she could not read or watch television, and over the last week her appetite had diminished to nil. Mo was not complaining, but Emily felt that I should see her and become more actively involved. Before I could ask Emily what she thought might be causing these changes, she told me that the previous week Dr. Campo had cut the Decadron dosage in half and was recommending that Mo be put in a nursing home for twenty-four-hour care. I was surprised, because the Decadron was a critical component of her current medical care.

"You know Mom. Always taking care of everybody. She'd do it for his sake. She'll do whatever her physician wants," she said, her voice full of frustration. "And Dr. Campo, he doesn't see my mom, he's just thinking that it will be easier for him. He only sees a medical situation, not a person."

I told Emily that I would come by later in the day and talk to her mother and, perhaps, adjust her medications. Mo was napping when I arrived. Emily, Bill, and Bud were in the kitchen doing dishes and talking quietly. The house smelled of tomato sauce and garlic. I sat at a faded Formica table under the window as they puttered.

"Do you think the tumor's growing?" Bill asked, as he dried the plates Emily handed him. "She's been good for so long, like a remission. Maybe it's started to grow again. We were going to eat out on the patio tonight. Mom loves to sit outside, but she couldn't get that far. She's really weak."

"Very possibly. These things can move in fits and spurts, with long periods of stability, then rampant growth. It also may be the smaller dose of Decadron," I replied. "Cause and effect are a little jumbled, but your mother certainly can steer the course of events here to some extent. Going back up on the Decadron dose might well buy some more time. Like the decision about chemotherapy, the medication and retirement home questions are up to her, and you. This is a personal decision for her and your family to make."

Bud, who was sitting on the other side of the table, chimed in. "Retirement home?! No way, Dr. Byock. We all think it's a stupid idea, and Dr. Campo only suggested it because he feels guilty over not diagnosing her sooner. Mom's staying right here."

"Would it help if she went back up on the Decadron?" Bud asked, as if to pin me down.

"It might. We'd have to see."

As if on cue, Mo called from the bedroom, and we all trooped in to see her. Curled up on her right side, she looked pale and frail, and had clearly lost weight. She was wearing a lightweight housecoat with a V-neck; it revealed the walnut-sized washable tattoos that Mary had given her of Betty Boop, hands on tilted hips, winking. Her room was minimally furnished and clear of clutter. A vase of orange marigolds decorated the dresser.

"Gee, Dr. Ira, what does a girl have to do to get a little attention around here?" she teased, and coquettishly batted her eyelashes.

"Just whistle, and I'll come running," I retorted.

She puckered up, but no sound came. "Oh, well," she sighed, "there goes another one of my talents out the window." I noticed she went back to chewing, and that the ever-present gum now helped to keep her mouth moist.

"Mom, we think you should reconsider your medication," Bud offered, as he sat on the edge of her bed and indicated a side chair for me. He was not a large man, but he had a strong, square face and bright blue eyes. He was an attorney in town and spoke with authority. Emily had left the room to see to Lindsey, and Bud leaned against the doorjamb.

Mo looked toward me for an answer. "According to your chart, Dr. Campo has halved your Decadron, and as I mentioned before, it can have a noticeable impact on how you feel," I said. "Tell me, Mo, how do you feel you are doing? How's the quality of your life these days?"

At first, she looked at me with the most somber expression I'd ever seen on her face. She appeared almost suddenly ill and older than I'd previously noticed. "I've been feeling pretty crappy these last couple of days. My head has started to ache, even to lift it, and I've been sick to my stomach unless I lie very still." She was quiet for a moment, and then looked up at me. Her eyes twinkled. "I have a good life visiting with my friends, and being around my children and watching little Lindsey. Yes, I have a good life," she said.

"I know the subject of a nursing home and radiation treatment have been raised. Are these things you want to do?" I tested. Emily had returned, but she hung back, possibly keeping an ear open for sounds of Lindsey.

"I don't want more treatment, Dr. Ira. I don't have much interest in dragging this out, and it seems to me that any new treatment would do that. The nursing home is another matter. I'm enough of a burden for these kids. I've already lived far beyond my time." Mo smiled at her three children, and I noticed a small line of tears rolling down her cheeks.

"Oh, Mom, don't say that!" Emily exclaimed.

"You all must be very tired of helping me to the bathroom and changing this confounded pee bag and cleaning up after me." Her voice trailed off, and for the first time, I saw Mo overcome with tears. Her children swarmed around her like bees protecting their queen, each reassuring her. I wanted to speak, but this was not the time; I waited until a look from Emily invited my help.

"Mo, I know you hate being a burden to your children." I spoke to the whole family. "I know you don't like being unable to do things for yourself. But in fact they need to care for you, for their own sake. They need to do it for their own grieving. This is an important part of how we grieve the loss of those we love. This is something you can give them, letting them take care of you. They love you very much, and want to do this. They *need* to do this."

"He's right, Mom," Bud said. "This is something we want to do. We love you, and we need to take care of you," he emphasized, picking up on my cue. "Think of all the years you wiped our noses and bandaged our scrapes and tucked us in. What's a couple of tubes and a little pee between friends? This way you can see how well you raised us! It's our turn, please." His voice trailed off.

"Yeah," Bill added. "And I'll make sure you get a Nut Whip every day!" We all burst out laughing, though Mo was still teary.

"You are dear children," she said sweetly, "but you have your own lives and your own children. You can't be always running over here to fuss over me."

"Mother!" Emily protested. "*We want to be here*. Really, nothing would make us happier. If you went to a nursing home, we'd be miserable, worrying about you all day, and having to take shifts to be with you there. I love living here with you. This has been the greatest summer of my life, the best time we've ever had together. Please, stop arguing. Let us be your children, let us love you."

Mo's assent was a simple smile and a steady stream of tears, as she and her children gazed lovingly at each other. They had decided to push on. "What a privilege to be here!" I thought, and I was aware that my own eyes were full. I wondered what the family must think of this doctor in their midst, as I wiped away tears with the back of my hand. For the moment, Mo's life seemed too rich to let it slip away. We revisited the options, I encouraged her to let me boost her Decadron and adjust her pain and nausea medications, and she readily agreed.

With these changes, Mo's condition temporarily improved; her discomfort diminished and her vision cleared. She again began to enjoy her days—and for several weeks the simple pleasures of visiting, answering letters with Emily's help, and holding Lindsey. In late September she again began to deteriorate significantly. The numbness in her left arm had graduated to nearly total paralysis on that side. She was wheelchair-bound and beset by dull, nuisance headaches. The weather was still warm enough, but she was now unable to sit outside under the spreading maple tree. Although her appetite was now nil, she still relished her daily spoonfuls of ice cream and other treats and regularly sipped juice or herbal tea. She was losing weight rapidly and sleeping much of the time.

When I stopped by the house on a Saturday morning, Mo was sleeping, and Emily nursed Lindsey while we talked. Emily's husband, Dean, who came down from Glacier Park every weekend, was outside changing the oil in their car. The sky was deep blue; it was a crystal clear day, and the living room was washed in sunlight. The metallic sound of Dean's wrench clanging inside the car could be heard. Also visiting were two harpists from the Chalice of Repose program at St. Patrick's Hospital. Trained to play for seriously ill patients and their families, they were here at hospice's request and with Mo's consent. The Chalice music is deeply soothing to many people who are anxious or distraught, and is always a gift of beauty. Its almost ethereal quality makes you understand why angels are often depicted playing harps.

Not wanting to interrupt, I stood at the door and listened until the harpists had completed their musical vigil.

"She's been sleeping a lot, but when she's awake, she seems pretty content," Emily explained. "She's cheerful and she smiles often, but she hasn't been saying much. You know, it reminds me of some of our Christmas mornings as a family. When we were kids, she was always Mom—in charge, organizing meals, and saying when we could open our packages. But as we got older she played less of the role of the parent, and more of just being there with us. She kind of stepped back into the background and just enjoyed watching us have a good time."

The memory of those times choked her up for a moment; she cleared her throat and continued. "She's stepping back now, too. At times, Mom seems detached and stares off into space, as if she's not here."

"That's not uncommon," I said. "It's like she's letting go of worldly attachments and focusing on someplace beyond."

Emily looked uncertain. "But every now and then, she perks up. This morning she woke up and announced she really wanted a cheeseburger with fries and a beer! And a Nut Whip, of course! It was wonderful. I've never seen Bud move so fast for the Dairy Queen!"

"Was she able to eat much of it?" I asked.

"Only a couple of bites, but she enjoyed them," she said.

"Emily, can you give me an idea of just how many hours a day she's sleeping?" I was trying to get a more complete picture of Mo's current status.

"At least fourteen or even eighteen hours for the last three days or so. At times it's hard to say whether she's actually sleeping. When she is awake she seems truly happy, as if she is gently floating. I thought she slept through the Chalice music, but she was just resting, and I saw in her eyes that she really liked it. She's awake now. I know she wants to see you."

Mo was in bed, curled up on her right side. She looked tiny and white, a wisp of a woman. It is a paradox of dying that a person can seem to grow strikingly in the realms of spirit and of soul as her physical self dramatically shrinks. I sat in the chair beside her bed; after three or four minutes, she opened her eyes. The Chalice harpists were quietly putting away their instruments. When I next turned around, they had left.

"Hi, Mo, you don't need to talk," I said softly. "I just wanted to come by and make sure you're all right."

She opened her eyes, which were still clear and brilliant. They seemed to be emanating light. We gazed into each other's eyes, and as she gave me a smile, her eyes teared up, and so did mine. She was radiant! I was half-crying and half-laughing in wonderment at this marvelous lady.

"Are you OK in there?" I asked, knowing the answer.

For a moment, she seemed to concentrate, as if grasping for the right answer. She began working her tongue and mouth. I wondered what she was trying to say. Her mouth opened, and there on the tip of her tongue was a small pink wad of gum! Mo still had her gum, and this was her way of letting me know that she was still "in there." While her body was barely alive, her spirit was strong and soaring.

I stayed for only twenty or thirty minutes. As I walked down the hall from Mo's room, I noticed a picture frame with a display of her collection of favorite sayings. I paused to read them, and one stuck with me: "Every death is a door opening on Creation's mystery." Mo was moving toward the mystery, and I knew she was well and unafraid.

Gail telephoned me later that afternoon. Mo had died fifteen minutes earlier, with Emily and Bill by her bedside. About an hour before she died, her breathing had become labored, each cycle a loud rattle and wheeze. I had ordered that a small amount of morphine be on hand for just such a purpose, and it promptly provided comfort. She rested, her breathing eased. Emily had just wiped her brow with a cool washcloth when Mo turned her head and quietly expired.

As much as any patient I have known, Mo personified the possibility of a joy within the process of letting go, transcending this world, and growing into an unexplored, spiritual realm. At the end of life, Mo had "self-actualized," to use Abraham Maslow's term, having mastered critical landmarks within the *inter*personal, *intra*personal and *trans*personal—or transcendent—realms of the self. She seemed to have achieved a sense of meaning about her own life and an inexpressible sense of meaning or profound appreciation about life in general.

A person dying may or may not use religious terms to describe this type of experience, but may speak of feelings of inner expansion and a connection to a whole that is elemental and absolute. Of course, for many people it is natural to describe themselves as feeling closer to God. These are not deathbed conversions; this deepened sense of connection typically occurs within the tradition in which one has been raised or has practiced. Emotionally, the person letting go of all that is worldly may feel exhilaration or a deep, still serenity. Outwardly, she may be joyful and, to the extent that strength allows, engaging. Or she may appear to withdraw, paying less attention to conversation and showing less interest in visiting, even with her closest loved ones. During this time a person may be quiet for long periods and, when asked, answer that she is in no pain or discomfort.

To family, as well as to caregivers who are unfamiliar with terminal care, people who have begun to focus on internal processes and concerns beyond their immediate world may appear confused. A person may seem to be watching or listening, and speaking, to others who died years earlier. These others, whom family and caregivers cannot see or hear, may or may not be real in some absolute sense. But they are certainly real to the person. This phenomenon of "nearing death awareness" is not rare. It has been beautifully explored and explicated by two experienced hospice nurses, Maggie Callanan and Patricia Kelly, in their book *Final Gifts*.

The taskwork that underlies the transcendent landmarks involves developing a new sense of self, a transformation from worldly person into a new spiritual identity. One's old self, including the pain of personal loss, drops away as one's focus shifts to matters of the spirit. The only taskwork necessary here may be to acknowledge that one is "new" and that one's experienced identity is fluid, evolving in an ever more meaningful direction.

Although she only alluded to it on occasion, Mo was helped in her journey by prayer. Her faith and religious conviction provided a foundation of confidence for moving toward the unknown without fear, ultimately allowing her to let go even of the pangs of loss. Perhaps her sister's daily visits to say the rosary strengthened her even further.

Religious beliefs and formal prayer are not the only source of spiritual guidance for people. In a manner similar to "nonintercessory" prayer, practices such as meditation can help a person to center his swirling thoughts and calm his emotions. From this plane of peace, one can begin to explore the transcendent realm of self. While meditation tends to be associated with Eastern spirituality, meditative practices are found within every religious faith. During meditation, a person's mind is alert and attentive yet still, grasping at nothing. By cultivating this skill of pure awareness, a person can develop the perspective of a witness, counter-balancing the sense of being an unwilling actor—or victim—in life's drama. The contemplative practice of prayer or meditation can provide a place of safety and distance—not from, but *within*, the experience. This ability to remain centered and "well within oneself" in the middle of distraction, doubt, anxiety, and bodily discomfort is recognized by many cultures and religious traditions as being critical preparation for the transition from life.

In addition, a number of what have come to be called alternative or complementary therapies are resources for inner growth. Hatha yoga can serve a purpose similar to meditation, through the gentle practice of holding postures. A variety of massage therapies can provide moments of peace and generate positive physical memories to balance the pain of illness. Therapeutic touch is an increasingly accepted nursing technique that projects the therapeutic intent of the practitioner to help unblock and move energy within the patient.

Insight therapy, a general term for a variety of talking therapies, can often help a person explore her spiritual depths. Dreamwork, for instance, can uncover rich and valuable material from the field of the unconscious. Breath work, which may range from the ancient yogic practice of pranayama to Holotropic Breathing, recently developed by Dr. Stanislav Grof, can allow access to otherwise hidden domains of personal and transcendent experience.

Each of these disciplines has its enthusiasts. A person's culture, values, beliefs, and temperament will all have an influence on which, if any, practice will be helpful. All these techniques and therapies foster a sense of composure and openness—"vulnerability" is perhaps a better word—despite the fact that lack of control is a dominant characteristic of dying. By relaxing body and mind, a person can become more open to the mystery that awaits: what a poet has called "the close and holy darkness." This tender vulnerability seems a prerequisite for the deepest tasks of inner development.

Death is the cosmic bell whose ring we hear, ever so faintly, even at the beginning of life. As its peal begins to ache in our ears and rattle our chest, how hard it must be to stay open! In my clinical work with people who are dying, I find that some form of contemplative practice is invaluable, if not essential, for myself as well. At some level of clinical care and counseling with dying persons, it is not what I do but rather *how I am* with a person that seems to matter most. In order to interact authentically and naturally with a dying person, while providing a space within which she can say—or not say—whatever she needs to, I, too, must cultivate some distance, not from, but *within*, the experience of impending mortality.

Of the various techniques just mentioned, I have direct familiarity only with meditation. For me, meditation is the quintessential practice in achieving comfort with chaos. Some days there is nothing so chaotic as sitting quietly and watching my mind—not following a particular train of thought or achieving any tangible goal, just watching and staying open.

Art is a natural expression and evocation of the deeper self that for many people provides another important source of guidance within the transcendent or spiritual aspects of life. "Good art" is good because it exposes and successfully conveys a valuable perspective or insight. Whether it is visual, theatrical, or musical, high art resonates within the viewer or listener. In being receptive to artistic works or expression, a person opens up and exposes a deeper self. Music can also evoke a sense of expansion and an experience of connection that, at times, gives rise to exhilaration. At its best, music can stir the spirit and soul, drawing the listener into a sense of connection that the composer or performers experienced at its creation. Similarly, participatory chants such as Hindu *kirtan* and Sufi singing and dancing invite direct experience of the transcendent.

In Missoula, the Chalice of Repose program provides musical guidance for a number of patients at this most critical time. The Chalice program is based on the work of Therese Schroeder-Sheker, a virtuoso harpist, vocalist, and accomplished medieval scholar, who has ministered at the bedside of dying persons for over two decades, offering gifts of profound, audible beauty and transcendent serenity. The clinical services of Chalice workers have become a valuable component of the care we provide for patients who are agitated or experiencing a pervasive sense of "dis-ease." We offer Chalice services for patients who we sense would benefit from a gift of beauty.

Doctors often seem unsettled by transcendent experiences and tend to regard them with some suspicion. A physician might not believe that Mo's ethereal state was real and might seek to explain it in terms of medications and metabolism. He might see her euphoria as a "toxic state" and thus discount it. Anyone who has been in the presence of someone in a state like Mo's knows that the question of whether or not the experience is "real" is irrelevant. Transcendence may well elude medical authentication. So what? Real or imagined, no one can deny the legitimacy and enormous value of euphoria for the patient who experiences it, and for the person's family.

At the edge of the transcendent—in the midst of "letting go"—a person who has completed the work of development does not disintegrate in dying. Rather, she *dissolves* out of life, becoming increasingly ephemeral—less dense or corporeal—but no less integrated, in the passage from life. Personhood becomes gauzy and translucent. Having completed and released the various realms and spheres of his or her previous self, the person who is surrendering to the transcendent is little more than the process itself. "Letting go" is all that is left.

Work on the realms of spirit and soul is, of course, influenced by one's culture, religious tradition, family life, philosophical perspective, and life experiences, but it is inherently intimate and deeply personal. In this last phase, as a person grows on out of life, there may be little for the family members or caregivers of a dying patient to contribute. Sometimes the best we can do is simply acknowledge the importance of the process, encouraging and protecting it by explaining the process to others whose own grief might interfere with the inner work of the dying person.

Maureen Riley's transcendence was surely aided by the way she had lived her life. Living well throughout her adult life provided invaluable preparation for dying well. Raising six children by herself, she chose early on to communicate fully and clearly with her children and friends. While nurturing her family, she did not neglect her inner self, her independence, and her identity as someone more than Mother of Six or Bargain Corner Volunteer. Mo was as complete a person as I have ever known. In dying, this completeness gave her freedom to let go of her self and grow on into pure spirit.

Twelve

Getting There from Here: Social and Cultural Dimensions

The stories in this book document the human capacity to experience meaning and value within the process of illness and dying. The fact that we all share this capacity, both as individuals and as members of our communities, has implications for our nation and for our culture. Some of us, like Maureen Riley, may find the ability to transcend suffering; others, like Douglas, can find meaning within the experience of suffering. Like Terry Matthews's and Michael Merseal's families, some will find that a community forms around their tragedy. We need to reflect on the meaning of these stories. Beyond their power as individual stories, they can teach us some public policy lessons and show us the need for changing our culture.

First, let's examine the social context of dying in America today. People who are told they have an incurable illness—whether cancer, ALS, or a relentless form of heart, lung, or kidney disease—suffer in fear, and their families suffer with them. Tragically, in America today, these fears are well founded. People fear tangible things related to when and how they will eventually die: being abandoned; becoming undignified in terms of what they do, how they look, and how they smell; being a burden to their families—not only a physical strain, but also a financial hardship; dying in pain. Studies confirm what people already know: Physical pain among the dying remains uncontrolled, often unaddressed, and certain groups of people are at much greater risk than others. In America, you have a greater chance of dying in pain if you don't speak English, and if you are black, Hispanic, poor, elderly, or a woman.

To make matters worse, the current health care crisis has caused many people to be pauperized simply because of being incurably ill and not dying quickly enough. Driven by Medicare and the insurance industry to reduce expenditures associated with the last year of life, hospitals, clinics, and HMOs have instituted an array of cost-containment measures reflecting a de facto strategy of "doing more with less." What this translates into, of course, is that the costs of care are being increasingly shifted onto the backs of the patients and families in need. Thus, in addition to the emotional stress of illness and dependency, the prospect of needing help with bathing, dressing, and meal preparation brings with it the real likelihood of serious financial strain for the patient and family. A comprehensive survey of the impact on the family of caring for a seriously ill loved one confirmed just that: 20 percent of families reported that a member had to quit work, delay his own medical care, or make another major life change to provide the needed care; 29 percent of families experienced the loss of most, or all, of their major source of income; and 31 percent reported the loss of most or all family savings.

When help is given by society, it is begrudging. To be terminally ill or elderly in America today is to be reminded frequently that you are a drain on the nation's resources. The reminders are communicated in myriad subtle and not-so-subtle ways through the media and in the statements of policymakers, and are reflected in the policies of insurance companies and the institutional requirements for health care, housing, and various aging services. The message to the elderly and the incurably ill is: Limit your use of resources and get out of the way to make room for those who are younger, vigorous, and still able to contribute to society.

These social realities directly impact the personal experience of dying. A dying father who feels that he is a drain on his family, physically and financially, will experience being a burden every moment of every day; that will be what his life has come to mean. Though his wife and children may affectionately acknowledge his years of love and selfless devotion, he will fret, feel worthless, and suffer.

Some of the causes of this crisis in end-of-life care are easily identified; others are deeper, more subtle, and more difficult to discern. Deficiencies in medical and nursing education are important contributing factors. Care for persons as they die is still inadequately taught; it rarely occupies more than a few hours within required course curriculums. Within the university teaching hospitals where doctors and nurses are trained, the culture of curative medicine is entrenched, and the values of caring are subordinate. Attention is directed toward preserving life at all costs—quite literally. Considerations of money, physical comfort, human dignity, and the quality of life experience are, at best, secondary. Commonly, when patients or their families raise questions about living wills and the avoidance of heroic measures, they are told that such concerns are premature, that there is "still so much that can be done." Oncology fellows, for instance, train in specialized referral medical centers where they learn that the optimal treatment for a patient who has "failed chemotherapy" is a clinical trial of ever more toxic regimens and all-out efforts to forestall death. Within this medical mind-set, the alternative of palliative care or home hospice care is rarely considered. People's medical training acts as a filter, through which too often they can see only curative or life-prolonging options. The problem is not that medical professionals are heartless, but rather that the goals of end-of-life care are often not well considered, if they are considered at all. Physicians and nurses remain strikingly unaware that alternative approaches to care for dying persons exist. When I explain end-of-life care, to church groups or service groups, such as Kiwanis or the Rotary, or to undergraduate students, they tend to get the idea immediately. It is not that they know more, but rather that they have to unlearn so much less.

Health care financing policies that limit resources for the dying also contribute to the crisis in end-of-life care. Trends in hospice funding and the resulting availability and quality of hospice care illustrate this problem and the fact that it cuts across race and class lines. Medicare and Medicaid reimbursement structures for hospice were set in the mid-1980s and have not been modified since their inception. With the advent of the HIV epidemic and with recent advances in palliative care, funding is now insufficient, and many community-based hospice programs are threatened with extinction. Within large profit-oriented health care corporations, a number of new hospice programs are emerging, but they tend to target patients whose care is less complicated and less expensive. Very few developing hospice programs are community based or are directed toward indigent patients, patients with AIDS, or others who require complex, costly care. This is not just a problem for the poor. The insufficient funding and access to robust hospice care impacts all of us.

Within the corporate cultures of insurance companies and managed care organizations, the essence of hospice care is often ignored. Insurance companies and prospective payment plans are interested in the bottom line. They know that hospice saves money, in some analyses as much as 30 percent, compared with care in its absence. Overlooking the effectiveness of the full hospice team, insurance carriers and HMOs often assume that the financial advantages of hospice are due solely to nurses visiting patients at home and keeping people out of the hospital. That's what they are most consistently willing to pay for—that is, assuming the visit is "medically necessary." The goals of addressing personal suffering and personal growth at life's end may be politely tolerated, as long as they are free. If the embracing of such goals requires staffing and related expenses, it is likely to be dismissed as unrealistic and not justifiable in the current financial climate. Already the quality of hospice care across the country is uneven. In some areas hospice is clinically sophisticated and strong, but in other cities and programs it remains unsophisticated or frankly inadequate.

Underpinning the crisis in end-of-life care are factors that lie deeper than deficiencies in medical education, misguided health care policies, and financing strategies. I believe that the root cause underlying the mistreatment and needless misery of the dying is that America, as a culture, has no positive vision and no sense of direction with regard to life's end. Without a position on the compass pointing the way, the health care professions' and society's approach to care for the dying has been confused, inconsistent, and frequently ill-considered. Often, despite the best of intentions, efforts to improve care have only made matters worse.

Currently, society has become fixated on the issue of assisted suicide as the solution to suffering at life's end. When I speak to people about the problems of end-of-life care, often the first question they ask is: "What do you think about physician-assisted suicide?" My thoughts on assisted suicide could fill another book; in brief, I mainly feel that it is the wrong question, the wrong way to frame our need as a society to respond to the crisis in end-of-life care. For one thing, while arguments in favor of legalizing assisted suicide are couched in terms of patient advocacy, they reinforce the message to the ill and frail elderly that their lives are no longer of value. In addition, the drive to legalize so-called "aid in dying" presents the crisis as black or white: "If only the doctor could legally end your life, you wouldn't have to suffer." In actuality there are many shades of gray.

The debate over legalizing physician-assisted suicide has diverted our attention from the more logical, humane, and lasting solutions to the crisis. For example, if and when physician-assisted suicide does become legal, our society will still have to contend with the suffering of large groups of patients who are presently excluded from any consideration of aid-in-dying. Children, the mentally retarded or developmentally disabled, the mentally ill, people with Alzheimer's disease or other acquired dementia, and those who are alert but paralyzed—that is, all those who are unable to participate in the suicidal act—are specifically excluded from proposals to legalize assisted suicide. To prevent abuses of assisted suicide, their particularly vulnerable status merits such exclusion. However, these people all have the potential for suffering in their dying. If death on demand is to be our society's compassionate response to the dying, is it not inevitable that society will have to extend this service to them as well? Stated another way, if assistance in suicide or euthanasia is deemed a right of persons who are dying, on what basis, and for how long, will society be able to deny that right to children, people who are paralyzed, or those who are mentally retarded or demented?

The stories that comprise this book argue that there are alternatives. Pain and other symptoms causing physical distress can be alleviated, even when they are severe. It is not always easy, but by being careful and comprehensive, and by being absolutely committed to do whatever is necessary to control physical distress, it can *always* be done. Personal suffering that derives from the experienced loss of meaning and from the feeling of impending disintegration can also be addressed. This, too, is not easy, but it can be done. How? One patient, one person, at a time.

Clinicians who are adept at working with dying persons know from experience that, in the midst of profound suffering, not only comfort, but also triumph and exhilaration, are possible. The separation between suffering and the sense of growth and transformation is but a membrane. The clinical skills required to help a person explore the boundaries of his unique suffering and pierce that membrane can be delicate, sophisticated, and sometimes subtle. But they are not mystical, and they can be taught. I hope that society and the medical profession of the twenty-first century allow those of us in palliative care to practice, deepen, and teach this level of clinical intervention.

If we, as a society, are to achieve a solution to the crisis, it must evolve slowly, one family at a time. Such a transformation cannot be legislated or implemented through policy alone. We can each have a role in that process by insisting that the wishes of our loved ones are respected, that expert medical care is brought to bear, that physical distress is eased, and that they are cared for in a dignified fashion.

The concept of dying well can provide a vision of a realistic and affirmative goal for life's end and a sense of direction to align our efforts with. Changes in medical practice and education, politics, and social policy are all necessary, but these by themselves will not suffice to provide a lasting solution to the crisis. Ultimately, a durable resolution of the crisis will require a transformation at the deepest level of American culture. Cultural values and expectations related to dying must shift away from the denial of death, and the viewing of dying as a time of inevitable emotional distress and barely avoidable physical suffering, toward an understanding of dying as a part of full, even healthy, living, and toward accepting care for the dying as a valuable part of the life of the community.

Dying persons deserve expert attention to their symptoms and emotional needs, but care for the dying is too important to be left to the experts. To be certain that the people we love do not become statistics of the crisis in end-of-life care, we family members and friends must retain responsibility to care for those we love as they die. We cannot ensure that dying will be easy or pretty—and it will never be fun—but we can ensure that people are not abandoned, that their basic human needs are provided for, and that their symptoms are addressed.

Collectively, as communities, we must take back responsibility for the care of our dying members. Currently, care for persons as they die is delegated to medical professionals and institutions: doctors, nurses, social workers, chaplains, therapists, hospitals, nursing homes, and hospices. Each has a critical role to play, but ultimately, as members of our communities, we all must retain the responsibility to see that the needs of dying persons are met.

Of the fundamental needs of persons as they die, only the need to control physical symptoms is uniquely medical. Their more basic needs are broader than the scope of medicine. They need shelter from the elements, a place to be. They need help with personal hygiene and assistance with elimination. They need nourishment or, as death comes close, sips of fluid to moisten their mouth and throat. They need companionship, and they need others to recognize their continued existence.

In recognizing these needs, we can say to the dying person with our words and, more importantly, with our actions: "We will keep you warm and we will keep you dry. We will keep you clean. We will help you with elimination, with your bowels and your bladder function. We will always offer you food and fluid. We will be with you. We will bear witness to your pain and your sorrows, your disappointments and your triumphs; we will listen to the stories of your life and will remember the story of your passing."

Individually and collectively, we can and must imagine a more enlightened, loving way to care for our grandparents, our parents, our brothers and sisters, and even our children in their dying. By demonstrating that care in practice, we enlist the imagination of others, heightening their own expectations. Imagination is key, because the crisis of terminal care has so many sources and so many manifestations that a piecemeal, mechanistic approach could never be enough. Only imagination, working on the level of shared values and expectations, has the power to effect the required cultural transformation.

By telling the stories of people who have died well, those of us who have cared for the dying, personally or professionally, can contribute in a vital way. The accounts of people from our communities who have grown personally and contributed to the growth of others in the process of their dying can serve as sparks within the tinder of our decaying health care system, igniting the imagination of Americans across our vast land and cultural landscape.

Years ago, Elisabeth Kübler-Ross envisioned a future in which dying was embraced as part of living and in which the care of the dying was an integral part of the life of the family and the life of the community:

> Children who have been exposed to these kinds of experiences—in a safe, secure, and loving environment—will then raise another generation of children who will, most likely, not even comprehend that we had to write books on death and dying and had to start special institutions for the dying patients; they will not understand why there was this overwhelming fear of death, which, for so long covered up the fear of living.
>
> This is my dream.

APPENDIX

Writing Your Family's Story: Questions and Answers

The stories in this book document the real experiences of real people dying. They also show what can be achieved in helping family and friends to die. People often ask me about difficult situations involving loved ones who are terminally ill. Perhaps a father is dying in pain, or a doctor persists with treatment that no one wants. In each case, of course, the specific answer depends on the people involved and the medical and community resources available, as well as the cultural and political climate of the hospital, nursing home, or community. I can, however, share some general guidelines that help me respond to questions I commonly hear.

I start by listening closely to the questions themselves, which can provide important insight into the attitudes and expectations of the person and family. For instance, asking "How can we make sure that Mom is getting the best care possible?" reveals the sense of responsibility family members feel and—this is key—their high expectations. In my mind, asking the question puts them halfway to the goal. Commitment and determination are the other essential ingredients they will need. Everything else is detail.

Family members rightly feel the responsibility to protect and nurture loved ones as they die. Whether or not you are related to a dying person by blood or marriage, if you have a special sense of connection to that person, you are family.

The "best care possible" will always be easier to arrange if the doctors, nurses, hospital, and nursing home and/or hospice program involved are skilled in palliative care and aligned with the goals of the patient and family. However, when it comes to end-of-life care, people should temper their trust in professionals with careful scrutiny. Reputations and board certifications mean nothing if the job isn't getting done. Ultimate responsibility for end-of-life care must remain with the dying person and the family. Enlist the help of the best doctors, institutions and support services you can find, but make certain your expectations are being met. Here is where commitment and determination come in.

Unfortunately, the current general quality of care for the dying in America is woefully low. Too often treatment goals are assumed and never made clear. Too often peoples' preferences in care are ignored. Too often their pain goes untreated. This sorry state of affairs must—*and will*—change. In the meantime, we must maintain high expectations for the care given our loved ones. You can and should expect that physicians and nurses will do whatever is necessary to relieve physical suffering. Beyond comfort, the care provided should enable the person to live as fully as possible in whatever time is left and should honor the tender, personal nature of dying. The process begins with asking your questions.

No set of questions could ever be complete; I have tried to focus on general approaches that may prove valuable to you and your family in your own, unique experience with dying.

Beginning to Talk About Dying

Q. My sister has advanced breast cancer, and no one in the family is talking about the fact that she's getting weaker and weaker. How do we begin to talk about dying?

A. Begin by being unembarrassed about the fact that eventually, everyone dies. I think conversation is easier when people approach the subject from an understanding that the experience is universal and no one can avoid it. Usually, when family members aren't talking about dying, one of two things is happening: There is an unwillingness on the part of the person or a family member to acknowledge that the illness is progressing, or dying is on everyone's mind, but there is a conspiracy of silence in a misplaced attempt to protect one another from discussing painful feelings and deepest fears.

Naturally, it is essential to be sensitive to your sister's feelings; in discussing her illness and treatment with her, follow her cues. You might begin by asking how she feels her treatments are going. What does her doctor say he is planning to do next? Or ask in an even more general way how she feels she is doing. If her answers reflect an optimism regarding cure that seems unlikely, given what you know of her condition, it may be best to let the matter rest, at least for awhile. Take care to avoid pushing your own agenda—this is first and foremost her dying. Trust your instincts. As her sister, you are probably in the best position to know how to proceed. One particularly gentle way to follow up on vague responses can be to inquire about events several months to a year in the future, such as where and how she wants to celebrate a birthday, Christmas, or other holiday, or if she is still planning a trip she mentioned previously.

Sometimes it is OK for sisters to be direct. While it is her illness and her dying, you are going through the experience, too. A lot of important questions can be asked without challenging her optimism. If, for instance, she responds to an open-ended "How are you doing?" by reporting that "Dr. Phillips says that the tests all look better," you might say something like "Do you mean there's hope to really beat this thing?" Her response will probably clarify whether she has avoided talking about not getting well to protect you or is focused on cure and, at present, emotionally unable to consider the alternative.

It's possible that your sister does want to talk about her dying. She may put out feelers to test you and others for their readiness to talk. Listen for discouraged or exasperated comments on the order of "I don't know why I'm going through all this!" or "I wish this would all be over with." These statements should be recognized as openings to important conversation. Dismissing such remarks ("Oh, you don't really mean that") or covering them over with simplistic reassurance ("You're going to get better, I just know it") effectively closes down conversation and isolates the person in despair. If your sister provides an opening, consider stating the obvious:

"What you're going through sounds awful"; and let her know you can listen: "I would love to hear how you're really doing."

In asking the hard questions, of course, you or your family must be willing to hear hard answers. Think about what you will do or say if she responds to your interest by openly confiding her darkest fears and fathomless sorrow. Sometimes what people need most is for someone they love to simply listen.

A valuable strategy for discussing these intimate and poignant subjects with your sister or with other family members is to use "I" statements, framing what you say in terms of what *you* are feeling. In talking with your other siblings or parents, avoid statements that sound as if you are telling others what they should be thinking, feeling, or saying ("We can all see Sherrie is getting sicker and we need to talk about her dying"). By sticking to "I" statements you can avoid intruding on your family's emotional space while saying the things that need to be said and that may, inevitably, provoke uncomfortable feelings in others. In talking privately with your mother or brother, for instance, you might say, "Sherrie looks weaker to me. I am worried about her." In this way you can open up the discussion without imposing an agenda. Similarly, in talking with your sister, it is almost always OK to tell her how you feel. "Sherrie, I love you so much, and I'm scared of losing you," is a very direct statement that, nevertheless, respects personal boundaries.

Q. Mom had a massive heart attack and is in a coma. How can she possibly die well?

A. When someone is in a coma it is hard to know exactly what they can hear, feel, and think. I choose to err on the side of assuming that a person in a coma can hear and feel. Thus, simple explanations, the human voice, and touch remain important elements of care.

Your mother is now beyond the ability to say the five things, but perhaps she can listen. Remember that the purpose of the five things is to complete relationships. It will do no harm and might be an extraordinary gift to tell her that you love her and that you will miss her. When there has been emotional conflict or turmoil within families, the impending death of a family member can be an opportunity for healing. What would your mother most have wanted to see happen before she died? If the answer is that she would have liked to see you and your father or sister forgive each other for past hurts, consider what a gift doing so could be to her. When they can be expressed honestly, feelings of forgiveness should be shared with your mom. Similarly, if she would be worried about you in the future, tell her that you can make it without her—you can. If there is a sense that she has been hanging on for some reason, at some point it may be helpful to tell her that it is OK to let go.

When people are incapacitated by illness, I try to think of ways not only to minimize bodily discomfort but also to gift them with physical pleasures. Music, gentle massage with fragrant oil, warm bathing, and hair-brushing are all simple pleasures to give to people who are unable to respond. In our culture, we reminisce and tell stories of our loved ones at funerals and memorial services that pay tribute to them and celebrate their lives. Why do we wait? Relatives and friends can begin that process, formally or informally, at your mom's bedside.

You cannot undo the tragic events of your mom's heart attack and coma, or the likelihood that she is beyond awareness. But if at the time of her death you are confident that she is comfortable and feel that she is loved—and even honored—in the care she has received, she will have died well.

Q. My mother and stepfather live in a distant state, and I have just found out that he is seriously ill and probably dying. How can I help him to die well?

A. There are a number of questions behind and within the one you asked: How involved should I be? How important is it for him to see me? Would I be able to take the stress of being involved? If I can only visit once, when should I go? What can I do from this distance?

Only you know the history and status of your relationship with your stepfather. If it has been loving and mutually supportive, I encourage you to stay involved, through frequent phone conversations with your stepfather, your mother, and the caregivers around them. If things between you have been distant, uneasy, or openly conflicted, take stock. Do you have things that you need to say to your stepfather? Is this a chance to write a happier ending to this chapter of your family's story? Does it matter to you whether the relationship ends well? If you made an attempt and it failed, would it matter to you to have tried? Be honest with yourself in asking these questions.

If you remain in doubt, I encourage you to lean toward being more involved. Make contact and offer whatever help you can while respecting your parents' privacy. Stay sensitive to how your interest and offers are received.

The distance and your own responsibilities may impose serious limitations on what you can do. If you decide that you want to make a trip, do so fairly early. If you wait, your stepfather may have less energy to really visit. Furthermore, if there is lasting value to be gained in your involvement, the sooner you start, the sooner the dividends begin flowing.

Even at a distance, there are things you can do. Stay in contact. Let your parents know you care. Send cards, and call—even during the day. This is not the time to worry about the phone bill. Remember, sometimes the most precious thing we can do for another person is to listen. The telephone can be an important resource in very practical ways as well. You may be able to participate in discussions with your parents and the doctor, home health, or hospice team seeing your parents. If they need help locally and are having trouble getting it, you may be able to find the services they need by being assertive and using the phone. Your local library may have the Yellow Pages for their town.

Can you take the stress of involvement? These days people walk around feeling they could not possibly deal with another ounce of stress. The real question is: Can you avoid it? The answer is no. You already know your stepfather is seriously ill. *You already own this pain.* Question the assumption that being uninvolved will lessen your discomfort. If you have work to do to complete your relationship with your stepfather and you choose to skirt it, the distress you feel may be less abrupt, but it is more likely to linger and gnaw at you over time. The question I recommend you consider is: Can any good come out of this bad situation?

APPENDIX

Helping Ease Symptoms and Bring Relief

Q. Mom has cancer, and she's having a lot of pain, despite the Darvon and ibuprofen the doctor is giving her. What else can be done?

A. Plenty. The right treatment will depend on what is causing the pain. Knowing what is likely to work best for an individual person in pain requires knowing about the pain and the person. Having a caring and careful doctor is crucial here. Only occasionally does evaluating pain in a person with cancer require elaborate testing. More often, a simple interview and gentle physical examination suffice.

Doctors are trained to diagnose pains by sorting through common patterns and causes of discomfort. A careful evaluation begins with basic questions: Where do you hurt? Is the pain constant or does it come and go? What makes it better? When is it worse? What type of pain is it: Sharp? Shooting? Pressurelike? Achy? Burning? Or boring? What else happens when you are hurting? Do you get short of breath? Sick to your stomach? It will help to begin keeping track of the type of pains your mother has, their qualities, and any associated symptoms. Make sure that the doctor and nurses who are managing her prescriptions are asking these sorts of questions.

Although propoxyphene (the generic name for Darvon and, with acetaminophen, Darvocet) is chemically related to morphine, codeine, and other "opioids," narcotics derived from the opium poppy, propoxyphene has relatively little pain-relieving power. Ibuprofen is probably the more potent of the two medications your mother is currently taking; it belongs to a class of drugs called nonsteroidal anti-inflammatory drugs (NSAIDs), which reduce pain by blocking the body's production of chemicals that mediate inflammation. These drugs are particularly effective at diminishing pain from metastatic cancers in bones. Thus, unless the ibuprofen is causing side-effects, such as stomach upset, it may be helpful to use doses in the higher range. However, don't increase the dose of ibuprofen, other NSAIDs, or any medications without speaking with her doctor, because some side-effects are silent yet dangerous.

Most people with cancer pain will eventually require treatment that includes a stronger opioid than propoxyphene. Alternatives include hydromorphone (Dilaudid), hydrocodone (with acetaminophen in Lortab,

Bancap, Vicodin, and others), oxycodone (Roxycodone, and with acetaminophen in Tylox, Percodan, Percocet, and Roxycet), fentanyl (Duragesic), and morphine. When they are needed, these medications should be used as part of a pain-relieving plan.

Still other medications may also be used to improve comfort. Steroids, such as prednisone or dexamethasone (Decadron), are often helpful. If bone pain is part of your mother's discomfort, radiation therapy may have an important pain-relieving role to play. Often brief courses of radiation therapy are enough.

When a person's pain persists despite the usual medications and interventions, more extensive diagnostic tests may be necessary to better define the cause of the discomfort and to guide therapies such as nerve blocks or intraspinal medication.

Q. I have advanced prostate cancer, and the doctor wants to start me on morphine. I am afraid that if I take it now, when the pain gets worse later, the medication will no longer work. What should I do?

A. The technical term for the effects of a medication wearing off over time is *tolerance*. While it is true that tolerance to narcotic medication can occur, it is never a significant problem in palliative care practice. During the course of a progressive illness like cancer, it is common for people to require intermittent increases in their dose of narcotic pain medication. Whether the required increase is due to tolerance, progression of the disease, or a combination of the two is usually a moot question. In any case, increasing the dose of the medication usually suffices. There is no maximum dose above which it is impossible to go. The right dose is the dose that works.

Q. My aunt has metastatic breast cancer and can't take narcotics because of a history of allergies to them. How do you treat severe pain when you have such an allergy?

A. People commonly use the word *allergy* to refer to side-effects that once required them to stop using a certain medication. For instance, a person may report being allergic to codeine and, when asked, describe a bad experience with nausea and vomiting suffered when it was prescribed after surgery years earlier. As awful as the bout of vomiting was, this was a typical initiation side-effect and not a true allergy. (Codeine is famous for causing nausea and is not often used in hospice practice.) True allergic reactions are usually marked by hives, blotchy rashes or, more seriously, the abrupt onset of swelling or shortness of breath following the first dose of a drug. Serious allergies, or anaphylaxis, with opioids or narcotics are quite rare. Even if a true allergy to one opioid medication exists, it is usually only necessary to prescribe a chemically different medication.

Q. My uncle has cancer; he has experienced so many side-effects of morphine that he decided it was preferable to live with his pain. Aren't there better medications?

A. Obviously, something must be done to allow your uncle to get relief. What that is will depend on the nature of the side-effects he is having. Somewhere around 25 percent of patients develop excessive sleepiness, confusion, or nausea when they begin taking scheduled doses of morphine or another narcotic. These initiation side-effects usually diminish or disappear within a few days to a week; in this regard, the phenomenon of tolerance is a beneficial feature of narcotic pharmacology. Unless and until the side-effects resolve, they can be treated in various ways.

One narcotic side-effect that consistently resists tolerance is constipation. Almost everyone who is taking narcotic pain medication requires a laxative of one sort or another to have adequate bowel movements. In practice, constipation is only a problem when it is not asked about and prevented or is not promptly attended to.

Everyone is an individual. If side-effects do not sufficiently diminish within a reasonable time, a change in medication is necessary. Reactions to one opioid, such as morphine, do not contraindicate the effective use of another. When side-effects persist, other medications can be added to achieve comfort. Antinausea medications, such as Compazine or Haldol, may be employed. Psychostimulants, such as methylphenidate (Ritalin) or dextroamphetamine (Dexedrine) may be utilized to counteract persistent sleepiness attendant on the needed doses of pain medication.

This may all seem complicated; I include this discussion simply to encourage high expectations and to assist you in identifying the sort of professional expertise to look for. Actually, the level of medical knowledge and technical skill required to treat pain is no more complicated than that demanded of internists, pediatricians, and family physicians in managing diabetes, a serious infection, or a hundred other medical conditions. You should insist on nothing less than expert medical help.

Q. My father has prostate cancer and a history of emphysema. He is taking sixty milligrams of long-acting morphine twice a day, which helps with the pain, but he is still uncomfortable. When he asked his urologist what to do, he said he was afraid to let my father take more pain medication because it could suppress his breathing. What would be the right dose in this situation?

A. The right dose is the dose that works. Doctors who are unfamiliar with modern palliative medicine sometimes worry about the respiratory depressant effects of narcotics. The notion that people who are taking narcotics for pain control might stop breathing if they take too much is simply not true. It is a clinical myth extrapolated from the fact that large doses of morphine given to a laboratory animal that is not in pain will depress the animal's breathing. And heroin addicts who are not in pain and who inject industrial quantities of narcotics do, occasionally, stop breathing. The respiratory drive is strong, and in both animals and humans it quickly overwhelms most of the respiratory depressant effect of narcotics. In other words, tolerance to the respiratory effects of narcotics develops rapidly. But even before tolerance sets in, pain is an effective antidote to respiratory depression.

Hospice research over the years has proven that, whatever the underlying neurochemical mechanisms, when morphine or other narcotics are used to treat pain, even in very large doses, there is no appreciable depression of breathing. On the contrary, by reducing anxiety and the physiologic "work of breathing," morphine has been repeatedly shown to improve respiration in patients with advanced lung disease.

Q. My thirty-two-year-old daughter is having more pain from her breast cancer. Her doctor wants to prescribe long-acting morphine pills, but in the past, whenever the pain was bad, pills never worked. The only time she was ever really comfortable was when she was in the hospital and had injections. Do injections work better than pills?

A. Not necessarily. Pills and injections basically work the same way, by delivering medication to the bloodstream. It's true that the level of morphine will initially rise more quickly with an injection, but the same concentration of morphine in the blood, and the same pain relief, can be achieved by either means. For cancer pain, it is almost always best to use medicine on a scheduled, round-the-clock basis, and oral long-acting morphine is well suited for this purpose. And immediate-release forms of oral morphine in liquid and pills are available for extra "rescue" doses of medication.

Recently, the narcotic fentanyl has become available as a transdermal (across the skin) patch under the brand name of Duragesic. Worn on the skin, Duragesic delivers a relatively constant level of fentanyl to the bloodstream for up to three days; it is useful for some people who have difficulty swallowing tablets or remembering to take their medication.

Injections are used in hospice care when people can no longer swallow pills or liquid medicines. An important trend has been away from intravenous (IV) injections, which require the insertion and maintenance of an IV line, and toward subcutaneous (SC) infusions, which use a fine-gauge needle placed in the loose connective tissue beneath the skin. In our hospice program we generally only use an IV route for pain medications when the person has previously had a surgically placed central IV line for chemotherapy. Subcutaneous infusions are well accepted by patients, easy to maintain, and provide a reliable way of delivering a steady baseline of medication as well as rapid-acting rescue doses.

Beware of intramuscular (IM) shots. They are rarely necessary in palliative care. Intramuscular injections hurt, and the rate of release of the drug from the muscle to the bloodstream is unpredictable. In my experience, the use of IM medications is a clue that the prescribing physician is unfamiliar with up-to-date symptom management techniques.

Q. The doctor wants to start Mom on narcotics for her breast cancer. Her sister was once addicted to drugs, and now she's worried about becoming addicted. Is this possible?

A. The myth that people in pain become addicted to narcotics is reinforced by the media's portrayal of addiction and street drug use. The "just say no" approach to illicit substance abuse has fostered a puritanical approach to taking pain medication and as a result many people with a legitimate need for narcotic medication have suffered needlessly in pain. Addiction is defined by the craving for a drug to achieve euphoria, drug-seeking in the absence of physical discomfort, and the manipulation of prescribers to obtain drugs. Clinical studies demonstrate that people who receive narcotics for the treatment of pain under the supervision of experienced doctors do not become addicted. Hospice experience bears this out. Following radiation therapy to an area of bone cancer, or in the case of localized pain, after the injection of a long-acting local anesthetic and chemical to destroy the nerve, pain commonly improves, and narcotic medication, such as morphine, can be reduced—and occasionally eliminated—without drug craving problems.

A more troubling phenomenon than addiction is prevalent in certain medical settings. A syndrome arises in which a patient's pain is continually undertreated and, in desperation, the person begins drug-seeking—lying to doctors and nurses and otherwise being manipulative—to obtain some relief. This pattern, called "pseudoaddiction," superficially resembles addictive behavior but has two distinguishing features. First, the person with pseudoaddiction is in pain; second, the drug-seeking behavior does not reflect some problem within the person but rather negligence on the part of the providers of medical care.

Of course, not all concerns regarding addiction can be dismissed as unfounded. Some people do have a history of serious addiction, which can directly or indirectly complicate the management of their terminal illness. Naturally, people who are addicted to drugs also have a right to have their pain treated as they die. When the dying person is known to be actively using heroin or crack cocaine or a similar potent nonprescribed drug, the pharmacological effects must be considered. In addition, there may be legitimate concerns about the diversion of drugs to others or the selling of prescribed drugs for profit.

If the patient has a history of serious addiction but is no longer using illicit drugs or alcohol, the issues are usually very different. In my experience, patients who are recovering drug addicts and alcoholics tend to be among those most resistant to taking pain medication in adequate doses. I try to emphasize to them that this is a medical, not a moral, issue and that taking medication for pain is not addiction. When patients with histories of drug abuse require narcotics after surgery, for instance, they rapidly return to abstinence as their wounds heal. When I am faced with an ardent "Twelve-Stepper" who needs, but is refusing to accept, a certain level of pain medication, I promise that I am prescribing only what is necessary and that, if and when their condition improves, I will reduce the dose.

In our culture, questions regarding drug abuse and addiction will continue to arise. It is important to air any worry about addiction with the doctor who will be in charge of treating your mom's pain. More than likely, it is an issue around which her doctor can be very reassuring.

Q. My brother is almost immobilized by pain, but every time the doctor asks about it, he says he's fine. What can I do?

A. Does your brother admit to you that he is in pain? If not, perhaps the place to begin is by gently remarking on his facial grimaces or stiff posture, or short temper, or whatever it is that makes you think he is in pain. Some people think it would be self-indulgent to complain or even admit to being in pain. "There are a lot of people a lot worse off than me," is a common sort of statement. My response to this is usually: "You're right. But so what? Don't you count, too?"

If your brother acknowledges having pain, ask him why he doesn't tell the doctor about it. Does he think that the doctor wouldn't be able to help anyway? Does he expect that he will simply have to put up with pain because of his illness? Is he feeling guilty about being ill ("I brought this cancer on myself by smoking") and, therefore, deserving of the pain? Some people, and some ethnic cultures, believe that pain is part of the healing or cleansing process.

Most commonly, people resist talking to the doctor about pain because of unspoken fears of addiction, or because of their desire to hold off on strong medications "until I really need it." Others deny increasing pain because they fear it means the disease is getting worse. Studies have shown that in medical encounters, such as may occur within busy cancer treatment clinics, patients may not want to take up time, or distract the doctor from "more important" issues, by bringing up their pain.

Encourage your brother to talk these issues out, first with you and other family and friends, second with his doctor. Pain is treatable and is best treated early. If the doctor doesn't seem to have time, ask for an additional appointment. If this doesn't work, ask for consultation with a specialist in pain or palliative care.

Q. My wife has always had problems with high cholesterol and insulin-dependent diabetes, and we are used to carefully controlling her diet. Now she is dying of lung cancer and losing weight. Do we have to keep watching her diet?

A. Probably not. Low-fat and diabetic diets are both intended to prevent long-term consequences of vascular (blood vessel) disease—particularly heart attacks, strokes, and kidney failure. The diagnosis of an incurable illness like your wife's lung cancer makes it likely that such prevention is no longer necessary. It is important that her insulin is adjusted to what she is eating, however, in order to prevent extreme levels of blood glucose or the onset of acidosis. Here again, working with your wife's doctor to liberalize her diet is essential.

Q. Mom has never wanted to be hooked up to a feeding tube. But because of her Alzheimer's, she is eating less and has been losing weight.

A. It is important to begin by asking why she is not eating. Sometimes people with Alzheimer's disease or other dementias stop eating because their dentures no longer fit or they have a sore in their mouth or because they have a toothache that they are unable to tell anyone about.

With advanced dementia, however, people may reach a point when they are neurologically not capable of eating. If this is the case, before inserting a feeding tube, it is important to ask "What purpose will the feeding tube serve?" If the answer is "I won't allow Mom to die of starvation," the subsequent question might be "What would it be acceptable for her to die of?" These are the real issues. Too often, questions of this sort are not asked. Families go along with, or insist on, feeding tubes and, whenever there is a fever, IV antibiotics. After many months, a family member may voice anguish over the plight of their loved one who "just won't die." In truth, at the end of a long illness people often stop eating; this seems to be part of the "wisdom of the body," and is, undoubtedly, one of the most peaceful and comfortable ways of dying.

Remember that placing and using a feeding tube are medical procedures that should meet defined, achievable clinical goals. I suggest that if your mother's condition is advanced, and a medical evaluation (including an oral examination) does not resolve the problem, she should be assisted in eating. A speech or occupational therapist skilled in eating disorders can provide invaluable help. If she resides in a nursing home, and you are not directly involved in her physical care, arrange to observe her at mealtimes. Is she being helped with eating? Determine in your own mind if the encouragement and assistance she is receiving are sufficient. On the other hand, make sure such assistance is not overly aggressive and does not border on force-feeding. Talk to her doctor. Get a second opinion. Talk to the local hospice program for its perspective.

Dealing with Doctors and the Medical System

Q. My grandfather has stomach cancer and lots of physical and emotional problems. I go with him to his doctor's appointments, but every time, we leave without having discussed what is bothering my grandfather most. The doctor always seems rushed and barely has enough time to talk about the lab tests and the next treatment. Without offending the doctor, how can we make sure that our problems are addressed and our questions answered?

A. Communication is absolutely essential in any doctor-patient relationship. Patients and family members have a right to expect that their physician will listen and try to answer their questions. There is no such thing as being too busy to listen: Appointments can be extended or new appointments made to address leftover issues. A physician who is consistently unable or unwilling to listen is probably not the person you want managing your grandfather's terminal care.

Most physicians can and do want to listen and are happy to answer questions. Keeping in mind that doctors do have tight schedules, a little preparation can go a long way. Before the next appointment talk with your grandfather about the questions you want to ask the doctor and write them down. At the beginning of the visit, let the doctor know that you have several questions you need to ask.

If there are a lot of concerns, organize the questions around topics such as treatment choices, medications, and side-effects; eating and meals; and help-at-home questions. The doctor may not answer every question herself, and, depending on your needs, she may refer you and your grandfather to a dietician or a social worker to answer some of them. Just make certain that you leave the doctor's office feeling confident that you know what you are to do regarding medications and general care or, if questions remain, that you know who you are to be in contact with next. Save the list of questions to refer to when you organize your thoughts for the next appointment.

Keep asking questions. It is critically important to have easy, open communication with the doctors and nurses helping to care for your grandfather. Do not settle for less.

Q. Mom is very old and becoming progressively incapacitated because of osteoporosis and spine fractures. She's living at home, but she can't take care of herself anymore. My sister and I have done our soul-searching, but we can't provide all the care she needs either. None of the nursing homes are places we could have our mom live. What should we do?

A. This is an extremely difficult question for which, at present, there are no good answers. The general level of nursing home care in America is unacceptable. You're right to feel as you do; you're in a bind. It's not that your expectations are too high, but that current standards are too low. My first advice is: Don't stop looking. Within the nursing home industry there are pockets of enlightenment and innovation scattered throughout the country. I have seen some excellent facilities, residential environments with a sense of community, places that feel alive in body and soul. Spend an hour in such a place, and you will get the sense that people *live* there. You will notice instances of honest solemnity as well as moments of genuine good cheer. The staff in these places tend to look you in the eye when they speak and address residents in a direct, authentic manner, without using diminutives.

The facilities that stand out in my mind are all places where the staff is carefully selected and adequately compensated, and ongoing training and education are valued. If you investigate an apparently better local nursing home and, after the tour and the sales pitch, aren't quite sure what to think, ask yourself this: Did the staff seem proud to work where they do?

In addition to nursing homes, ask the local community, hospital, or hospice social worker about *personal care homes* or other *assisted-living* arrangements. Some retirement communities that require long-term investment have integrated assisted-living, skilled nursing, and hospice services for members. If one exists in your area, it is worth inquiring if there is any provision for which your mom may qualify.

Hiring help in the home may be another option. Most areas have agencies that provide private duty services. Some insurance and government medical plans will partially cover this expense. A social worker is invaluable at working through the particular maze. If you have the means, another, informal option may be to place a classified ad requesting someone to live with your mom. This requires a commitment on your part to interview and carefully screen the respondents and carefully supervise whomever is chosen.

Keep looking. You'll know the right situation when you find it. Whichever situation you settle on, stay involved and, unless you are delighted with the care, stay alert for better alternatives. As you are doing so, continue to look ahead and prepare for a time when your mom may need more care. Keep her doctor involved. If her relocation forces her to change physicians, interview more than one and find one with whom you and your mom feel comfortable.

Wherever your mom lives, build a working relationship with the people who are directly caring for her. Learn their names and treat them with respect. Ask as many questions as you have about her condition and treatments. Let the staff know by what you say and by your interactions with your mom that you really care and will make certain things are done right. Be pleasant and persistent, but if you have to choose, be persistent.

Look for ways to work in partnership with the facility staff and to augment their care in ways that bring some pleasure into your mom's life.

Enlist her favorite nurse or aide to help you think of ways to enrich her daily routine or to celebrate various occasions.

When her condition warrants it, ask for hospice to become involved. Know that wherever she is living, if you think that hospice may help your mother, she has the right to a formal hospice evaluation. Hospice programs routinely see patients in nursing homes, personal care homes, and various other living arrangements. Be advised, however, that some nursing homes will discourage hospice involvement, reacting as if the request for hospice care is an affront to their capabilities. In fact, hospice programs represent a team of specialized services that are not otherwise available. When you are evaluating nursing homes or assisted-living facilities, ask if they have a working relationship with one or more local hospice programs. Is it common for residents to be served by hospice as they progressively decline?

Q. Our mother had a stroke a year ago. She is comatose and on a feeding tube. She never wanted to be kept alive artificially, and my brother and I want the tube removed. Her doctor and nursing home are making us feel like we want to kill her. Would it be cruel to remove her tube?

A. No, it is not cruel; in some circumstances it may be the most merciful thing to do. Keeping a tube in a person's nose or directly into her stomach for no reason other than artificially prolonging her life can be senseless and inhumane. Are her hands restrained so that she does not reflexively pull at the tubes? Has she had pneumonias or other complications from the feedings? Is she more comfortable or less comfortable because of the feedings?

Dying of a progressive inability to eat is probably one of the most natural and physiologically gentle ways to expire. In the context of advanced illness, hunger is rarely, if ever, a source of discomfort. The same is true with thirst. Hospice patients who are dehydrated are regularly asked if they are thirsty; most answer no, but those who say yes are consistently and fully relieved by having their mouth and throat moistened. A recent study confirmed this experience. "Thirst," for people with advanced illness and dehydration, is a feeling of dryness, not the familiar sensation that can be quenched only by drinking substantial amounts of fluid. In any event, the discomfort associated with dehydration is easily prevented.

Most important is your resolve to ask what is really right for your mother. Given that her death from this stroke is inevitable, think about how it might occur in a way that would honor and celebrate her. If tube feedings are stopped, the time remaining should be one of heightened care and attention. Think about simple rituals to mark this passage that would have meaning for her. Keeping a candle burning in her room or bringing a group of her friends and family together to read to her or sing to her—or simply to hold vigil—can be tangible ways of honoring her. The possibilities are limited only by your imagination.

Q. My wife was in a car accident and is in a vegetative state. Her living will specifies that she does not want artificial nutrition. The nursing home director says that the institution cannot allow removal of the tube. Isn't this a violation of my wife's rights?

A. It's more than likely that this is, indeed, a violation of your wife's rights. Only a few states, notably Illinois and Missouri, impose statutory limits on a person's right to refuse artificial nutrition through a living will. There is general agreement that tube feeding is a medical procedure that can be refused by the patient either directly or, as in your wife's case, through an advance directive document. Nursing homes must either comply or cooperate with the transfer of care to another, willing facility.

The situation is often more difficult when there is no living will or durable power attorney for health care, or if the document signed by the patient does not specify a preference regarding tube feedings or intravenous hydration. Some nursing homes and hospitals still contend that any form of nutrition is basic care and resist all attempts to remove feeding tubes. While the sentiment is nice, the indiscriminate requirement to deliver calories and fluid frequently results in medically mandated assault on the person dying. Everyone dies of something, and there are far less comfortable ways to die than by wasting away.

If you see a conflict brewing with the nursing home, step back for a few days or a week; avoid confrontation, at least until you are well prepared and have contingency plans. Talk with an attorney who is knowledgeable about health policy and law in your state. Ask the attorney about having a family member formally appointed as your wife's guardian. Contact a local hospice program and ask for its advice. It may well have dealt with similar situations and know of an informal way around this problem. Maybe transferring her to a different location would resolve the dilemma. Perhaps there is an inpatient hospice facility to which she could be transferred. Is there any possibility of taking your wife home for the time she has left? At home, restrictive policy and procedural concerns will not apply.

Q. My dad is having constant pain from his colon cancer. When we asked his oncologist to do something, he said he was already prescribing morphine, and that Dad was doing as well as could be expected. Is there something else we can do?

A. If your dad is in pain, there is always something else that can and should be done. You need to get medical help. The exact approach to your father's pain will be determined by a number of specifics: the details of his illness, the cause (or causes) of his various pains, any additional serious medical conditions, his previous experience with medications, his current dose of medications, and so on. All this is not especially complicated, as medical treatments go, but it clearly requires some expertise. Ask for, or seek out, a consultation with a physician experienced with hospice or palliative care. You might ask a local hospice program to conduct an admission evaluation or ask for a consultation with a hospice nurse. Whether or not your father is eligible for hospice at this time, useful suggestions are likely to come from the evaluation, and it will lay some groundwork for the future.

Q. My mother has advanced breast cancer and horrible back and leg pains. Her doctor referred her to a pain clinic. How is this different from hospice?

A. Many pain clinics are directed by anesthesiologists and focus exclusively on the physical components of pain. These centers are procedure oriented; as such, they are important resources when nerve-numbing injections or implantable narcotic infusion pumps are called for. But they are not hospices. Only occasionally does a patient's pain require surgically implanted devices or neurolytic injections. In the majority of situations, simpler treatments and medications can be used. Hospice programs consciously look at the bigger picture, attending to pain but also paying attention to the person's medical and nonmedical needs.

Q. My father is a disabled veteran and always goes to the Veterans Administration hospital and clinics. Now he is dying of lung cancer and languishing in a VA hospital forty miles from our town. He is only occasionally seen by a doctor, is often short of breath, and spends most of his day just lying in bed alone. He seems lost in the system. How can I improve his care?

A. In this situation, getting hospice involved may be essential. If your father's doctor acknowledges that care is palliative in nature, you can and should insist on a quality of care that meets hospice standards. The VA has a formal policy that calls for the development of hospice programs throughout the VA system. Unfortunately, this policy was adopted during an era of budget-cutting that threatens existing departments and entire VA facilities. It is not surprising that reality has not met expectations. In several regional veterans' hospitals, palliative care programs have been expanded, and in several others, exciting new programs have come into being; but more commonly, endless delays betray a de facto policy of ignoring the mandate.

You might start by asking if your father's VA hospital has a hospice program and, if so, if the hospice team is involved in his care. If hospice is involved, meet with your dad's hospice nurse or "case manager" and find out what are they doing for him. Ask if he has been evaluated for a treatable depression. Does the hospice have a counselor who can see him? Has the hospice chaplain seen him? Ask what the hospice team is doing—and what you can do—to make your father's remaining life more full. Who is the hospice medical director, and could she become your father's primary physician?

If there is no hospice program at the VA, ask to have a local hospice program from the community come and see him. As a health insurer, the VA is very reluctant to pay for home services, but it has been known to do so. It could possibly even be convinced to pay for hospice care in your own community. The old saying about the squeaky wheel applies here. If all else fails, make noise. Call your own or your father's congressional representative and complain. Your father deserves the best care possible. If he is dying, that includes hospice. Insist on it.

What other things you can do to improve the quality of your father's life depends on what sorts of things currently bother him or what things interest him. If, for instance, he suffers from boredom, ask the facility about books on tape, reading services, and similar activities. If he would enjoy more company, consider enlisting visits from members of a veterans' group, congregation, or civic organization your dad has an affinity with. Ideally, the staff will have anticipated some of these possibilities, but if not, it is better for you to bring them up than not to have them considered.

Q. My sister has a rare lung disease and is dying of progressive respiratory failure. Her pulmonary specialist said that he didn't think she would qualify for hospice, because she didn't have cancer. Why isn't she eligible for hospice?

A. She is. Hospice programs care for people who are dying, regardless of diagnosis. The misconception that hospice is primarily for people with cancer is regrettable.

During the early 1970s, as hospice was developing in England and America, most patients referred to hospice had cancer. In recent years, more and more patients with progressive neurologic diseases or heart, kidney, or respiratory failure are being served by hospice. A large and growing number of people are living with advanced HIV/AIDS; each one deserves the sort of services that hospice represents. Unfortunately, in the United States, the bureaucracy and payment system of Medicare, Medicaid, and many insurance plans work against patients who need a hospice level of service but whose diagnosis does not lend itself to a reliable prediction of when they might die. Some hospice programs are reluctant, for financial reasons, to accept patients with AIDS, who may require very expensive medications, or patients with heart disease or emphysema, who may stabilize between crises and live many months. In our program's experience, patients with advanced lung disease have been well suited and seem to especially benefit from hospice care.

If you meet initial resistance from the doctor, ask for a second opinion. If there is resistance from the local hospice program, persist. Appropriateness for hospice is determined by prognosis, not diagnosis. Ask to meet with the hospice executive director or the medical director. Is there another, competing hospice program in the area?

Q. Dad has been told that his diabetes and the heart and kidney disease it has caused are incurable. Is it time to talk with hospice? If not, how will we know when it is?

A. Part of the answer to this question relates to your father's functional status. Usually people raise this question when the person has recently been losing weight and/or the ability to get around or care for himself in basic ways. If the trend in his general health and function is clearly downward, it is worthwhile to talk with hospice.

At least as important, however, are your father's preferences and expectations regarding his care. Does he want to live as long as possible, and would he welcome aggressive treatments (such as CPR and artificial ventilation) aimed solely at prolonging life? A closely related question is: How does he experience his current quality of life? I have learned that it is a mistake to assume that because a person can no longer do things for himself or, perhaps, can no longer read the newspaper, that his quality of life is poor. I have to ask.

In general I choose to err on the side of encouraging people to talk early on about hospice, pick up some hospice information, and meet with someone from a local program. Sometimes, if family members wait until they are absolutely certain their loved one is ready, the referral comes too late. The sort of work described in the stories in this book takes time. Relationships build over time, as does confidence and trust. It works both ways. Even with all the education and clinical training our hospice team has, each person and family is unique. We can only develop real expertise one case at a time.

Q. My brother has had most of his medical care at the university medical center, and he sees many doctors. Which doctor should manage his pain?

A. This is an example in which identifying the problem and asking the question comprise two-thirds of the solution. One doctor should primarily manage your brother's pain treatment and symptomatic medications. That physician should be skilled in symptom management and easy to talk with. When she is not available, there must be a clearly delineated call system or backup plan. At intervals ask whether your brother's various doctors are receiving (and reading) notes from the other doctors involved in his care. As his condition changes, it should always be clear who is the medical "captain" of the physician team, and who is responsible for comfort measures, if it is not the captain.

Q. Is there any certification or licensing for doctors who specialize in palliative medicine? If not, how do I evaluate a hospice doctor?

A. Palliative medicine, the field of care that hospice physicians practice, is a recognized medical specialty in England and Australia. Development of formal specialty status is well under way in Canada. In the United States, the National Board of Certified Hospice Nurses has begun administering an examination and offering certification. The American Board of Hospice and Palliative Medicine began offering a certification examination for physicians in 1996. Formal recognition of palliative medicine as an American medical specialty is, however, a number of years in the distance.

At present, there is no simple answer to your question. Ask the local hospice program in your area to suggest physicians who are knowledgeable in palliative medicine. You can call the American Academy of Hospice and Palliative Medicine and ask about member physicians in your area. Of course, it may be sufficient to ask your doctor if he has any special knowledge or training in this area. If symptom management problems occur, always consider obtaining a consultation with another physician or a formal consultation with a hospice nurse.

Q. Dad has congestive heart failure, and the doctor says he probably won't live beyond a year. The hospice program says Dad is not eligible, because his doctor won't certify that he has less than six months to live. I think both parents would benefit from hospice care. Is there any way Dad might qualify?

A. The criterion of a "six months or less" life expectancy is often misunderstood and does not need to be a barrier to hospice care. Medicare established the six-month criterion for payment purposes, and it has been adopted by virtually all government and private health payers who cover hospice services. There is, however, considerable flexibility within the actual regulations and Medicare's official "interpretative guidelines." Most hospice programs talk in terms of a "limited life expectancy" as criterion for admission. Recent studies have shown that determining the life expectancy of any single patient remains a very inexact science, even when physicians' best estimates are bolstered by sophisticated computer models. Therefore, using the figure of six months as anything more than a rough guideline is inappropriate.

In practice, it is more important whether your father's orientation is toward living as long as possible and desiring continued life-saving care or toward the completion of his affairs and living as comfortably and fully as possible in whatever time is left. If his condition and preferences make hospice seem appropriate, the program could admit him with the understanding that he will be reevaluated at regular intervals, and that if he stabilizes or his preferences regarding care shift, hospice could back out—at least for a time. Before they did, however, the hospice team would have helped to devise a plan of care, which would improve your parents' ability and confidence to perform self-care at home.

Q. My mother is at home and cared for by a hospice program. Still, she is in pain much of the time. Is the hospice not doing its job?

A. I don't know, but if your mother is in a lot of pain, something is wrong. How often has the hospice nurse been seeing her? Does your mother, or do you, tell the nurse that she is in pain? Does your mother take her medicine regularly? Does she have medicine to take as "rescue" doses, and does she know how much she can take and how often?

If you sense that the hospice team is not as involved as it should be, ask hard questions. Why is Mom still in pain? What are we supposed to do when she hurts and it is not yet time for her next dose? If the nurse seems evasive or refers you back to your doctor for these questions, consider this an indication that your mother's doctor may be the problem. Ask the hospice nurse directly if your mother's doctor is easy to work with.

Not all hospices are created equal. Your mother's pain is a serious problem that merits serious, ongoing attention. If the hospice team is not responding with the frequency and intensity that the problem deserves, begin by asking that the hospice medical director do a formal consultation. If the nurse says something like "Oh, our doctor doesn't do that," complain loudly or change hospices. Having a medical director who is available to deal with problems of uncontrolled symptoms is a minimal requirement for hospice program certification.

Q. We got hospice involved because we needed someone to change Dad's dressing. Now they want us to talk to the hospice chaplain and the social worker and to let a volunteer visit. We don't feel ready for it. Aren't they rushing it?

A. It's OK to take some time, but my bias is to encourage you to at least meet the people suggested. Hospice care is genuinely a specialized team process; in this regard, it differs from routine home health care. Your preconceptions about what the social worker or chaplain will say or do could keep you from meeting people who might surprise you in pleasant ways. At the very least, meeting the members of the hospice team now will build familiarity, which can be a comfort later when more services are needed.

When the Dying Is Your Own

Q. I have cancer, and I am not ready to talk about dying, but my family bought me this damn book. I feel like they're pushing me into the grave. Why can't they just leave me alone?

A. I can't speak to the wisdom of them giving you this book, but as long as you asked, there are reasons why they can't just leave you alone. Even in dying you are stuck with family. Like it or not, you didn't stop being part of your family when you became ill. And belonging to your family still involves give and take. Being sick certainly changes your roles and diminishes your responsibilities within your family, but responsibilities do not simply go away.

From the tone of your question, I can almost hear your response: "Responsibilities, for Christ sakes. Just let me be!" Sorry, you're not dead yet, and, while your responsibilities aren't onerous, they are real. My best advice is: Relax! It will all happen naturally if and when you can accept the fact that you are still connected to your family. For instance, you have a responsibility to tell your family what you need and what you want. Unless you do, they may well not know. If you don't want to talk about dying, tell them so. But don't do it out of bravado or in silent suffering; it just causes everyone more pain.

It's not dying that people need to talk with each other about, but the living they've shared and their relationships. I think people who are dying have a responsibility to help reconcile strained relations they have with family and previously close friends. In other words, if a relative or friend is open, it seems irresponsible to ignore the chance to heal wounded relationships before one's death.

Dying is fundamentally a personal experience; if it is truly your choice, it is also your right to be "left alone." Recognize, however, that your relatives and friends each have their own personal experience with regard to your dying. You can't change that fact, and it's not your fault, but you can help them with their own emotional distress. They may suffer because of the isolation from you. Acknowledging another's pain by simply offering a kind word or a hug can be an enormous gift to people who love you.

Q. I have AIDS. Though I currently feel well physically, I know that I will eventually die of the disease. I have transferred important property, prepared my will, and assigned a durable power of attorney for health care decisions. But I still do not feel ready to die. What can I do to prepare myself emotionally?

A. My guess is that you have already done much of the work you need to do at this point in time. Since your financial and legal affairs sound like they are in order, ask yourself about affairs in other areas of your life. Are your relationships also "in order"? It may not be time to say goodbye, but to say "forgive me" and "I forgive you," and to express appreciation and affection to the people closest to you, means less will need to be said later.

For some people, questions of meaning are what underlie a sense of unreadiness. These are not merely intellectual issues of philosophy or religion but rather genuine, wrenching struggles to understand why certain things turned out the way they did in your life. If you are someone for whom it is essential to get a sense of meaning about your disease, an event in your past, or life in general, honor this need and make this illness an opportunity to search for answers that make sense to you.

Now that the disease is a fact and you are who you are, what does life hold? What matters most to you in life? Listen carefully to your answers; they will point the way to where your work lies. Of course, this sort of inquiry and introspection can have value at any time in our adult lives. Preparation for dying need not be separate from living. Do the work you are drawn to do, but keep the focus on living.

Q. I'm not married, I have no brothers or sisters, and my parents died many years ago. Now I am terminally ill. The stories in this book stress the importance of family. Can I die well without family?

A. The dying experience represents an opportunity for a person to achieve a sense of reconciliation, completion, and closure in relationships with family. This sense of completion is internal and can be achieved even after someone has died. If you have been previously married and have unreconciled feelings toward your former spouse, or if you feel that your relationship with your deceased parents or living relations was incomplete when they died, it is worth talking about these feelings with a member of a hospice team or a counselor.

As I have stated earlier, I think of family as a process; family is marked by feelings of mutual connection, appreciation, and caring. When I use the word *family*, I mean both relatives and loving friends. Almost certainly, you have a group of friends who qualify as family in this sense of the word. Notice who shows up and who you miss when they don't. In my years of hospice work, I have witnessed family dynamics emerging around even the most isolated individuals. When people have been utterly alone for years, it may be nurses or aides in a nursing home, or perhaps hospice volunteers, who become family to the person dying.

Finally, as important as family is, there are other aspects of our personhood that are equally important. In what ways might it be important for you to change or grow, as a person, during the life that lies ahead?

Q. I'm dying of lung and brain cancer and can't do anything I used to enjoy. I'm feeling hopeless, and every day feels like an ordeal. Why should I go on living?

A. Your question resounds with pain. It is awful to feel this bad. I don't know specifically why you should go on living, but I know that while you are living, there is relief to be had from your despair. It is normal to be sad and have a sense of loss at this time, but feelings of hopelessness and unworthiness are not inevitable—although it may feel that way at present—and are often markers of clinical depression. Effective medications and counseling exist. There is a way through. Don't give up; get help.

Assisted Suicide

Q. My grandfather has been in a nursing home for years and hasn't recognized anyone in the family for at least two years. It seems like he's in the hospital every couple of months for an infection. Wouldn't it be kinder to put him out of his misery?

A. Perhaps, but what misery is he in? Is he in pain, or does he spend his days frightened and agitated? If so, these treatable conditions must be attended to.

At times when this question is asked, "the misery" is actually the family's. The patient is in no distress and may actually enjoy most days, but he is "no longer the person we know."

If, on the other hand, his daily life is miserable, and it is consistent with his previous wishes, I firmly agree that he should be allowed to die. Are there ways in which his present care is keeping him alive unnecessarily? Is he being fed by a tube? What was the goal of treating his infections? Discomfort can be managed without reversing the underlying condition. If the desire is to invite death, these treatments should be reconsidered. Malnutrition and infection are two of the most natural ways for people with dementia and general debilitation to die. By "letting nature take its course" you can remain loving and pampering in your care of your grandfather without feeling that you have caused his demise.

Q. My friend has advanced AIDS and has been asking me to help him plan his suicide. I love him and want to help him, but I can't bear to talk about suicide. What should I do?

A. This is delicate turf. You are right to feel uncomfortable with this request. Yet it is wonderful that your friend trusts you enough to talk about suicide openly, and I encourage you to allow him to air his feelings.

People who are contemplating suicide typically feel hopeless, worthless, and burdensome. In helping him plan his suicide, you risk reinforcing these impressions. The request for help in suicide is often a way of expressing deep despair. Try to respond in ways that speak to his continued worth in your eyes. Tell him you love him and that caring for him is a burden you want to shoulder.

If your friend persists in his request, discuss his plans openly with him, but acknowledge that the decision and actions should be his own. Your friend already has the ability to end his life. People with AIDS and opportunistic infections need only stop taking their various antibiotics, and complications of the disease will soon carry them away. The same carbon monoxide that Dr. Kevorkian provides is available from the back of any car. While this may sound awful, it is a mode of death that is available to him and is without pain. Additionally, because of your friend's condition, it is unlikely that he would be bothered by hunger were he to stop eating. In fact, refusing to eat is probably the most common and age-old way for people who are fed up with life to hasten death. Were he to do so, you could stand by him, continuing to love him, nurture him, and testify to his inherent worth.

Q. What should I do if my friend decides to go ahead with the suicide and wants me to be with him?

A. Naturally, there are legal issues to consider. If you are the one to actually administer the lethal drug or carbon monoxide or to place a plastic bag over his head, you will be at some legal risk.

If, however, what your friend intends is genuinely a suicide, in the current social climate your legal risk is probably slight. Still, the issues of legality and of unwelcome publicity should be carefully weighed.

Ultimately the decision will be a deeply personal one that only you can make. In whatever you do, try to express your continued love and your sense of his continued worth. Do not become complicit with his feelings of being unworthy and solely a burden. If you decide to be present, share your feelings with him. Our loved ones should know they are being reluctantly released from our arms as they die.

Caring for a Dying Child

Q. My three-year-old daughter has a brain tumor, which is growing again after surgery and radiation therapy. We want her to be at home when she eventually dies, but all the specialists work through the university medical center. Is there any way she can be at home when she dies?

A. Yes, in all likelihood there is. Unless you live in the same city as the university hospital, you can work with a pediatrician or family doctor in your own community who can stay in close contact with the pediatric oncologists.

Most hospice programs readily accept children as patients, and a number of larger communities have special pediatric hospice teams. The hospice team can work with your local physician, as well as helping to coordinate care with the university-based specialists. If you do not have an established relationship with a doctor near your home, you might call a hospice first and ask for suggestions.

The National Hospice Organization, Children's Hospice International, and the American Academy of Hospice and Palliative Medicine may each be a resource in helping to locate needed services in your community. Their addresses and phone numbers are listed in the appendix.

Q. My child has leukemia. The treatments keep getting more aggressive. I hate seeing him in such distress and would rather lose him than watch him suffer. What can we do?

A. Childhood leukemias are often curable; even in fairly late-stage disease, aggressive therapy sometimes results in long-term survival. Before deciding to stop therapy, be sure that everything possible is being done to ensure your son's comfort. Is he being adequately medicated in advance of painful procedures? Initial pain medication can be given by mouth, avoiding the anticipatory fear of the first needle stick. In many pediatric centers, topical anesthetic cream has become routine before starting IVs or doing any procedures involving needles.

Young patients may need to be held still for various procedures. However, except in true emergencies, it is no longer acceptable to hold a child down rather than medicate him for pain. Do not be intimidated by nurses or doctors who tell you otherwise. Insist that adequate comfort measures are routinely performed. If your child is frequently in pain, or has other physical distress that is not being actively addressed, complain loudly. And keep complaining until things change.

Q. Our six-year-old boy has a brain tumor and requires pain and antiseizure medication. He hates any kind of shots. What else can we do, if and when he is unable to take oral pills and liquids?

A. Many medications come in concentrated form that requires only that a few drops of liquid be placed under the tongue or in sips of juice. In some circumstances it is preferable to use suppositories or pills that are placed rectally. Research has shown that such pills, properly placed, are absorbed as completely and as quickly as if they were swallowed.

If injections do become unavoidable, ask about subcutaneous infusions, which are the easiest to begin and tend to be very well tolerated.

Q. Our little four-year-old girl is dying, and it is hard to imagine any possible value in this experience. How can we possibly find anything worthwhile in this awful time?

A. It seems profane to even consider the possibility of anything worthwhile coming out of your daughter's dying. If this time does have value, it may only be apparent years from now as you look back. Attempting to find meaning in the illness and death of a child can become a trap for parents. There will probably never be satisfactory answers for why this has occurred. The loss of a child may be truly meaningless.

Perhaps the tragedy of a child's death is only outweighed by the miracle of her birth. More than one grieving parent has found meaning in balancing the sense of tragedy by considering the time they had together as a precious gift.

The developmental landmarks that I have already discussed apply in different ways with young children. The key landmarks have to do with achieving self-acceptance, self-worth, a love of self, and the capacity to feel the love of others. These landmarks are more readily accessible to children; the younger they are, the less they have to unlearn. Children are, by nature, innocents. They are not burdened by accumulations of regret, remorse, or guilt, and thus have much less to let go of. Tenderness, vulnerability, and trust, which can be so difficult for adults to achieve, come naturally to them. This ability is an aspect of their inherent wisdom, and is one reason why children tend to teach adults so much even as they die.

Be kind to yourself. Stop looking for meaning and searching for value. This is the most difficult time imaginable. It is enough, for the present, to put one foot in front of the other and remember to breathe. Do it all with a loving attitude; toward your daughter, your other children, your spouse, and yourself.

Q. My five-year-old son has had leukemia since he was about one, and it keeps recurring, despite aggressive treatment. How can I begin talking to him about dying?

A. A child's understanding of what dying means will be different from what we might think as adults. The monumental existential issues of loss and finality very often have little power for children. Instead your child may be most concerned about separation from you, in an immediate, physical sense. In whatever you say, therefore, be certain to include reassurance that you will always be there to comfort and care for him.

Children deserve to be treated honestly. It is only fair to tell them when treatments have stopped working. But it is certainly acceptable to balance the bad news with some good. When a decision has been made to halt further chemotherapy, for instance, it is OK to emphasize that he won't have to go to the hospital nearly as often, that there won't be so many needle sticks anymore, and that your family will be spending a lot more time together at home and having some fun.

Your pediatrician, the cancer program, or the local hospice will be able to help and will have some age-appropriate storybooks to help begin talking about dying. A child may understand dying in terms of heaven and the afterlife. Unless such notions are unacceptable within your family's religious tradition, the belief that you will all eventually be back together can be enormously comforting for him.

RESOURCES

Addresses

Academy of Hospice Nurses
32478 Dunford Rd.
Farmington Hills, MI 48334
(303) 432-5482

Access Project
AIDS Treatment Data Network
611 Broadway, Suite 613
New York, NY 10012-2608
1-800-734-7104
(212) 260-8868
E-mail: AIDSTreatD@aol.com

American Academy of Hospice and Palliative Medicine
P.O. Box 14288
Gainesville, FL 32604-2288
(352) 377-8900
General e-mail: ahp@ahp.org
Web site: http://www.ahp.org

American Board of Hospice and Palliative Medicine
P.O. Box 14288
Gainesville, FL 32604-2288
(352) 377-8900

American Cancer Society
1599 Clifton Rd., N.E.
Atlanta, GA 30329
1-800-227-2345

American Hospice Foundation
1130 Connecticut Ave., N.W., Suite 700
Washington, DC 20036-4101
(202) 223-0204

Cancer Information Service for the Pacific Northwest
1124 Columbia St., MP-951
Seattle, WA 98104
1-800-4-CANCER
(206) 667-4682

Candlelighters Childhood Cancer Foundation
7910 Woodmont Ave., Suite 460
Bethesda, MD 20814
1-800-366-2223
(301) 657-8401

Children's Hospice International
901 N. Washington St.
Alexandria, VA 22314
1-800-242-4453
(703) 684-0330

Choice in Dying, Inc.
200 Varick St.
New York, NY 10014-4810
1-800-939-WILL
(212) 366-5540, ext. 242
General e-mail: cid@choices.org
Web site: http://www.choices.org

Delta Society
Pet Partners Program
289 Perimeter Rd. East
Renton, WA 98055
1-800-869-6898

Federal Centers for Disease Control
National AIDS Hotline
1600 Clifton Rd., N.E.
Atlanta, GA 30333
1-800-342-2437

Hospice Education Institute
Five Essex Square
P.O. Box 713
Essex, CT 06426
Hotline: 1-800-331-1620
(203) 767-1620 ("Hospice Link")

Hospice Association of America
519 C St., N.E.
Stanton Park
Washington, DC 20002-5809
(202) 546-4759

Hospice Nurses Association, National Office
5512 Northumberland St.
Pittsburgh, PA 15217
(412) 687-3231

National Association of People with AIDS
1413 K St., N.W., Tenth Floor
Washington, DC 20005
(202) 898-0414

National Board for Certification of Hospice Nurses
5512 Northumberland St.
Pittsburgh, PA 15217-1131
(412) 687-3231

National Cancer Institute
Cancer Information Services
P.O. Box 24128
Baltimore, MD 21227
1-800-422-6237

National Hospice Organization
1901 N. Moore St., Suite 901
Arlington, VA 22209
1-800-658-8898
(703) 243-5900

National Institute for Jewish Hospice
8723 Alden Dr., Suite 652
Los Angeles, CA 90048
1-800-446-4448
In California: (213) 467-7423

National Prison Hospice Association
P.O. Box 941
Boulder, CO 80306
(303) 666-9638

People with AIDS Coalition
31 W. 26th St.
New York, NY 10010
1-800-828-3280
(212) 532-0568

Robert Wood Johnson Foundation Last Acts Resource Directory
℅ Barksdale Ballard
8027 Leesburg Pike, Suite 200
Vienna, VA 22182
(703) 827-8771
web site: http://www.rwjf.org

Further Reading

Michael Appleton and Todd Henschell, *At Home with Terminal Illness: A Family Guide to Hospice in the Home.* Englewood Cliffs, N.J.: Prentice-Hall, 1995.

Sandra L. Bertman, *Facing Death: Images, Insights, and Interventions.* Bristol, Penn.: Taylor & Francis, 1991.

Anne Brener, *Mourning and Mitzvah: A Guided Journal for Walking the Mourner's Path Through Grief to Healing.* Woodstock, Vt.: Jewish Lights Publishing, 1993.

Gail Cason-Reiser, Michael Demoratz, and Richard Reiser, *Dying 101: A Short Course on Living for the Terminally Ill.* Laguna Beach, Calif.: Pushing the Envelope Publications, 1995.

Eric J. Cassell, *The Nature of Suffering and the Goals of Medicine.* New York: Oxford University Press, 1991.

Charles Corr, Clyde Nabe, and Donna Corr, *Death and Dying, Life and Living.* Pacific Grove, Calif.: Brooks/Cole Publishing, 1994.

David Feinstein and Peg Elliott Mayo, *Rituals for Living and Dying.* New York: HarperCollins, 1990.

Victor Frankl, *Man's Search for Meaning.* New York: Washington Square Press, 1984.

Kathy Kalina, *Midwife for Souls.* Boston: St. Paul's Books and Media, 1989.

Verena Kast, *Joy, Inspiration and Hope.* College Station: Texas A & M University Press, 1991.

Patricia Kelley and Maggie Callanan, *Final Gifts.* New York: Poseidon Press, 1992.

Elisabeth Kübler-Ross and Mal Warshaw, *To Live Until We Say Goodbye.* New York: Simon & Schuster, 1978.

Susan Lang and Richard Patt, *You Don't Have to Suffer.* New York: Oxford University Press, 1994.

Dale Larson, *The Helper's Journey: Working with People Facing Grief, Loss, and Life-Threatening Illness.* Champaign, Ill.: Research Press, 1993.

Stephen Levine, *Meetings at the Edge.* New York: Anchor Doubleday, 1984.

———, *Who Dies: An Investigation of Conscious Living and Conscious Dying.* Garden City, N.Y.: Anchor Books, 1982.

Katie Maxwell, *Beside Manners: A Practical Guide to Visiting the Ill.* Grand Rapids, Mich.: Baker Book House, 1990.

Catherine Ray, *I'm Here to Help.* Mound, Mont.: Hospice Handouts, 1992.

Sogyal Rinpoche, *The Tibetan Book of Living and Dying.* New York: HarperCollins, 1992.

Andrea Sankar, *Dying at Home.* Baltimore: Johns Hopkins University Press, 1991.

Hannelore Wass, ed., *Dying: Facing the Facts.* New York: Hemisphere Publishing, 1979.

ACKNOWLEDGMENTS

For several years Pat Kelley, co-author of *Final Gifts* and a dear friend, had been encouraging me—actually nagging me—to write a book. "Ira, you really need to write a book. You should talk with my agent. You'd really like my agent." It seemed that the last thing I needed to do was write a book, so I always thanked her and ignored her. But Pat is persistent and she was right. When I finally did contact her fabled agent, Gail Ross, I liked her immediately. Thank you, Pat.

Gail believed that there was a valuable book within my work and writings. More important, she made me believe it. Her vision and insight pervade this project. In coming to know a bit of what Gail does I've become aware of her pivotal role in creating and nurturing contemporary nonfiction, a role the public will never know.

When it became clear that the proposal for *Dying Well* was more than just another project on my cluttered desk, I knew I needed help. Lisa Berger, whose accomplishments as an author include *Under Observation,* the acclaimed portrayal of McLean Psychiatric Hospital, could have written her own book about death and dying. Instead, to my great good fortune, she agreed to help me write mine. Lisa was writing coach, task master, in-house (*in-head!*) editor. She lived and breathed this book with me. What began as a relationship of author to hired talent evolved into a collaboration of friends. The stories, thoughts, and words of *Dying Well* are mine, but the contributions of Lisa's craft to the quality and cohesion of this book are apparent in every page.

Enormous credit for the final manuscript belongs to Jane Isay, my editor at Riverhead. Jane recognized the potential of this project on first reading the proposal. She never flagged in her enthusiasm. Working with Jane has been a wonderful experience. She provided direction as a sage Zen brush painter might, in broad perfect strokes, while supporting me as only a Jewish mother could, with affection and confidence in my abilities that drew from me the best I could give.

My colleagues in hospice in Missoula warrant recognition for so much of the content of this book. Although the narration of this book is written in the first-person singular, many, many times "we" would have been more accurate. Caring is a "team sport," and as team members in our work we are natural extensions of one another. It is a privilege to work with the people I do.

I am indebted to Mary Molloy Beaulieu, office manager of the Palliative Care Service. Mary's affliction for order, attention to detail, and pride in all she does makes what I do possible. Somehow she manages to meet chaos with composure, handle me with humor, and make me look good. Thank you, Mary.

Sincere appreciation also goes to the staff at the Institute of Medicine and Humanities, the Ridge Library at St. Patrick Hospital, and the Mansfield Library at the University of Montana. The resources these institutions in Missoula offer make it possible for me to do the writing and research I do.

My thanks to Martha Ramsey, my copyeditor, for the meticulous attention to detail and obvious sensitivity to the subject that is apparent in the polishing of the manuscript.

Dan Baum, another "Son of Sy," is someone without whom I might not have begun writing in earnest. Dan is a dear friend whose editing gives new meaning to the term "tough love." Over the years, the fact that he would edit my work at all has provided crucial encouragement to keep trying. Along with his co-conspirators Meg Knox and Bill Chaloupka, Dan forms an inner circle of real writers whose take on the cultural and political scene keeps me grounded. Without their counsel, prodding, and belief in me, this book would not have been written.

I feel gratitude to Anita Doyle for her years of friendship, intellectual discernment, and editorial support.

Among the most influential people in my early professional development have been colleagues and teachers, including Harvey Horne, Claus Bahnson, Sally Medrano, Kimberley Dougherty, John Blossom, William Lammers, and Josephina Magno.

My further professional evolution has been nurtured in discussions and work with colleagues who comprise the American Academy of Hospice and Palliative Medicine, especially its board of directors; the warmest, least pretentious collection of serious people I have ever known.

Virtually all of the theory or insights I have and can offer herein I have learned from reading or hearing the work of teachers in the field. I am indebted to them all. I feel a special gratitude for and wish to recognize the following teachers:

> Dr. Balfour Mount, for repeatedly inspiring me; for being my deepest and most enduring mentor; for challenging me, provoking me, and befriending me.
>
> Dr. Elisabeth Kübler-Ross, for demonstrating in her practice that dying is, indeed, a part of living.
>
> Ram Dass, for making the wisdom of the East accessible and relevant in an American context and for adding his own compelling insights and humor.
>
> Dame Cicely Saunders, for inspiring and mentoring us all.

Sincere thanks are due my mother, Ruth Byock, and sister, Molly, for the openness and willingness to share Sy's story. Thank you for your love.

My daughters, Lila and Satya, have put up with a great deal. Over the years they have had to donate too much of their Dad to the cause of end-of-life care. Without their love, support, and encouragement this book could not have been written. Like so much of what I do, in many ways this book is really for them.

Finally and most profoundly, I want to deeply thank and honor the patients whose stories I have shared. Their openness and vulnerability was freely given so that I and others might learn from their experiences. Other patients and families were interviewed for stories that must await being fully told. I thank them, too, for extending to me their trust.

INDEX

Addiction, questions of, 260–61
Advance directives, 267–68
AIDS patients
  and assisted suicide, 278–79
  hospice case, 160–71
  hospice programs and, 270
  preparations for death by, 275–76
Allergies, and pain medication, 256–57
ALS. *See* Amyotrophic lateral sclerosis
Alternative therapies, 236
Alzheimer's disease, 87, 262–63
  hospice case of, 110–17
America
  dying in, 241–42, 244–46
  end-of-life care in, 250
American Academy of Hospice and Palliative Medicine, 272, 279
Americans, and death, xiii
Amyotrophic lateral sclerosis (ALS), 88–98
Anger, 162
  at terminal illness, 61, 65–82, 195–96
Antibiotics, 263
  refusal of, 278
Antinausea medications, 257
Anxiety, 148–49, 152–53
Art, 237
Artificial feeding, 179–80
  refusal of, 267–68
  See also Food, refusal of
Assertive pain management, 60
Assisted-living arrangements, 265–66
Assisted suicide, 60, 179, 244–45, 277–79
  See also Euthanasia

Bancap, 256
Barbiturates, 208–9, 215
  intravenous, 187
Bone pain, radiation therapy for, 256
Brain disease, of child, 173–92
Brain tumor, 62–66, 82
  hospice case of, 219–39
Brannigan, Susan, 130
Breast cancer, pain from, 258–60
Breath work, 236

Names in italics are pseudonymous cases

Bronchitis, chronic, 141
Brown, Bonnie, 66, 73, 81–82
Buddhism, and suffering, 83
Burden, terminal care as, 159–60
Burke, Wallace, 87–98
Byock, Seymour, 3–24, 85–86

Callanan, Maggie. *See Final Gifts*
Cancer
  of colon, 36–41
  of kidney, 193–216
  of lung, 61–84
  pain relief for, 255–59, 268
  of pancreas, 3, 5, 8–9, 12–15
Carbon monoxide, 278–79
Cardiopulmonary resuscitation (CPR), 14, 27
Caregivers, ordeals of, 159
Care of dying persons, 42, 96–98, 246
  acceptance of, 167
  burden of, as gift, 159–71
Caring, values of, medical profession and, 243
Cassell, Eric. *See The Nature of Suffering and the Goals of Medicine*
Chalice of Repose program, 116–17, 136, 150, 152, 232–33, 237–38
Changes, dying and, 33
  spiritual, 31–32
Child, dying, care of, 173–92, 279–82
Childhood leukemia, 280
Children, and love of parents, 71, 77
Children's Hospice International, 279
Christianity, and suffering, 83
Chronic obstructive pulmonary disease (COPD), 140–58
Clinical depression, 101, 277
Codeine, 256–57
Colon cancer, 36–41
Comatose state, 252–53, 266–67
Comfort One, 199–200
Commitment, for end-of-life care, 250
Community, 96–98, 175, 241
  and care for dying members, 246–48
Community-based hospice programs, 243–44
Compazine, 257
Complementary therapies, 236
Completion of relationships, 120–21, 133, 158, 252
  five things for, 140, 146, 151, 157–58, 252
Constipation, narcotics and, 257
COPD. *See* Chronic obstructive pulmonary disease
Costs, of terminal care, 242
CPR. *See* Cardiopulmonary resuscitation
Curative medicine, 243

Darvocet, 255
Darvon, 255
Daughter, relationship with, 45–46, 53
Davis, Harriet, 127–29
Day, Lily, 130
Death, 237
  Americans and, xiii
  of child, value in, 280–81
  doctors and, 35–36
  experience of, 30–32
  at home, 48–49
  and lifelong development, 32–33
  preparations for, 275–76
  as problem, 26–28
  timing of, 225
Decadron (dexamethasone), 256
Decisions
  end-of-life, 137
  about life-prolonging treatments, 115, 116–17, 129, 135
Defiance of death, 200
Degenerative polio dystrophy, 174
Dehydration, 179, 266
Dementia, 86–87, 262–63
  hospice case, 110–17
Denial of impending death, 197, 200
Dependency, 141, 159
  dignity and, 97–98
  physical, 86–87
    acceptance of, 22–23
  terminal illness and, 84, 85–86

INDEX

Depression, 277
  terminal illness and, 101
Determination, for end-of-life care, 250
Development, lifelong, 32–33
Dexamethasone. *See* Decadron
Dexedrine (dextroamphetamine), 257
Diabetic diets, 262
Diagnosis
  and hospice eligibility, 270–71
  of pain, 255
Diet, in terminal illness, 262
Dignity, 72
  loss of, 85–86
  maintenance of, 86–117
Dilaudid (hydromorphone), 255
Distant relations, dying, 253–54
DNR (do not resuscitate) order, 14
  See also Comfort One
Doctor-patient relationship, communication in, 263–64
Doctors. *See* Physicians
Dougherty, Kimberly, 29
Dramatic attempts to save life, 26–27
Dreamwork, 236
Dreiling, Andi, 43–44, 52–57, 151, 153–54, 166, 168–71, 207
  and Michael Merseal, 174, 181–82, 187, 189–91
Drug abuse, and narcotic medications, 260–61
Duragesic. *See* Fentanyl
Dying, xiv
  American society and, 241–42, 244–46
  child's understanding of, 281–82
  experience of, xiv, 30–32, 57, 275
  home care for, 16–17
  process of, 35–36, 218
  suffering of, 59–60
  talking about, 250–52
Dying patients, 42
  hospital treatment, 27–29
Dying well, 32–34, 36, 139, 213, 246, 253
  without family, 276–77
  living well and, 238–39
  suffering and, 84

Eating
  inability of, 266
  stopping of, 92, 263, 278
  See also Food
Edwards, Jake, 159–71
Eligibility for hospice programs, 272–73
Embarrassment at illness, 8–9
Emergency room (ER), death in, 27–28
Emotional distress of dying, 214
Emphysema, 141
  hospice programs and, 270
End of life
  decisions, 137
  experience of, desirable, 32
  goals of, 34
  taskwork of, 32, 78
End-of-life care
  crisis in, 242–44
    assisted suicide and, 244–45
  medical profession and, 243, 250
Esperenza Care Cooperative, 16, 29–31
Ethics committee, and Merseal case, 187–89
Euphoria, 238
Euthanasia, 60, 192, 208, 216
  right to, 245
  See also Assisted suicide
Experience of dying, xiv, 30–32, 57, 275

Family
  relationships with, 276–77
  responsibility for dying members of, 249–50
  and terminal illness, 84, 242, 274–75
  See also Home-centered care for the dying
Father, death of, 1–26, 85–86
Fatherhood, terminal illness and, 63–64
Fears, of dying process, 241–42
Feeding tubes, 115, 262–63
  refusal of, 267–68
  removal of, 266–67
  See also Food
Fentanyl (Duragesic), 256, 259

Final Gifts (Callanan and Kelly), 235
Financial impact of terminal care, 242
Financing of hospice programs, 90, 243
Five things of relationship completion, 140, 146, 151, 157–58, 252
Food
  lack of, 266
  refusal of, 92, 278
  withholding of, 179, 262–63
Forgiveness, 26, 253
Fragile X syndrome, 174
Frankl, Victor. See *Man's Search for Meaning*
Functional decline, dignity and, 86–87
Functional status, and hospice eligibility, 271
Future, possession of, 60

Gifts, from children, 199
Glioblastoma, 220–39
Goals
  of dying persons, 120–21, 225
  of medical profession, 35
  survival as, 45–46
Good art, 237
Goodbyes, 218
Good deaths, 30–32
Grandmother, death of, 17
Grief, 170
  caregiving and, 231
  and clinical depression, 101
  family and, 201
  at imminent death, 49
Grof, Stanislav, 236
Groth, Kenneth, 205
Growth
  death of child and, 175, 192
  through death of loved one, 26
  in dying, 32, 160, 213, 246
    personal, 80–81, 140
  dying well and, 33–34
Guggenheim, Mary Anne, 173–77, 184–85
Guthrie, Woody, 119

Haldeman, Janelle, 119–37
Haldol, 257
Hardships in life, 104
Hardy, Bruce, 174, 175, 177
Hatha yoga, 236
Healing
  and dying, 32
  within families, 252–53
  of relationships, 53
Health care, medical profession and, 35
Health care corporations, profit-oriented, and hospice programs, 243–44
Health care crisis, 242–43
Health care professionals, and cost controls, 242
Heart disease, hospice programs and, 270
Heatherfield Nursing Home, 111–17, 121–36
Help, hired, at home, 265
Helplessness, 44
Heroic measures, avoidance of, 243
Heroism, 139
Hindu *kirtan*, 237
HIV epidemic, and hospice funding, 243
Holotropic Breathing, 236
Home Box Office, Merseal story, 188
Home-centered care for the dying, 16–18, 21–24, 48–49
  hospice and, 89–90
Home health nurses, 28
Hopelessness, 44, 277
Hospice House, Missoula, 89–90, 93
Hospice physicians, licensing for, 272
Hospice programs, 27, 28–29, 266, 268–69
  case histories of
    AIDS patient, 161–71
    amyotrophic lateral sclerosis, 88–98
    brain tumor, 222–39
    childhood brain disease, 175–92
    colon cancer, 43–57
    dementia, 111–17
    Huntington's chorea, 129–37
    kidney cancer, 199–216
    lung cancer, 61–84
    lung disease, 144–58
    multiple sclerosis, 99–110

children as patients in, 279–80
eligibility for, 270–71, 272–73
Esperenza Care Cooperative, 29–31
functioning of, 161
as team process, 274
weekly conferences, 165–66
funding for, 90, 243–44
medical treatment and, 181–82
and pain management, 59–60, 268, 273–74
successful, 31–32
timing of, 271
Veterans Administration and, 269–70
Hospitals
death in, 21, 22, 26–29
and hospice programs, 30
psychiatric unit of, 75–79
Human development, lifelong, 32–33
Hunger, 266, 278
See also Food
Huntington's chorea, 119–37
Hydrocodone, 255
Hydromorphone. *See* Dilaudid

Ibuprofen, 255
Identity
loss of, in dying, 85
new, 235–36
suffering and, 84
terminal illness and, 61
Imaginary conversations, 105–6
Incurable illness, and suffering, 59–60
Infections, death from, 278
Injections
alternatives to, 280
pain relief from, 259
Innocence of children, 281
Insight therapy, 236
Insurance industry
and cost controls, 242
and hospice programs, 90, 244, 270
Intimacy, imminent death and, 25–26
Intramuscular (IM) injections, 259
Intravenous injections, 259
of antibiotics, 263
Introspection, 276
Involvement, stress of, 254
"I" statements, 252

Jaundice, painless, 3
Joy of letting go, 234–35
Judaism, and suffering, 83

Kammerer, Vickie, 43, 50–51, 145, 151, 153–54, 166–68, 199, 211–12
Kearney, Douglas, 60–84
Keller, Helen, 49
Kelly, Patricia. *See Final Gifts*
Kerscher, Gail, 227
Kidney cancer, 193–216
King, Tom, 165, 166, 169, 182, 187, 189–91
Kirtan, 237
Kübler-Ross, Elisabeth, 247–48

Labor of dying, 23
Lagrange, Marcel, 13, 18
Landmarks of dying, 33–34, 46
Legal risk, suicide and, 279
Lessons, from death of child, 174–75
Letters, for children in future, 198
Letting go, 217–18
process of, 234–35, 238–39
Letting Go: A Hospice Journey (film), xv
Leukemia, in childhood, 280
Life, fighting for, 193
Life expectancy, determination of, 273
Lifelong development, 32–33
Life-prolonging treatments, 26–27
decisions about, 115, 116–17, 129, 135
Listening
need for, 252
physicians and, 263–64
as therapy, 103
Live-in paid caregivers, 265
Living well, dying well and, 238–39
Living wills
compliance with, 267–68
medical profession and, 243
Lortab, 255

Lou Gehrig's disease. *See* Amyotrophic lateral sclerosis (ALS)
Love, expression of, 23, 71, 77, 109–10, 137, 158, 252
  through care, 160, 168
  grief as, 170
Loved ones, need to care for, 22–23
Low-fat diets, 262
Lung cancer, 61–84
Lung disease, and hospice care, 270

McCall, Mary, 106, 108–9, 203–4, 221, 222
Malnourishment, 179–80
  death from, 278
  See also Food
Managed care organizations, and hospice programs, 244
Man's Search for Meaning (Frankl), 83
Maslow, Abraham, 234
Massage therapies, 236
Matthews, Terry, 193–216
May, Gerald, 170
Meaning
  in death of child, 281
  in dying, xiv, 121, 241
  loss of, and suffering, 83
  questions of, 276
Medicaid, and hospice programs, 90, 243, 270
Medical care, advances in, 21
Medical education, and terminal care, 243
Medical profession
  and communications, 263–64
  and dying patients, 181–82
  and health care, 35
  and pain management, 60
  and serious illness, 26–28
Medicare
  cost controls, 242
  and hospice programs, 90, 243, 270, 273
Meditation, 236, 237
Mental pain, 60
Methylphenidate. *See* Ritalin
Missoula, Montana, 70, 160–61
  Hospice House, 88–90, 93
  hospice team, 34
Missoulian, 222
  and Merseal story, 188, 189
Montana health directive, Comfort One, 199–200
Morphine, 256
  dosages, 259
  and respiration, 258
  side effects of, 257
  tolerance to, 256
Morris, Steve, 139–58
Multiple sclerosis, 99–110
Music, 237
  See also Chalice of Repose program
Narcotic medications
  fear of addiction to, 260–61
  respiratory depressant effects of, 258
  tolerance to, 256, 257
National Board of Certified Hospice Nurses, 272
National Cancer Institute, 63
National Hospice Organization, 279
Nature of Suffering and the Goals of Medicine, The (Cassell), 60
Nearing death awareness, 235
Needs of dying persons, 247
Neurological disease, 86
Nietzsche, Friedrich, 83
Nonintercessory prayer, 235–36
Nonsteroidal anti-inflammatory drugs (NSAIDs), 255
Nurses, public health, 28
Nursing homes, 264–66
  and dying patients, 27

Oxycodone, 256

Pain, of dying person, 214
  denial of, 261–62

mental, 60
physical
alleviation of, xiv, 245, 250, 255–63, 268, 271–72
and death, 241–42
hospice care and, 273–74
and suffering, 59–60
unbearable, and suicide thoughts, 44
undertreatment of, 260
Pain clinics, 268–69
Painless jaundice, 3
Palliative care, 59–60, 206, 214–16
and hospice funding, 243
licensing for specialty, 272
medical profession and, 243, 258, 268
in Veterans Administration hospitals, 269
Pancreas, cancer of, 3, 5, 8–9, 12–15
Parker, Jim, 114, 116
Participatory chants, 237
Peace, in dying, xiv
Pediatric development, 33
Pediatric hospice programs, 279
People, enjoyment of, 4–5
Percocet, 256
Percodan, 256
Personal care homes, 265
Personal distress, dying and, 82–83
Personal experience of dying, 57
Personhood, 86, 277
loss of, 60
terminal illness and, 85
and transcendence, 238
Physical care of dying person, benefits from, 31
Physical pain, 215
alleviation of, 59–60, 250, 255–63, 268, 271–72
and death, 241–42
Physicians
communications with, 263–64
and death, 35–36
and pain relief, 255, 271–72
and palliative medicine, 258
and suicide, 244–45
and transcendent experiences, 238
Pills, pain relief from, 259
Pleasures, for comatose persons, 253
Pomeroy, Stella, 99, 101, 106
Possessions, disposal of, 42–44
Prayer, 235–36
Predictions of disease course, 201
Prednisone, 256
Pride, illness and, 9
Process of dying, 218
Propoxyphene, 255
Prostate cancer, pain of, 256, 258
Pseudoaddiction, 260
Psychiatric unit, 73–79
Psychology of smoking, 141
Psychostimulants, 257
Public health system, 28
Purpose in life, suffering and, 83

Quality-of-life considerations, 271
Questions
about end-of-life care, 250–82
physicians and, 263–64

Radiation therapy, for bone pain, 256
Recording of stories, 113–14, 146
Relationships
anger and, 66–72
completion of, 53, 120–21, 133, 158, 252
five things in, 140, 146, 151, 157–58
death and, 31
difficult, 104
father-son, 6–8
ordering of, 275–76
Relaxation, 145–46
Religions, and suffering, 83
Religious faith, 235–36
Renal cell carcinoma, 193–216
Residential hospice, 89–90, 93
Resources, 283–85
Respiration, narcotics and, 258

Responsibility
for dying family members, 249–50
of dying person, 275
Retirement communities, 265
Riley, Maureen, 217–39
Ritalin (methylphenidate), 48, 257
Rituals of dying, 267
Rosauer, Julia, 98–110
Roxycet, 256
Roxycodone, 256

Sadness, 101, 162
acceptance of, 78–80, 84
acknowledgement of, 72, 82
sharing of, 77
St. Patrick's Hospital, Missoula, 61–62, 204, 220–21
psychiatric unit of, 75–79
SC (subcutaneous) infusions, 259, 280
Schroeder-Sheker, Therese, 237–38
Sedation of terminal patients, 207–9, 215
Self
feeling good about, 105
sense of
incurable illness and, 83–84
letting go of, 218
loss of, 60
Self-actualization, 234
Self-esteem, dying and, 86
Self-image, and dignity, 98–110
Self-worth, dying and, 86
Side effects of pain medications, 256–57
Simon, Linda, 199, 203
Sky View Nursing Home, 152–54
Smith, Gerritt, 14–15, 18
Smoking
and lung cancer, 62, 80
as self-nurture, 141
Social workers, 265
Society, American
and dignity, 86
and dying, 241–42, 244–46
Spirituality of dying person, 233–36
Stegner, Karen, 221–23
Steroids, to relieve pain, 256
Stevens, Jack, 205–6, 207
Stohlberg, Larry, 29
Stories
of death, xiv-xv
of dying experiences, 249
recording of, 113–14, 146
Subcutaneous (SC) infusions, 259, 280
Sudden deaths, 53
Suffering, 82–83
from impending death, 245–46
incurable illness and, 59–60
and loss of dignity, 85–86
meaning in, 241
physical, xiv, 215
See also Pain, of dying person
Sufi singing, 237
Suicide
assisted, 60, 179, 244–45, 277–79
thoughts of, 44, 144
Suppositories, medicated, 280
Symptom management, 59–60, 215

Talking about dying, 250–52
Talking therapies, 236
Taskwork, at end of life, 32, 78, 235
Taylor, Jane, 195, 198, 210
Television, Merseal story, 188
Terminal illness
costs of, 242
and loss of personhood, 60
medical approach to, 35–36
and pain, 59–60
progressive, 120
Therapeutic touch, 236
Thirst, 266
Thomas, Dylan, 193
Tolerance to narcotic medications, 256, 257
Transcendence
of dying, 237–38
of suffering, 241

Transdermal narcotic, 259
Transitional phase of dying, 23
Treatments, decisions against, 222–23
Tylox, 256

Unconscious person, death of, 192
Undertreatment of pain, 260
Universality of dying, 250

Valley Medical Center (VMC), Fresno, California, 12, 18–19, 28
  emergency room of, 26–27
  and hospice program, 29–30

Value, in child's death, 280–81
Versed, 180–82, 186–87
Veterans Administration hospitals, 269–70
Vicodin, 256
Visiting nurse service, 29
Visscher, Hap, 110–17
Vulnerability, 236–37
  of children, 281

Well-being, in dying, xiv, 30, 32, 34
Wilson, Anne-Marie, 35–57
Wisdom, of children, 281

ABOUT THE AUTHOR

Dr. Ira Byock was trained in family practice and has specialized in caring for the dying for the past seventeen years. He is Director of a Robert Wood Johnson Foundation National Program to improve end-of-life care. Dr. Byock serves as President of the American Academy of Hospice and Palliative Medicine. He lives with his two daughters in Missoula, Montana.